sports challenge
Eagles Edition

Trivia, Puzzles & Interesting Facts about the Eagles

Introduction by
Anthony Gargano

ELI KOWALSKI

Cover Designed by Delaney-Designs

The following individuals and organizations generously gave permission to
reproduce photographs in this book:

Urban Archives, Temple University Libraries, pages 20, 25, 49, 50, 60, 101,
120, 125, 129, 154, 161, 162, 169, 176, 185, 203, 209, 210, 212, 262, 325,
326, 330, 334, 339, 340

Mitch Rosenberg, pages 258, 259, 321

Photo Credit: Bobby Mansure, page 89

Illustrations by Bob Carroll, pages 236, 237, 238, 239, 240, 241, 242, 244,
245, 246, 247, 248, 249

First Published 2006

Publisher
Sports Challenge Network
Philadelphia, PA 19102

www.sportschallengenetwork.com

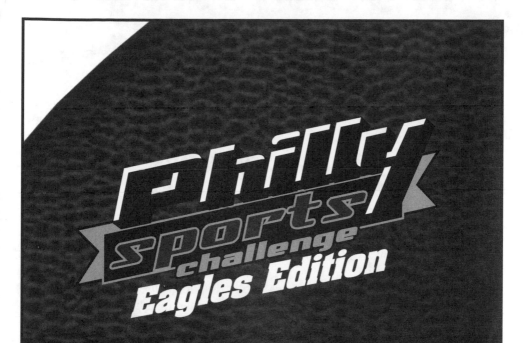

Philly Sports Challenge
Eagles Edition

Questions by

ELI KOWALSKI

Introduction by

Anthony Gargano

ACKNOWLEDGEMENTS

I would like to express my sincere gratitude to the following for their enormous contributions to this book.

To Jim Gallagher, retired Eagles Public Relations Director for his interest in this project and all of his time and insight that he generously gave me.

To Ray Didinger, Hall of Famer, co-author of the Eagles Encyclopedia and Emmy Award writer and producer at NFL Films, for allowing me access over the years to his vast knowledge on the Eagles and all of his courtesies and encouragements.

To Anthony Gargano, sportscaster and writer, for generously giving his time in writing the books introduction and for his encouragement and support on this project with his insight about the Eagles.

To Amy Korba, for her assistance in proofing and editing this prolonged project.

To my family, for having the patience in what has taken me a long time to complete, throughout all my good days and bad ones. My sincere thanks for their generous support and love.

CONTENTS

ROSTERS

questions / answers

ON THE FIELD

questions / answers

HONORS

questions / answers

POSTSEASONS

questions / answers

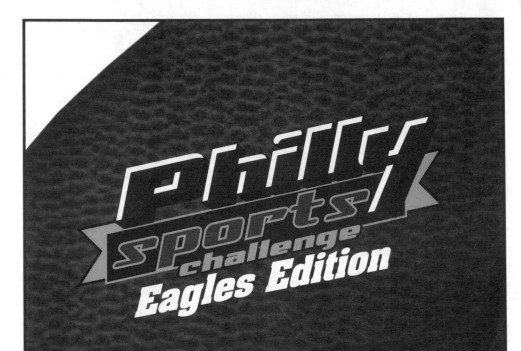

Introduction

INTRODUCTION

In Philadelphia, we are more literal than literary. The profound nature that we prefer is served in a shot glass, bullish and harsh. It's out there, with no need of subjective meandering or hidden meaning. We are an Old Soul, Old School City for a baby nation, steeped in its own ways.

It's why Philadelphia is one of the rare old East Coast cities that connects more with football than baseball. There is nothing pastoral about football. There is no elegant metaphor for football.

It's just football.

And our football is green. Such a dull color otherwise, it conjures the richness of the game here.

For it's always Eagles Green in Philadelphia.

It's Randall and Reggie and Jaws and Wilbert and Concrete Charlie and Tommy and Harold and Donovan and Trot and Vai and Doooce, and all of those Sundays spent with them, our heart on the line. It's the Fog Bowl and the House of Pain Game and 4th and 26 and Wilbert's Run and the Body Bag Game and every delicious victory over the Cowboys.

And here we know our Eagles history like we know our nation's (I give the benefit of the doubt here, as the Birds probably trump). We flex our knowledge here. We parade it, the ultimate barometer of fandom. Because you're not a true fan if you can't answer:

Who holds the record for the longest punt made in Eagles history?

So finally, in this book, we have our Birds Bible to test our knowledge, study for the big test of fandom and be first team among the flock.

- Anthony Gargano

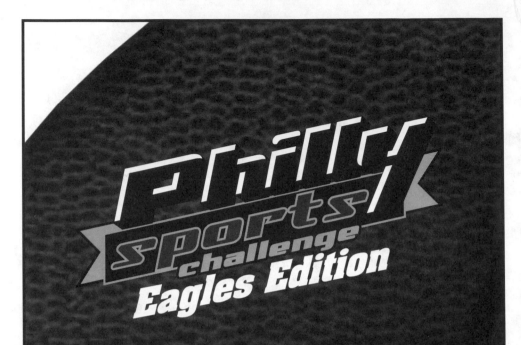

Philly sports challenge
Eagles Edition

The Thirties:
Depressing Eagles

THE THIRTIES: DEPRESSING EAGLES

1. During the 1933 season, how many bye weeks did the Eagles have before they actually played their first game?

    a. 1
    b. 2
    c. 4
    d. None

2. What was the combined score of the Eagles' first three games of the 1933 season, in which they lost all three games?

    a. 116-9
    b. 87-24
    c. 135-56
    d. 91-35

3. In which year did the Eagles end their regular season with three consecutive bye weeks?

    a. 1933
    b. 1935
    c. 1937
    d. 1939

4. In the 1934 season, how many total bye weeks did the Eagles have?

    a. 2
    b. 3
    c. 4
    d. 5

5. Who did the Eagles defeat in the last game of the '34 season?

    a. New York Giants
    b. Brooklyn Dodgers
    c. Boston Redskins
    d. Cincinnati Reds

6. During the 1936 season, how many times were the birds shut out?

    a. 3
    b. 5
    c. 6
    d. 8

7. The Eagles only had one win during the 1936 season. Who did they defeat?

    a. Chicago Bears
    b. Boston Redskins
    c. Brooklyn Dodgers
    d. New York Giants

8. In the 1937 season, the Eagles only won two games. The first win was against Washington; who else did they defeat that year?

    a. Brooklyn Dodgers
    b. Pittsburgh Pirates
    c. Cleveland Rams
    d. New York Giants

9. In 1937, the Eagles played five games in October. How many did they win?

    a. 1
    b. 2
    c. 3
    d. 4

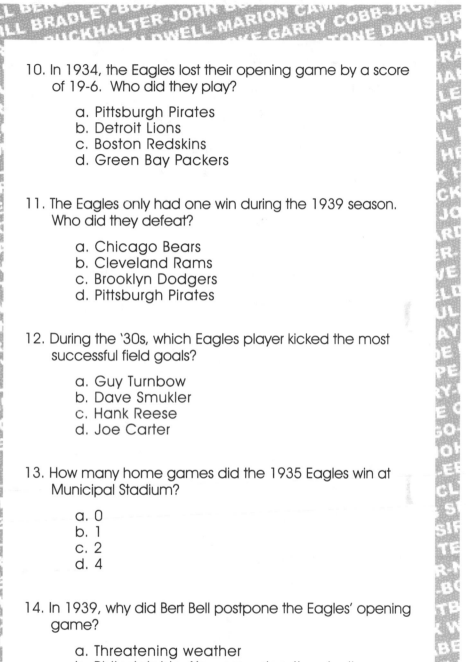

10. In 1934, the Eagles lost their opening game by a score of 19-6. Who did they play?

    a. Pittsburgh Pirates
    b. Detroit Lions
    c. Boston Redskins
    d. Green Bay Packers

11. The Eagles only had one win during the 1939 season. Who did they defeat?

    a. Chicago Bears
    b. Cleveland Rams
    c. Brooklyn Dodgers
    d. Pittsburgh Pirates

12. During the '30s, which Eagles player kicked the most successful field goals?

    a. Guy Turnbow
    b. Dave Smukler
    c. Hank Reese
    d. Joe Carter

13. How many home games did the 1935 Eagles win at Municipal Stadium?

    a. 0
    b. 1
    c. 2
    d. 4

14. In 1939, why did Bert Bell postpone the Eagles' opening game?

    a. Threatening weather
    b. Philadelphia A's were using the stadium
    c. Fire at the stadium
    d. Uniforms did not arrive

15. During the 1936 season, who scored the Eagles' only touchdown in their win against the New York Giants?

    a. Jim Leonard
    b. Ed Manske
    c. John Kusko
    d. Joe Carter

16. The 1936 season was the Eagles' worst season in franchise history. How many total touchdowns did the team score?

    a. 3
    b. 5
    c. 7
    d. 9

17. In 1937, who was the Eagles' leading scorer?

    a. Bill Hewitt
    b. Joe Carter
    c. Swede Hanson
    d. Jay Arnold

18. How many games did the Eagles win in their first decade?

    a. 15
    b. 18
    c. 21
    d. 27

19. Who did the Eagles play in the last game of the decade (1930s)?

    a. Chicago Bears
    b. Pittsburgh Pirates
    c. Brooklyn Dodgers
    d. Cleveland Rams

20. In 1933, when did the Eagles make their first successful field goal?

    a. First game
    b. Third game
    c. Fifth game
    d. Didn't make one that year

21. In which year during the thirties did the Eagles only score 51 points for the entire season?

    a. 1933
    b. 1934
    c. 1936
    d. 1939

22. Which one of the following Eagles players was not an attorney when not playing football?

    a. Jack Roberts
    b. Henry O'Boyle
    c. Lee Woodruff
    d. Joe Kresky

answers on page 364

THE FORTIES: EAGLES UPLIFTED

1. The '49 Eagles had only one loss. Which team beat them?

    a. New York Bulldogs
    b. Chicago Bears
    c. New York Giants
    d. Detroit Lions

2. In 1948, which one of the following teams did the Eagles not shut out when they scored 45 points?

    a. Boston Yanks
    b. New York Giants
    c. Washington Redskins
    d. Detroit Lions

3. In how many games during the '48 season did the Eagles score 45 points or more?

    a. 2
    b. 3
    c. 4
    d. 5

4. To start the '40s decade, how many wins did the Eagles achieve during the 1940 season?

    a. 1
    b. 3
    c. 5
    d. 0 wins, 1 tie

5. In 1942, after winning their first game, how many games did the Eagles lose before winning another game that season?

    a. 4
    b. 6
    c. 8
    d. 10

6. In 1940, which Eagle led the NFL in pass receptions?

    a. Red Ramsey
    b. Don Looney
    c. Les McDonald
    d. Joe Carter

7. In what year did the Eagles finally have their first winning season?

    a. 1941
    b. 1943
    c. 1945
    d. 1949

8. How many consecutive home games did the Eagles win between December 14,1947, and December 11, 1949?

    a. 9
    b. 11
    c. 14
    d. 17

9. In 1949, which Eagles player broke an NFL record by converting seven points-after-touchdowns in a single game?

    a. Joe Muha
    b. Frank Reagan
    c. Jim Parmer
    d. Cliff Patton

10. When the Eagles and Steelers merged in 1943 to form the Steagles what was their season record?

    a. 5-4-1
    b. 4-5-1
    c. 6-3-1
    d. 3-6-1

11. Who was the Eagles captain on the '49 squad which
    won the National League Football title shown here
    receiving a gilded football from Ralph Kelly president of
    the Philadelphia Chamber of Commerce?

    a. Tommy Thompson
    b. Steve Van Buren
    c. Al Wistert
    d. Russ Craft

answers on page 365

'50s PRO BOWLERS

```
C B R B K U E L K B U A O D S R G O E
W M P E T E P I H O S U E L R P Y H R
S T A R I A R T U B T R A A K S N W M
P T P N E H N B L B A K A N E E E B N
U H E A E D S O F Y A A O O N N T R T
N B T T E R Y K U T N T B D F R K N F
K O E B I T U N O H R A K C A A A Y A
I T R L U I R B S O A I E M R B I B R
N A E M C C N E N M R K K Y R R K L C
E A T N W T K Y T A U B F M A E E C S
B O Z R E I R L N S V L M M G T R M S
A P L S U R L D A O I M T O U L T U U
B E A Y E O E L E N B W R T T A D O R
E N F J S B E I E J S T L O J W I Y M
P L F L K K U M S Y M F K A N P K H R
N B U C K O K I L R O Y O A K N U H U
U K U L O M R A J E K I M R N R U O T
R H A D M E K R U B N A I R D A S R R
C W O D N T I D E K R N D S B S T R R
```

AdrianBurk	AlWistert	BobbyThomason	BuckLansford
BuckoKilroy	ChuckBednarik	JerryNorton	KenFarragut
LumSnyder	MikeJarmoluk	NormVanBuren	NormWilley
PetePihos	PeteRetzlaff	RussCraft	TomBrookshier
TommyMcDonald	WalterBarnes		

answers on page 420

THE FIFTIES: FLY EAGLES FLY

1. The 1955 Eagles had a season record of 4-7-1. Which team did they tie that season?

    a. Pittsburgh Steelers
    b. Chicago Cardinals
    c. Los Angeles Rams
    d. Cleveland Browns

2. Which offensive formation did the Eagles primarily run during the '50s?

    a. I-formation
    b. Single wing
    c. T- formation
    d. Double wing

3. Former Eagles owner and NFL commissioner Bert Bell suffered a fatal heart attack while watching the Eagles play which team?

    a. Cleveland Browns
    b. Pittsburgh Steelers
    c. New York Giants
    d. Baltimore Colts

4. In 1958, to who did the Eagles offer the head coaching job but never closed the deal?

    a. Paul Bryant
    b. Frank Howard
    c. John Madden
    d. Vince Lombardi

5. The worst defeat of the decade occurred in 1952, when which team defeated the Eagles by the score 49-7?

    a. Cleveland Browns
    b. Washington Redskins
    c. San Francisco 49ers
    d. Green Bay Packers

6. The Eagles had their best defensive season of the decade in 1950 when they held their opponents to the fewest points in the league. How many total points did they allow that year?

    a. 133
    b. 137
    c. 141
    d. 149

7. The first 200-yard receiving game of the decade occurred when Eagle Bud Grant caught 11 passes against which team?

    a. Cleveland Browns
    b. Dallas Texans
    c. St. Louis Rams
    d. New York Giants

8. The largest margin of victory in the decade occurred in 1953, when the Eagles destroyed which team by the score of 56-17?

    a. Los Angeles Rams
    b. Detroit Lions
    c. Chicago Cardinals
    d. Pittsburgh Steelers

9. Whom did Eagle quarterback Norm Van Brocklin connect with on a 91-yard touchdown pass?

a. Pete Pihos
b. Tommy McDonald
c. Al Wistert
d. Bobby Walston

10. Which Eagle set a club record by scoring 25 points in a single game?

a. Don Johnson
b. Jerry Williams
c. Pete Pihos
d. Bobby Walston

11. The '53 Eagles ruined a perfect season for which NFL team by defeating them on the last game of the season?

a. Baltimore Colts
b. Cleveland Browns
c. Washington Redskins
d. Chicago Cardinals

12. After the first game of the '55 season, which Eagles player suffered a career-ending injury and ended his record of starting *101 consecutive games?*

a. Bucko Kilroy
b. Russ Carroccio
c. Hal Giancanelli
d. Bibbles Bawel

13. The '56 Eagles only won three games that year. Which team did they defeat twice?

a. Washington Redskins
b. Pittsburgh Steelers
c. New York Giants
d. Chicago Cardinals

14. How many of the 110 games played during the 1950s did the Eagles win?

    a. 46
    b. 51
    c. 57
    d. 63

15. During the '59 season, which Eagle scored on an 81-yard punt return?

    a. Dick Bielski
    b. Clarence Peaks
    c. Tommy McDonald
    d. Art Powell

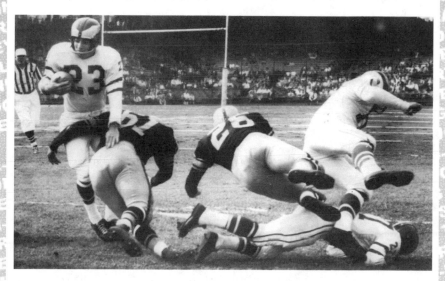

16. Which Eagles player was the leading rusher on the '56 squad?

    a. Don Schaefer
    b. Hal Giancanelli
    c. Dick Bielski
    d. Ken Keller

17. In 1953, against which team did Chuck Bednarik score his only Eagles career touchdown?

    a. San Francisco 49ers
    b. Baltimore Colts
    c. Cleveland Browns
    d. Pittsburgh Steelers

answers on page 365

THE SIXTIES: ON THE ROAD TO VICTORY

1. In their 1960 Championship season, who led the Eagles in both receptions and receiving yards?

    a. Bobby Walston
    b. Pete Retzlaff
    c. Jerry Wilson
    d. Tommy McDonald

2. During the 1968 season, how many consecutive games did the Eagles lose?

    a. 7
    b. 9
    c. 11
    d. 13

3. During the 1960s how many touchdowns did Eagle Don Burroughs score off of his 29 interceptions?

    a. 0
    b. 3
    c. 9
    d. 11

4. How many different head coaches did the Eagles have during the '60s decade?

    a. 3
    b. 4
    c. 5
    d. 6

5. In 1968 Eagles running back Harry Jones carried the ball 22 times for how many yards?

    a. 24
    b. 87
    c. 191
    d. 237

6. In what year did Jerry Wolman sell the Eagles franchise to Leonard Tose?

    a. 1963
    b. 1965
    c. 1967
    d. 1969

7. To whom did the Eagles lose their first game of the 1960 season, who later went on to win the championship?

    a. Pittsburgh Steelers
    b. Dallas Cowboys
    c. Cleveland Browns
    d. St. Louis Cardinals

8. The Eagles were triumphant in how many fourth-quarter comebacks during their 1960 championship season?

    a. 3
    b. 5
    c. 6
    d. 8

9. Which Eagle scored a total of 62 touchdowns during the 1960s?

    a. Pete Retzlaff
    b. Tommy McDonald
    c. Ollie Matson
    d. Tim Brown

10. Which Eagles player got injured, allowing Chuck Bednarik to become the legendary 60-minute man?

    a. Bob Pellegrini
    b. Joe Robb
    c. John Wilcox
    d. Maxie Baughan

11. Which Eagles head coach won the most games in the sixties?

    a. Ed Khayat
    b. Nick Skorich
    c. Joe Kuharich
    d. Jerry Williams

12. Which Eagle ran back the opening kickoff for a touchdown to start the '61 season?

    a. Irv Cross
    b. Ted Dean
    c. Clarence Peaks
    d. Tim Brown

13. Chuck Bednarik played his last game in an Eagles uniform against which team?

    a. New York Giants
    b. Dallas Cowboys
    c. St. Louis Cardinals
    d. Detroit Lions

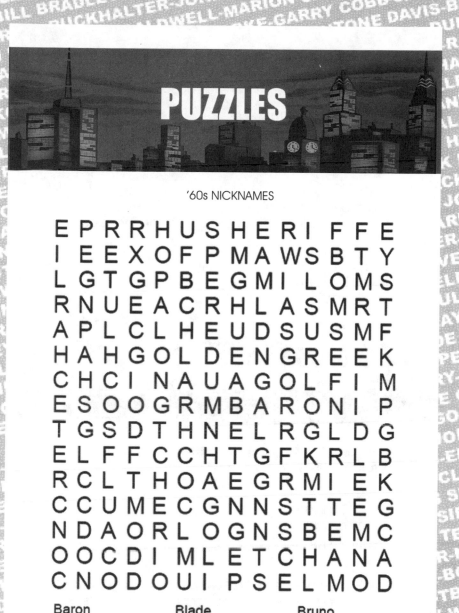

PUZZLES

'60s NICKNAMES

```
E P R R H U S H E R I F F E
I E E X O F P M A W S B T Y
L G T G P B E G M I L O M S
R N U E A C R H L A S M R T
A P L C L H E U D S U S M F
H A H G O L D E N G R E E K
C H C I N A U A G O L F I M
E S O O G R M B A R O N I P
T G S D T H N E L R G L D G
E L F F C C H T G F K R L B
R C L T H O A E G R M I E K
C C U M E C G N N S T T E G
N D A O R L O G N S B E M C
O O C D I M L E T C H A N A
C N O D O U I P S E L M O D
```

Baron	Blade	Bruno
Bullet	ConcreteCharlie	Dutchman
GoldenGreek	Goose	Gummy
High	Hopalong	King
Messiah	Sheriff	SwampFox

answers on page 421

29

14. During the '68 season the Eagles lost their first eleven consecutive games. Which team did the Eagles finally defeat for their first win of the season?

    a. Detroit Lions
    b. New Orleans Saints
    c. Minnesota Vikings
    d. Green Bay Packers

15. Which one of the following Eagles players did not complete at least one pass during the '66 season?

    a. Earl Gros
    b. King Hill
    c. Izzy Lang
    d. Jack Concannon

answers on page 366

THE SEVENTIES: EAGLES TAKE A DIVE

1. The Eagles began the 1970 season with how many straight losses?

    a. 3 games
    b. 5 games
    c. 6 games
    d. 7 games

2. The Eagles had only three wins during the 1970 season. Which one of the following teams did the Eagles not defeat that season?

    a. Pittsburgh Steelers
    b. Miami Dolphins
    c. New York Giants
    d. Washington Redskins

3. For the start of the 1972 Eagles season, who was the starting quarterback?

    a. Jim Ward
    b. Ron Powlus
    c. George Mira
    d. Pete Liske

4. How many Eagles veterans crossed the picket line during the 1974 players' strike?

    a. 12 players
    b. 17 players
    c. 20 players
    d. 28 players

5. In 1976, against which team did the Eagles play their only overtime game of the season?

    a. Washington Redskins
    b. New York Giants
    c. Atlanta Falcons
    d. Green Bay Packers

6. In the 1971 season, against who did Eagles Head Coach Ed Khayat earn his first win?

    a. Denver Broncos
    b. Washington Redskins
    c. St. Louis Cardinals
    d. New York Giants

7. The Eagles were known during the seventies for losing five consecutive games several times. In which year did they actually lose six consecutive games?

    a. 1971
    b. 1972
    c. 1974
    d. 1976

8. Which Eagles player's daughter suffered from leukemia which sparked Eagles owner Leonard Tose and GM Jim Murray to start 'THE EAGLES FLY FOR LEUKEMIA' charity?

    a. Ron Porter
    b. Tim Rossovich
    c. Fred Hill
    d. Ben Hawkins

9. In the 1970s, whom were the Eagles playing when their opponent's fans booed the officials for about 18 minutes because of bad calls?

    a. New Orleans Saints
    b. Pittsburgh Steelers
    c. Baltimore Colts
    d. St. Louis Cardinals

10. The Eagles played the Dallas Cowboys twenty times during the '70s decade. How many of those games did the Eagles win?

    a. 3
    b. 5
    c. 9
    d. 11

11. In the '70s, who became the Eagles first soccer-style kicker?

    a. Ove Johansson
    b. Nick Mike-Mayer
    c. Horst Muhlmann
    d. Tom Dempsey

12. In 1974 Eagles backup quarterback Mike Boryla won the last three games of the season. Which one of the following Eagles quarterbacks won their first three starts?

    a. Roman Gabriel
    b. Norm Snead
    c. Adrian Burk
    d. Pete Liske

13. In 1977 who caught Eagles quarterback Ron Jaworski's first touchdown pass?

    a. Charlie Smith
    b. Keith Krepfle
    c. Tom Sullivan
    d. Harold Carmichael

14. The first winning season of the '70s decade happened in which year?

    a. 1973
    b. 1975
    c. 1976
    d. 1978

15. In 1979 which team did the Eagles defeat by 37 points?

    a. St. Louis Cardinals
    b. Cleveland Browns
    c. Detroit Lions
    d. Houston Oilers

answers on page 367

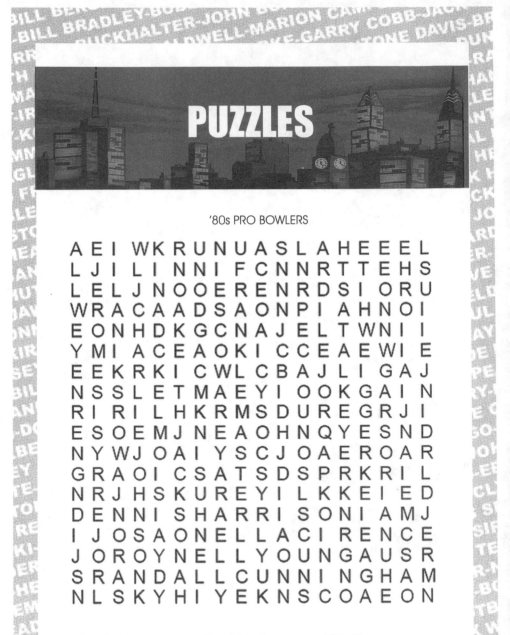

PUZZLES

'80s PRO BOWLERS

```
A E I W K R U N U A S L A H E E E L
L J I L I N N I F C N N R T T E H S
L E L J N O O E R E N R D S I O R U
W R A C A A D S A O N P I A H N O I
E O N H D K G C N A J E L T W N I I
Y M I A C E A O K I C C E A E W I E
E E K R K I C W L C B A J L I G A J
N S S L E T M A E Y I O O K G A I N
R I R I L H K R M S D U R E G R J I
E S O E M J N E A O H N Q Y E S N D
N Y W J O A I Y S C J O A E R O A R
G R A O I C S A T S D S P R K R I L
N R J H S K U R E Y I L K K E I E D
D E N N I S H A R R I S O N I A M J
I J O S A O N E L L A C I R E N C E
J O R O Y N E L L Y O U N G A U S R
S R A N D A L L C U N N I N G H A M
N L S K Y H I Y E K N S C O A E O N
```

CharlieJohnson	DennisHarrison	EricAllen
FrankLeMaster	HaroldCarmichael	JerryRobinson
JerrySisemore	KeithJackson	MikeQuick
RandallCunningham	RandyLogan	ReggieWhite
RonJaworski	RoynellYoung	WesHopkins

answers on page 422

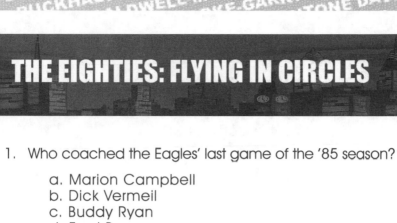

THE EIGHTIES: FLYING IN CIRCLES

1. Who coached the Eagles' last game of the '85 season?

   a. Marion Campbell
   b. Dick Vermeil
   c. Buddy Ryan
   d. Fred Bruney

2. The Eagles began the 1986 season with how many straight losses?

   a. 2 games
   b. 3 games
   c. 4 games
   d. 5 games

3. During the 1986 season, which one of the following teams did the Eagles not play in overtime?

   a. Chicago Bears
   b. Los Angeles Raiders
   c. St. Louis Cardinals
   d. Seattle Seahawks

4. Which of the following years did the Eagles not have a playoff appearance?

   a. 1981
   b. 1985
   c. 1988
   d. 1989

5. In 1981, which team did the Eagles embarrass when they defeated them by 42 points?

  a. Washington Redskins
  b. New Orleans Saints
  c. St. Louis Cardinals
  d. Baltimore Colts

6. In 1980 the Eagles set a team record by winning how many regular season games?

  a. 10
  b. 11
  c. 12
  d. 13

7. In 1983, whom did the Eagles defeat for their lone home game victory?

  a. Chicago Bears
  b. Washington Redskins
  c. Baltimore Colts
  d. Los Angeles Rams

8. In 1985, against which team did Eagles quarterback Ron Jaworski come back and start after his broken leg injury?

  a. St. Louis Cardinals
  b. Dallas Cowboys
  c. New Orleans Saints
  d. Buffalo Bills

9. In the eighties, which team did the Eagles defeat for their first overtime win?

  a. New York Giants
  b. Detroit Lions
  c. New Orleans Saints
  d. Atlanta Falcons

10. 1986 was Buddy Ryan's first year as the Eagles head coach. Which team did the Eagles defeat with a shutout victory?

      a. San Diego Chargers
      b. Chicago Bears
      c. Atlanta Falcons
      d. Los Angeles Rams

11. Which Eagles head coach won the most games during the eighties?

      a. Fred Bruney
      b. Dick Vermeil
      c. Marion Campbell
      d. Buddy Ryan

12. Which team did the Eagles shut out during the '81 season?

      a. St. Louis Cardinals
      b. Tampa Bay Buccaneers
      c. Miami Dolphins
      d. Buffalo Bills

13. In 1989, which Dallas Cowboys player accused Eagles Head Coach Buddy Ryan of putting a bounty on him?

      a. Michael Irvin
      b. Garry Cobb
      c. Luis Zendejas
      d. Troy Aikman

14. In 1980, whom did the Eagles play when Harold Carmichael failed to catch a pass, breaking his streak of 127 consecutive games with a reception?

a. San Diego Chargers
b. Dallas Cowboys
c. Atlanta Falcons
d. Minnesota Vikings

15. In 1983, against which team did Ron Jaworski throw an 83-yard touchdown pass to Mike Quick on the first play of the game (and the Eagles still lost)?

a. Chicago Bears
b. St. Louis Cardinals
c. Dallas Cowboys
d. Baltimore Colts

answers on page 367

THE NINETIES: WATCH OUR EAGLES SOAR

1. During the '98 season, who was the leading tackler for the Eagles?

a. Michael Zordich
b. James Willis
c. William Thomas
d. Brian Dawkins

2. The Eagles had numerous playoff appearances during the nineties. Which one of the following years did they not make it to the playoffs?

a. 1990
b. 1992
c. 1996
d. 1998

3. Which Eagles head coach won the most games during the nineties?

   a. Buddy Ryan
   b. Rich Kotite
   c. Ray Rhodes
   d. Andy Reid

4. In which year did the Eagles start using the West Coast offense?

   a. 1991
   b. 1993
   c. 1995
   d. 1997

5. Which team defeated the Eagles by the score of 38-0 to give the Eagles their largest margin of defeat for the decade?

   a. Green Bay Packers
   b. Seattle Seahawks
   c. San Francisco 49ers
   d. Houston Oilers

6. In which year did the Eagles change their uniforms to a midnight green with a screaming Eagle?

   a. 1995
   b. 1996
   c. 1998
   d. 1999

7. In 1990 the Eagles led the NFC in points scored. How many points did they score?

   a. 396
   b. 417
   c. 436
   d. 452

8. How many Redskins were forced to leave the game caused by injuries in what was dubbed 'The Body Bag Game'?

    a. 4
    b. 5
    c. 6
    d. 8

9. Which team did the Eagles defeat for the team's first home shutout of the decade?

    a. Green Bay Packers
    b. Indianapolis Colts
    c. Buffalo Bills
    d. Phoenix Cardinals

10. In 1992 the Eagles finished the regular season 11-5. Including this season, how many consecutive regular seasons did the Eagles win ten games or more?

    a. 4
    b. 5
    c. 7
    d. 8

11. When Andy Reid succeeded Ray Rhodes as the Eagles head coach, how many rookies were on the roster?

    a. 9
    b. 12
    c. 14
    d. 17

12. In the nineties, what year did the Eagles lose 13 games for the worst regular season in the team's history?

a. 1993
b. 1995
c. 1996
d. 1998

13. Who was the Eagles' head coach when Jeffrey Lure purchased the team?

    a. Andy Reid
    b. Rich Kotite
    c. Buddy Ryan
    d. Ray Rhodes

14. The Eagles had a dry spell from 1996-1999, winning no road games until the birds finally defeated which team in 1999 for their first road win since '96?

    a. Chicago Bears
    b. Buffalo Bills
    c. New York Giants
    d. Carolina Panthers

15. Which one of the following Eagles players was not part of the so-called 'Bergey Bunch'?

    a. Kevin Reilly
    b. Ray Phillips
    c. Frank LeMaster
    d. Tom Ehlers

answers on page 368

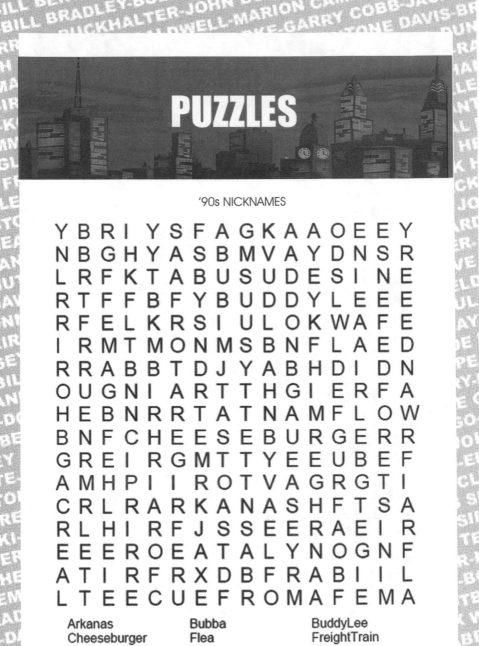

PUZZLES

'90s NICKNAMES

```
Y B R I Y S F A G K A A O E E Y
N B G H Y A S B M V A Y D N S R
L R F K T A B U S U D E S I N E
R T F F B F Y B U D D Y L E E E
R F E L K R S I U L O K W A F E
I R M T M O N M S B N F L A E D
R R A B B T D J Y A B H D I D N
O U G N I A R T T H G I E R F A
H E B N R R T A T N A M F L O W
B N F C H E E S E B U R G E R R
G R E I R G M T T Y E E U B E F
A M H P I I R O T V A G R G T I
C R L R A R K A N A S H F T S A
R L H I R F J S S E E R A E I R
E E E R O E A T A L Y N O G N F
A T I R F R X D B F R A B I I L
L T E E C U E F R O M A F E M A
```

Arkanas	Bubba	BuddyLee
Cheeseburger	Flea	FreightTrain
Kjax	MinisterofDefense	Money
Muddy	PrettyBoy	Refrigerator
Rev	Silk	Tank
Toast	Tra	Wolfman

answers on page 423

THE NEW MILLENNIUM
Road to the Super Bowl

1. How many times was Eagles quarterback Donovan McNabb sacked during the 2001 season?

   a. 26
   b. 32
   c. 39
   d. 47

2. During the 2002 season, how many different Eagles attempted to throw a pass?

   a. 3
   b. 5
   c. 7
   d. 9

3. During the 2003 season, Eagle L.J. Smith led all rookie tight ends in which category?

   a. Blocks
   b. Dropped passes
   c. Yards per catch
   d. Receptions

4. Through the 2003 season, who caught the most touchdown passes from quarterback Donovan McNabb?

   a. James Thrash
   b. Todd Pinkston
   c. Charles Johnson
   d. Chad Lewis

5. During the 2003 season, how many turnovers did the Eagles give up in their own red zone?

    a. 0
    b. 2
    c. 4
    d. 7

6. The Eagles started the 2004 season 4-0. When was the last time they did that?

    a. 1987
    b. 1993
    c. 1998
    d. 2001

7. In 2004, the Eagles' defensive line gave up how many completions that were 40 yards or longer?

    a. 0
    b. 1
    c. 3
    d. 5

8. To whom did Eagles quarterback Donovan McNabb throw the first pass of the 2004 regular season?

    a. Terrell Owens
    b. Freddie Mitchell
    c. L.J. Smith
    d. Chad Lewis

9. In 2005, which player did the Eagles release because he would not sign his franchise-tag tender?

    a. Terrell Owens
    b. Corey Simon
    c. Hugh Douglas
    d. Dirk Johnson

10. In 2005, Eagle Jeremiah Trotter was ejected prior to the opening kick-off for getting involved in an altercation with which Atlanta Falcons player?

    a. DeAngelo Hall
    b. Robert Redd
    c. Bryan Scott
    d. Kevin Mathis

11. During the 2003 season, which of the following Eagles players was not part of the 'Three Headed Monster'?

    a. Freddie Mitchell
    b. Duce Staley
    c. Brian Westbrook
    d. Correll Buckhalter

12. Which one of the following Eagles quarterbacks won his first four starts in the new millennium?

    a. Koy Detmer
    b. A.J. Feeley
    c. Doug Pederson
    d. Bobby Hoying

answers on page 369

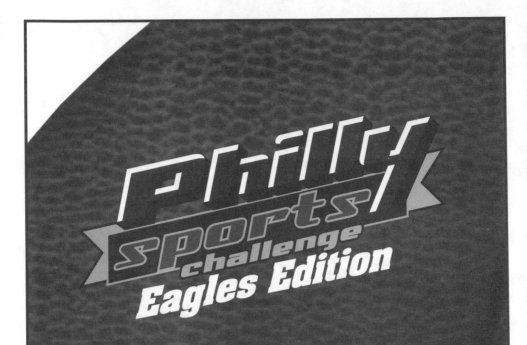

Watching Over the Nest

FRONT OFFICE

1. What is former Eagle Harold Carmichael's position with the Eagles organization?

   a. Director of Player Relations
   b. Wide Receivers Coach
   c. College Scout
   d. Director of Fan Development

2. From whom did Leonard Tose buy the Eagles football franchise?

   a. Jeffery Lurie
   b. Lud Wray
   c. Norman Braman
   d. Jerry Wolman

3. Before being promoted to head coach, Rich Kotite held what position with the Eagles?

   a. Defensive Coordinator
   b. Offensive Coordinator
   c. Quarterback Coach
   d. Running Back Coach

4. When was the Philadelphia Eagles team founded?

   a. 1927
   b. 1933
   c. 1939
   d. 1942

5. Who once owned both the Eagles and the Yellow Cab Company of Philadelphia?

a. Leonard Tose
b. Jay Snider
c. Jerry Wolman
d. Pete Retzlaff

6. In what year did Eagles owner and general manager Bert Bell propose the concept of an annual college draft?

a. 1924
b. 1927
c. 1931
d. 1935

7. Eagles owner Norman Braman was offered what position in President Ronald Reagan's first administration?

a. Commissioner of Trademarks/Patents
b. Commissioner of Federal Communications Commission
c. Commissioner of Federal Trade Commission
d. Commissioner of Immigration and Naturalization Service

8. Eagles owner Alexis Thompson competed on which US Olympic team?

a. Bobsledding
b. Field hockey
c. Ski jump
d. Lacrosse

9. Which Eagles owner helped established the Philadelphia City All-Star football game?

a. Jerry Wolman
b. Leonard Tose
c. Norman Braman
d. Alexis Thompson

10. Which one of the following candidates did Eagles owner Leonard Tose not interview for the Eagles head coaching job?

    a. Jimmy Johnson
    b. Dick Vermeil
    c. Joe Paterno
    d. Hank Stram

11. Which one of the following Eagles owners was also part of the '100 Brothers' ownership?

    a. Jerry Wolman
    b. Leonard Tose
    c. Norman Braman
    d. Joe Kuharich

12. For which radio station did Eagles president Joe Banner once hold a position as a producer?

    a. WIP
    b. WPEN
    c. WCAU
    d. WFIL

13. Eagles owner Alexis Thompson opened the first permanent NFL preseason training facility. What was it called?

    a. The NFL Experience
    b. The Eagle's Nest

c. The Eagle Lodge
d. The Eagle's Retreat

14. In 1957, Frank McNamee took over as the Eagles' team president. What high-ranking position did he hold with the city of Philadelphia?

    a. Police Commissioner
    b. Department of Streets Commissioner
    c. Fire Commissioner
    d. City Council President

15. After his playing days were over with the Eagles, what position did Hugh Douglas hold with the birds?

    a. College Scout
    b. Team Ambassador
    c. Marketing Assistant
    d. Director of Fan Relations

16. When Leonard Tose purchased the Eagles, which former Eagles player did he hire to be his general manager?

    a. Jerry Williams
    b. Pete Retzlaff
    c. Wayne Robinson
    d. Eddie Khayat

17. Which city did Leonard Tose try to negotiate to move the Eagles franchise?

    a. Los Angeles
    b. Tempe
    c. Flagstaff
    d. Phoenix

answers on page 369

PUZZLES

EAGLES HEAD COACHES

```
K B H N B U C K S H A W U I M S Y
K E U I B E R Y L I R H L W E A G
I C G D M V R R L I O Y A D R L E
J I H D D I I T E D E Y O W O I D
I O D I R Y K A B A N H D U H I E
M C E C R A R E P E R U Y I E H I
T R V K K N R Y M Y L U S R L C O
R H O V U W I I A C A L Y K A I H
I J R E Y H L R C N C D E R E R I
M O E R E L A I N I N O D J N O N
B H W M N I Y R O A H S R I Y K L
L D J E R R Y W I L L I A M S S E
E I R I A M K M R C R K D C A K N
S A C L E O I H A R H M T D E C M
J L E S B R I E M N K A E N R I K
R I C H K O T I T E N A D S G N S
T O T O M E C A C I L Y B A L I L
T A Y A H K D E N S M M L C M K R
```

AndyReid	BertBell	BuckShaw
BuddyRyan	DickVermeil	EdKhayat
GreasyNeale	HughDevore	JerryWilliams
JimTrimble	JoeKuharich	LudWray
MarionCampbell	MikeMcCormack	NickSkorich
RayRhodes	RichKotite	WayneMillner

answers on page 427

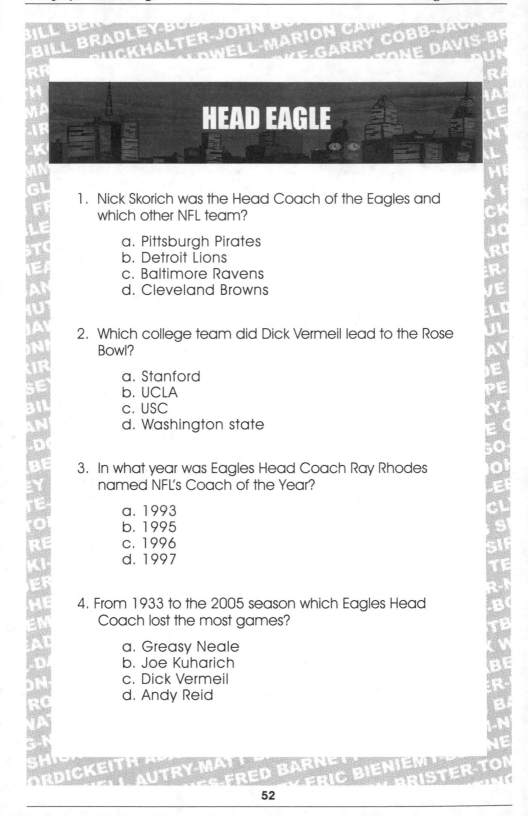

HEAD EAGLE

1. Nick Skorich was the Head Coach of the Eagles and which other NFL team?

    a. Pittsburgh Pirates
    b. Detroit Lions
    c. Baltimore Ravens
    d. Cleveland Browns

2. Which college team did Dick Vermeil lead to the Rose Bowl?

    a. Stanford
    b. UCLA
    c. USC
    d. Washington state

3. In what year was Eagles Head Coach Ray Rhodes named NFL's Coach of the Year?

    a. 1993
    b. 1995
    c. 1996
    d. 1997

4. From 1933 to the 2005 season which Eagles Head Coach lost the most games?

    a. Greasy Neale
    b. Joe Kuharich
    c. Dick Vermeil
    d. Andy Reid

5. What former Eagles coach played with the Phillies?

   a. Buddy Ryan
   b. Greasy Neale
   c. Buck Shaw
   d. Bert Bell

6. Which Eagles Head Coach had a 1-11-0 losing season?

   a. Lud Wray
   b. Ed Khayat
   c. Nick Skorich
   d. Bert Bell

7. Which one of the following Eagles Head Coaches won more than 10 games?

   a. Hugh Devore
   b. Nick Skorich
   c. Jerry Williams
   d. Ed Khayat

8. In his four years as Head Coach of the Eagles, how many total wins did Ray Rhodes achieve?

   a. 27 wins
   b. 29 wins
   c. 31 wins
   d. 35 wins

9. Defensive Coordinator Bud Carson worked under which Eagles Head Coach?

   a. Buddy Ryan
   b. Dick Vermeil
   c. Rich Kotite
   d. Marion Campbell

10. Against which NFL team did Andy Reid record his first win as the Eagles' Head Coach?

    a. Dallas Cowboys
    b. Cleveland Browns
    c. New York Giants
    d. Baltimore Ravens

11. When the Philadelphia and Pittsburgh football franchises merged in 1943 the team had two head coaches. Greasy Neale was from Philadelphia. Name the Pittsburgh coach.

    a. Walt Kiesling
    b. Jim McMurdo
    c. Bo McMillin
    d. Frank Bausch

12. Prior to being hired as the Eagles' Head Coach, for what team was Buddy Ryan Defensive Coordinator?

    a. Oakland Raiders
    b. Chicago Bears
    c. Houston Oilers
    d. St. Louis Cardinals

13. In his first five years as Head Coach, what was Andy Reid's win/loss record?

    a. 48-32-0
    b. 51-29-0
    c. 54-26-0
    d. 46-32-2

14. After leaving the Eagles, where did Mike McCormack become the Head Coach?

    a. Arizona Cardinals
    b. Baltimore Colts
    c. Cleveland Browns
    d. Seattle Seahawks

15. How old was Dick Vermeil when he became the Eagles'
    Head Coach?

    a. 39
    b. 42
    c. 45
    d. 48

16. Which Eagles Head Coach traded Tommy McDonald?

    a. Jerry Williams
    b. Joe Kuharich
    c. Eddie Khayat
    d. Marion Campbell

17. In 1951, which Eagles Head Coach retired after the
    second game due to illness?

    a. Walt Kiesling
    b. Hugh Devore
    c. Bo McMillin
    d. Fred Bruney

18. Which one of the following Eagles Head Coaches never
    won the 'Coach of the Year' award?

    a. Greasy Neale
    b. Bert Bell
    c. Dick Vermeil
    d. Buck Shaw

19. Who was the head coach that led the Eagles to the
    NFL Championship in 1960?

    a. Nick Skorich
    b. Hugh Devore
    c. Buck Shaw
    d. Jim Trimble

20. How long was Joe Kuharich's contract when he signed on as the Eagles' coach and general manager?

    a. 5 years
    b. 7 years
    c. 10 years
    d. 15 years

21. What NFL team did Marion Campbell coach for besides the Philadelphia Eagles?

    a. Baltimore Colts
    b. Detroit Lions
    c. Atlanta Falcons
    d. San Francisco 49ers

22. After leaving the Eagles, where did Buddy Ryan go on to be Head Coach?

    a. Arizona Cardinals
    b. Baltimore Ravens
    c. Cincinnati Bengals
    d. Denver Broncos

23. How many former Eagles players became head coaches for the birds?

    a. 2
    b. 3
    c. 6
    d. 8

24. Prior to becoming the Eagles' Head Coach, which other NFL team did Hugh Devore coach?

    a. Chicago Cardinals
    b. Pittsburgh Steelers
    c. Green Bay Packers
    d. Cleveland Browns

25. Several years after leaving the Eagles, which team did Nick Skorich end up coaching?

    a. San Francisco 49ers
    b. Buffalo Bills
    c. Baltimore Colts
    d. Cleveland Browns

26. After leaving the Eagles, Rich Kotite went on to coach the New York Jets. How many wins did he record in his two years as their head coach?

    a. 4
    b. 7
    c. 9
    d. 12

27. Jim Trimble was fired by the Eagles in 1955 and went on to coach which Canadian football team?

    a. Edmonton Eskimos
    b. Toronto Argonauts
    c. Calgary Stampedes
    d. Hamilton Tiger-Cats

28. Which one of the following Eagles coaches was never the head coach of Notre Dame's football team?

    a. Hugh Devore
    b. Buck Shaw
    c. Joe Kuharich
    d. Mike McCormack

29. Which Eagles Head Coach is credited with bringing the West Coast offense to Philadelphia?

    a. Dick Vermeil
    b. Rich Kotite
    c. Ray Rhodes
    d. Buddy Ryan

30. Which Eagles Head Coach was also the first football coach for the Air Force Academy's football team?

    a. Buck Shaw
    b. Jim Trimble
    c. Hugh Devore
    d. Bo McMillin

31. In 1976 against which team were the Eagles playing when Head Coach Dick Vermeil won his first game?

    a. Dallas Cowboys
    b. New York Giants
    c. Atlanta Falcons
    d. Washington Redskins

32. During the thirties, how many games did Eagles Head Coach Bert Bell win?

    a. 6
    b. 9
    c. 14
    d. 17

answers on page 370

EAGLE COACHES

1. Which Eagles coach played on the 1987 arena football league champion Denver Dynamite?

    a. Marty Mornhinweg
    b. John Harbaugh
    c. Pat Shurmur
    d. Juan Castillo

2. What position did Eagles coordinator Jim Johnson play in college?

   a. Quarterback
   b. Cornerback
   c. Tight end
   d. Safety

3. Former Eagles Defensive Coordinator Bud Carson was once the Head Coach of which NFL team?

   a. Atlanta Falcons
   b. Baltimore Ravens
   c. Cleveland Browns
   d. Denver Broncos

4. On which college football team did Eagles special Teams' Coordinator John Harbaugh play?

   a. Miami of Ohio
   b. Western Michigan
   c. Morehead State
   d. Western Kentucky

5. Eagles Offensive Line Coach Juan Castillo played for which USFL team?

   a. Houston Gamblers
   b. Oakland Invaders
   c. Denver Gold
   d. San Antonio Gunslingers

6. For which NFL team was Jim Johnson a player?

   a. New York Jets
   b. St. Louis Cardinals
   c. Buffalo Bills
   d. Baltimore Colts

7. Before being promoted to Head Coach, what type of coach was Marion Campbell with the Eagles?

    a. Defensive Coordinator
    b. Quarterbacks
    c. Tight ends
    d. Offensive Line

8. After leaving the Eagles, coach Brad Childress got his first head coaching job with which NFL team?

    a. Buffalo Bills
    b. Minnesota Vikings
    c. St. Louis Rams
    d. Kansas City Chiefs

9. Which one of the following was not an Eagles Quarterbacks Coach?

    a. Sid Gillman
    b. Doug Scovil
    c. Bobby Thomason
    d. Bill Walsh

10. Marv Levy had his first NFL coaching position with the Eagles. What type of coach was he?

a. Linebackers
b. Special Teams
c. Offensive Coordinator
d. Quarterbacks

11. Which one of the following was not an Eagles Special Teams Coordinator?

a. Frank Reagan
b. John Harbaugh
c. Dave Atkins
d. Dave Toub

12. Eagles defensive coordinator Jim Johnson was once the head coach of which football team?

a. Oklahoma Outlaws
b. Jacksonville Bulls
c. Univ. Of Indiana
d. Missouri Southern

13. Prior to becoming the Eagles' Head Coach Nick Skorich was what type of coach under Buck Shaw?

a. Linebackers
b. Special Teams
c. Line
d. Backfield

14. Which one of the following was not an Eagles Offensive Coordinator?

a. John Ralston
b. Jon Gruden
c. Emmitt Thomas
d. Ted Marchibroda

BROADCASTERS

```
K C I U Q E K I M A O R T E M R S
A B L S R E T L A W N A T S C L C
I O B N B T Y J R I L L S E L H A
N E B I I A L I B I L L S E A R S
R I R S L Y S S R I I R J R U B H
A M B I L L C A M P B E L L D L Q
B E M E B O B W E R U I L L E R Y
M L B M E R R R G B E H R I H O T
I B B R R G S A A S E S S R A B A
J B K C G R R R W N R K N R R E L
A B O B E A R I B O S O T E I E A
R I R B Y N F J G S B O M M N F B
I C R L H T M A S T G R M A G B T
L S A M A A S M U R Y B S E L E E
R R A E L L L A N D Y M U S S E R
A A B E S E M L A L N O N B A A J
L E S B M K Y B O E K T L E O N F
```

AndyMusser	BillBergey	BillBransome	BillCampbell
BillSears	BobHall	ByrumSaam	CharlieSwift
ClaudeHaring	JimBarniak	MerrillReese	MikeQuick
StanWalters	TaylorGrant	TomBrookshier	

answers on page 424

15. Sid Gillman was an experienced head coach for many years in the NFL. What was his role under coach Dick Vermeil?

    a. Defensive Coordinator
    b. Assistant Coach
    c. Quarterbacks Coach
    d. Receivers Coach

16. Which Eagles coach played high school football under Mike Holmgren?

    a. Bill Shuey
    b. Ted Williams
    c. John Harbaugh
    d. Marty Mornhinweg

answers on page 371

CALL OF THE EAGLES

1. In what year did Bill Campbell start broadcasting the play-by-play action of Eagles games?

    a. 1944
    b. 1949
    c. 1954
    d. 1956

2. In what year did Merrill Reese start calling the play-by-play action for Eagles games?

    a. 1969
    b. 1974
    c. 1977
    d. 1978

3. Who was the Eagles' play-by-play broadcaster when Merrill Reese joined the booth as the team's color analyst?

    a. Charlie Swift
    b. Andy Musser
    c. Bill Campbell
    d. Byrum Saam

4. In what year did former Eagle Mike Quick join Merrill Reese in the broadcast booth as the color analyst?

    a. 1996
    b. 1998
    c. 2000
    d. 2002

5. Which of the following players wasn't an Eagles color analyst?

    a. Bobby Thomason
    b. Joe Pisarcik
    c. Tom Brookshier
    d. Clarence Peaks

6. Which former city councilman was once an Eagles color analyst?

    a. Frank Rizzo
    b. Jack Kelly
    c. James Tayoun
    d. Thatcher Longstreth

7. Who was the Eagles' play-by-play broadcaster when Stan Hochman joined the booth as the team's color analyst?

    a. Byrum Saam
    b. Andy Musser
    c. Bill Campbell
    d. Charlie Swift

8. Who was the Eagles' first radio broadcaster to do the team's play-by-play?

    a. Bob Hall
    b. Chuck Thompson
    c. Taylor Grant
    d. Byrum Saam

9. Which Philadelphia radio station has broadcasted the most Eagles games?

    a. 1210 WCAU
    b. 610 WIP
    c. WIBG99
    d. 94.1 WYSP

10. Who was the first ex-player to work for the Eagles radio network as a color analyst?

    a. Ron Jaworski
    b. Tom Brookshier
    c. Don Burroughs
    d. Bobby Walston

answers on page 372

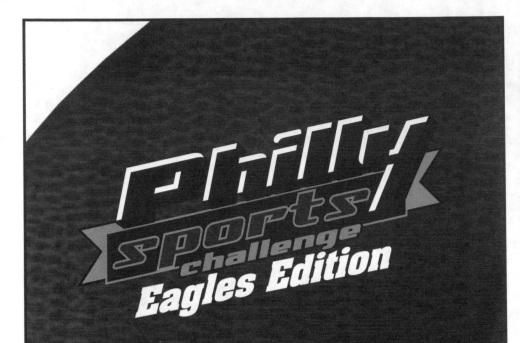

Phillips sports challenge
Eagles Edition

What's In A Name

A BIRD BY ANY OTHER NAME

1. What was Eagles quarterback Sonny Jurgensen's real first name?

   a. Howard
   b. Ray
   c. Christian
   d. Frank

2. What was Eagles guard Bubba Miller's real first name?

   a. Stephen
   b. David
   c. William
   d. James

3. What was Eagles tackle Ira Thomas's real first name?

   a. Troy
   b. Markus
   c. William
   d. Tyrone

4. We knew this Eagles player by the name Swede Hanson, but what was his real first name?

   a. George
   b. James
   c. Chuck
   d. Thomas

5. What was Eagles kicker Happy Feller's real first name?

a. James
b. Brian
c. George
d. Roger

6. What was Eagle Pete Perot's real first name?

a. Dennis
b. Charles
c. Kevin
d. Edwin

7. What was Eagles head coach Buck Shaw's real first name?

a. Lawrence
b. William
c. James
d. Donald

8. What was Eagle A.J. Feeley's real first name?

a. Aaron
b. Adam
c. Alex
d. Anthony

9. Which Eagles player's real first name is 'Sateki'?

a. Dhani Jones
b. Thomas Tapeh
c. Reno Mahe
d. Eric McCoo

10. What was Eagle Bud Grant's real first name?

a. Victor
b. Harold
c. David
d. Allen

11. What was Eagle Alabama Pitts's real first name?

    a. Gerald
    b. Derrick
    c. Edwin
    d. Monty

12. We knew him as Sam Baker but what was this Eagles player's real first name?

    a. Oliver
    b. Loris
    c. Donald
    d. Kent

13. What was Eagle Po James's real first name?

    a. Leroy
    b. Pernell
    c. Ron
    d. Fred

14. As the Eagles Head Coach he was called Greasy Neale, but what was his real first name?

    a. Henry
    b. Milton
    c. Earle
    d. Granville

15. We knew this Eagles player by the name Bosh Pritchard, but what was his real first name?

    a. Byron
    b. Calvin
    c. Benjamin
    d. Abisha

answers on page 372

NICKNAMES FROM THE '30s

1. Which Eagles back was nicknamed 'The Ripper'?

   a. Nick Prisco
   b. John Roberts
   c. Herald Frahm
   d. John Cole

2. What was Eagle Mike Sebastian's nickname?

   a. Freight Train
   b. Speedy
   c. Cannonball
   d. The Sharon Express

3. Which Eagles back was nicknamed 'Dynamite'?

   a. Lee Woodruff
   b. Albert Weiner
   c. Dave Smukler
   d. Richard Thornton

4. Which Eagles player was nicknamed 'Aimee'?

   a. Howard Bailey
   b. Carl Jorgenson
   c. Howard Aver
   d. Forrest McPherson

5. What was Eagle Osborne Willson's nickname?

   a. Diddie
   b. Ozzie
   c. Stormin
   d. Ollie

6. Which Eagles end was nicknamed 'Mousie'?

   a. Herbert Roton
   b. Burle Robinson
   c. George Rado
   d. Herschel Ramsey

7. Which Eagles player was nicknamed 'King'?

   a. John Cole
   b. Elwood Dow
   c. Glenn Frey
   d. Swede Hanson

8. Which Eagles player was nicknamed 'Stumpy'?

   a. Mike Sebastian
   b. Clarence Thomason
   c. Laf Russell
   d. Dick Riffle

9. Which Eagles player was nicknamed 'Wackie'?

   a. Don Jackson
   b. George Kavel
   c. Irv Kupcinet
   d. Glenn Frey

10. Which Eagles player was nicknamed 'Stinky'?

    a. Rankin Britt
    b. George Mulligan
    c. Bill Hewitt
    d. Everitt Rowan

11. What was Eagle Charles Leyendecker's nickname?

    a. Stuffy
    b. Tex
    c. Husky
    d. Professor

12. Which Eagles player was nicknamed 'The Muke'?

    a. Charles Hajek
    b. Carl Kane
    c. Herschel Stockton
    d. Bob Pylman

13. What was Eagle Maurice Harper's nickname?

    a. Moose
    b. Munchkin
    c. Mouse
    d. Mo

14. Which Eagles player was nicknamed 'Bummie'?

    a. Paul Cuba
    b. Bob Gonya
    c. Allen Keen
    d. Herbert Roton

15. What was Eagle Joe Pivarnick's nickname?

    a. Stumpy
    b. Rebel
    c. Butch
    d. Flash

answers on page 373

NICKNAMES FROM THE '40s

1. Which Eagles guard was nicknamed 'Piggy'?

    a. Walter Barnes
    b. Don Weedon
    c. Eberle Schultz
    d. Ben Agajanian

2. Which Eagles guard was nicknamed 'Walking Billboard'?

    a. Henry Benson
    b. Enio Conti
    c. Rocco Canale
    d. Bree Cuppoletti

3. Which Eagles player was nicknamed 'Flippin'?

    a. Jack Banta
    b. Foster Watkins
    c. Mel Bleeker
    d. Jim Castiglia

4. Which Eagle was nicknamed 'The Crooning Halfback'?

    a. Bosh Pritchard
    b. Keith Byars
    c. Darnell Autry
    d. James Joseph

5. Which Eagles player was nicknamed 'Big Ox'?

    a. Al Wistert
    b. Ernie Steele
    c. Jim Kekeris
    d. Walt Nowak

6. Which Eagles center was nicknamed 'Moose'?

    a. Robert Bjorklund
    b. Chuck Cherundolo
    c. Lyle Graham
    d. Maurice Harper

7. Which Eagles player was nicknamed 'One Man Gang'?

    a. Steve Sader
    b. Elmer Hackney
    c. Pat McHugh
    d. James Lankas

8. Which Eagles player was nicknamed '20 Grand'?

    a. Dan DeSantis
    b. Franklin Emmons
    c. William Jefferson
    d. Bob Davis

9. Which Eagles player was nicknamed 'Man O' War'?

    a. Jack Hinkle
    b. Lou Tomasetti
    c. Albert Johnson
    d. Robert Thurbon

10. What was Eagle Pete Pihos's nickname?

    a. Tank
    b. Horse
    c. The Golden Greek
    d. Money

11. What was Eagle Steve Van Buren's nickname?

    a. Bulldog
    b. Movin' Van
    c. Bubba
    d. Truck Driver

12. Which Eagle was nicknamed 'Banana Hands'?

    a. Dick Humbert
    b. Bill Hewitt
    c. Wes Hopkins
    d. Toy Ledbetter

13. Which Eagles player in the '40s was nicknamed 'Tubby'?

    a. Bill Hewitt
    b. Al Thacker
    c. Ted Williams
    d. Tommy Thompson

14. Which Eagles player was nicknamed 'Rebel'?

    a. Milt Trost
    b. Ray Graves
    c. Joe Carter
    d. Wes McAfee

15. Which Eagles player was nicknamed 'Slingshot'?

    a. Davey O'Brien
    b. Vic Sears
    c. Joe Muha
    d. Cliff Patton   answers on page 373

NICKNAMES FROM THE '50s

1. Which Eagles defensive tackle was nicknamed 'Swamp Fox'?

    a. Ed Khayat
    b. Jess Richardson
    c. Marion Campbell
    d. Erwin Will

2. Which Eagles player was nicknamed 'The Sheriff'?

    a. Bobby Walston
    b. Ed Cooke
    c. Billy Hix
    d. Joe Restic

3. Which Eagles player was nicknamed 'Abe'?

    a. Bobby Thomason
    b. George Taliaferro
    c. John Rauch
    d. Adrian Burk

4. What was Eagle Pete Retzlaff's nickname?

    a. The Baron
    b. Reds
    c. The Bullet
    d. The Comish

5. What was Eagle Norm Willey's nickname?

    a. The Plow
    b. Wild Man
    c. The Horse
    d. Bull

6. What was Eagle Willie Irvin's nickname?

    a. Sunshine
    b. Truck Driver
    c. Big Train
    d. Bubba

7. What was Eagle Ed Meadow's nickname?

    a. Tank
    b. Country
    c. Bulldog
    d. Rocket

8. Which Eagles player was nicknamed 'Rocky'?

    a. John Ryan
    b. Bill Stribling
    c. Jerry Wilson
    d. John Bredice

9. Which Eagles player was nicknamed 'Killer'?

    a. Bill Koman
    b. Ken Keller
    c. Don King
    d. Bob Kelley

10. Which Eagle player was nicknamed 'Bullet'?

     a. Billy Barnes
     b. Clyde Scott
     c. Jack Ferrante
     d. Walt Stickel

11. Which Eagles player was nicknamed 'Smackover'?

     a. Frank Ziegler
     b. Buist Warren
     c. Clyde Scott
     d. Alvin Thacker

12. Which Eagles player was nicknamed 'Gummy'?

     a. Jim Carr
     b. Tommy McDonald
     c. Clyde Scott
     d. Don Stevens

13. What was Eagle Clarence Peaks's nickname?

     a. Gumby
     b. Slick
     c. High
     d. Felix

14. Which Eagles player was nicknamed 'Lum'?

     a. Ken Snyder
     b. Al Pollard
     c. Jerry Norton
     d. Adrian Burk

15. Which Eagles player was nicknamed 'Jumbo'?

     a. Mike Jarmoluk
     b. Neil Worden
     c. John Huzvar   answers on page 374
     d. Frank Wydo

NICKNAMES FROM THE '60s

1. What was Eagle Bob Brown's nickname?

     a. Bulldozer
     b. Brick
     c. Blaze
     d. Boomer

2. Which Eagles player was nicknamed 'Concrete Charlie'?

     a. Billy Barnes
     b. Chuck Bednarik
     c. Chuck Weber
     d. Chuck Hughes

3. Which Eagles player was nicknamed 'Iron Mike'?

     a. Mike Clark
     b. Mike Dirks
     c. Mike McClellan
     d. Mike Ditka

4. What was Eagle Bobby Walston's nickname?

     a. The Sheriff
     b. The Rustler
     c. Wrangler
     d. Maverick

5. Which Eagles player was nicknamed 'Juggie'?

     a. Ed Blaine
     b. Lynn Hoyem
     c. Alvin Haymond
     d. Jim Nettles

6. Which Eagles player was nicknamed 'Hopalong'?

    a. Ernie Calloway
    b. Howard Cassady
    c. Bill Hobbs
    d. Harry Wilson

7. What was Eagle Norman Snead's nickname?

    a. Nutty
    b. Crusin'
    c. Foreman
    d. Stormin'

8. Which Eagles player was nicknamed 'Blade'?

    a. Ben Hawkins
    b. Tim Brown
    c. Don Burroughs
    d. Ed Blaine

9. What was Eagle Mike Clark's nickname?

    a. Onside
    b. Hammer
    c. Bark
    d. Sweetness

10. Which Eagles player was nicknamed 'Goose'?

    a. Bob Freeman
    b. Earl Gros
    c. Ollie Matson
    d. George Tarasovic

11. What was Eagle Ron Blye's nickname?

    a. Birdie
    b. Super Fly
    c. Die Hard
    d. Bye Bye

12. Which Eagles player was nicknamed 'Golden Greek'?

    a. Dick Chapura
    b. John Mellekas
    c. Lou Ghecas
    d. Ben Agajanian

13. What was Eagle Glenn Glass's nickname?

    a. Brick
    b. Red
    c. Gigi
    d. Bubble

12. What was Eagle Dwight Kelley's nickname?

    a. Iron Man
    b. Cyclone
    c. Duke
    d. Ike   answers on page 374

NICKNAMES FROM THE '70S

1. Who is credited with giving Eagle Ron Jaworski with the nickname 'Jaws'?

    a. Doug Collins
    b. Dick Vermeil
    c. Charlie Young
    d. Bill Bergey

2. Bill Dunstan played for the Eagles from 1973 through 1976. What was his nickname?

    a. Popeye
    b. The Destroyer
    c. The Fridge
    d. Bull Dog

3. Which Eagles player was nicknamed 'Big Foot'?

    a. Mike Horan
    b. Tony Franklin
    c. Dennis Harrison
    d. Ray Ellis

4. What was Eagle Tom Sullivan's nickname?

    a. Sly
    b. Slick
    c. Silky
    d. Silver Bullet

5. Which Eagle was nicknamed 'Big Bird'?

    a. Joe Lavender
    b. Joe Pisarcik
    c. Alex Wojciechowicz
    d. Clyde Simmons

6. What was Eagle Charles Young's nickname?

    a. Spring
    b. Tree
    c. Tank
    d. Hawk

7. Which Eagles player was nicknamed 'Panther'?

    a. Tony Baker
    b. Leroy Keyes
    c. Sonny Davis
    d. Richard Harris

8. Which Eagles player was nicknamed 'Bubba'?

    a. Harold Jackson
    b. John Spagnola
    c. Bill Bergey
    d. Scott Fitzkee

9. Which Eagles player was nicknamed 'Frito Bandito'?

    a. John Bunting
    b. Dick Hart
    c. Vince Papale
    d. Joe Jones

10. Which Eagles player was nicknamed 'T-Bone'?

    a. Stan Walters
    b. Jerry Sisemore
    c. Artimus Parker
    d. Nate Ramsey   answers on page 375

NICKNAMES FROM THE '80s

1. Which Eagles player was nicknamed 'Pillsbury Doughboy'?

    a. Ron Solt
    b. David Alexander
    c. Evan Cooper
    d. Todd Bell

2. Which Eagles player was nicknamed 'Silk'?

    a. Gregg Garrity
    b. Dale Dawson
    c. Ray Ellis
    d. Mike Quick

3. Which Eagles player was nicknamed 'Gizmo'?

    a. Dave Little
    b. Ken Reeves
    c. Henry Williams
    d. Elbert Foules

4. What was Eagle Mike Reichenbach's nickname?

    a. Rock'em Sock'em
    b. Rock'em Back
    c. Rocky
    d. Rock star

5. Which Eagles player was nicknamed 'Big Foot'?

    a. Alonzo Johnson
    b. Paul McFadden
    c. Rusty Russell
    d. Dennis Harrison

6. Which Eagles player was nicknamed 'Hoagie'?

    a. Charlie Johnson
    b. Harold Carmichael
    c. Randy Logan
    d. Wes Hopkins

7. Prior to being known as 'Jaws,' what was Eagles quarterback Ron Jaworski's nickname?

    a. Loud mouth
    b. Polish rifle
    c. Heat
    d. Bum

8. Which Eagles player was nicknamed 'Trash'?

    a. Gregg Garrity
    b. Carl Hairston
    c. Ken Clarke
    d. Ray Ellis

9. What was Eagle Rich Kraynak's nickname?

    a. Big Foot
    b. Destroyer
    c. Mule
    d. Conan

10. Which Eagle was nicknamed 'Groucho'?

    a. Wally Henry
    b. Cris Carter
    c. Melvin Hoover
    d. Bill Campfield

11. His most famous nickname was 'Minister of Defense, but what other nickname was Reggie White called?

    a. Rev
    b. Freight Train
    c. Big Dog
    d. The Punisher

12. In his short stay as an Eagle what was Bill Cowher's nickname?

    a. Face
    b. Beast
    c. Mule
    d. Brusier

answers on page 375

NICKNAMES FROM THE '90s

1. Which Eagles player was nicknamed 'Mr. Automatic'?

    a. David Akers
    b. Roger Ruzek
    c. Matt Bahr
    d. Gary Anderson

2. What was Eagle Irving Fryar's nickname?

    a. Slick
    b. Hands
    c. Rev
    d. Money

3. Which Eagles player was nicknamed 'Money'?

    a. Eddie Murray
    b. Chris Boniol
    c. Tom Hutton
    d. Matt Bahr

4. Which Eagles player was nicknamed 'The FLea'?

    a. Fred Barnett
    b. Eric Allen
    c. Al Harris
    d. Michael Zordich

5. What was Eagle Vaughn Hebron's nickname?

    a. Silk
    b. Pretty Boy
    c. Trash
    d. Blade

6. Which Eagles player was nicknamed 'Refrigerator'?

    a. Andy Harmon
    b. Jermane Mayberry
    c. William Perry
    d. Bernard Williams

7. Which Eagle was nicknamed 'Troup?'

    a. Ed Jasper
    b. Tim Harris
    c. Frank Cornish
    d. Michael Samson

8. Which Eagles player was nicknamed 'K-Mart'?

    a. Kevin Turner
    b. Eddie Murray
    c. Cecil Martin
    d. Kelvin Martin

9. What was Eagle Heath Sherman's nickname?

  a. Wolfman
  b. Moose
  c. Rock
  d. Tank

10. Which Eagles player was nicknamed 'Cheeseburger'?

  a. Hugh Douglas
  b. William Perry
  c. Al Harris
  d. Chad Lewis

11. What was Eagle Izell Jenkins's nickname?

  a. Slick
  b. Rock-n-Roll
  c. Toast
  d. Smackover

12. Which Eagles player was nicknamed 'Freight Train'?

  a. Jerome Brown
  b. Seth Joyner
  c. Charlie Garner
  d. Troy Vincent

13. Which Eagles player was nicknamed 'Buddy Lee'?

  a. Seth Joyner
  b. Dennis McKnight
  c. Duce Staley
  d. Al Harris

answers on page 376

NICKNAMES OF THE 21st CENTURY

1. Which Eagles player nicknamed Hank Fraley with the name 'Honey Buns'?

   a. Mike Bartrum
   b. Paul Grasmanis
   c. Hugh Douglas
   d. Tra Thomas

2. What is Eagle David Akers's nickname?

   a. Money
   b. Clutch
   c. Green
   d. Steady

3. What is Eagle Nate Wayne's nickname?

   a. Bumps
   b. Tank
   c. Freight Train
   d. Meat

4. What is Eagle Jevon Kearse's nickname?

   a. The Bull
   b. The Freak
   c. Wildman
   d. Sack Attack

5. What was Eagle Corey Simon's nickname?

   a. Pooh Bear
   b. Mack Truck
   c. Bulldozer
   d. Bubba

6. What is Eagle Sam Rayburn's nickname?

    a. Sam I Am
    b. Truck Driver
    c. Beast
    d. Ray O Sack

7. Which Eagles player is nicknamed 'Full Throttle'?

    a. Calvin Williams
    b. Jason Short
    c. Andre Waters
    d. David Alexander

8. What was Eagle Brian Mitchell's nickname?

    a. Twinkle Toes
    b. Speedster
    c. Mitch
    d. Mr. Bigglesworth

9. Which Eagles player had the nicknamed 'He Hate Me'?

    a. Freddie Mitchell
    b. Terrell Owens
    c. Rod Smart
    d. Todd Pinkston

10. Which Eagles player was nicknamed 'The Axeman'?

    a. Ike Reese
    b. Jeremiah Trotter
    c. Paul Grasmanis
    d. Tim Hauck

11. Which Eagles player was nicknamed 'The General' by ESPN's Chris Berman?

    a. Reggie Brown
    b. Jon Runyan

c. Mike Bartrum
d. Correll Buckhalter

12. What was Eagle Dorsey Levens's nickname?

a. Horse
b. Ox
c. Tank
d. Bulldozer

13. What is Eagles head coach Andy Reid's nickname?

a. Buns
b. Barrel
c. Brutis
d. Big Red

14. What is the nickname of these four guys?

a. The Eagle-ettes
b. The 700 level guys
c. The Iggles Nest
d. The Eagles Pep Band

answers on page 376

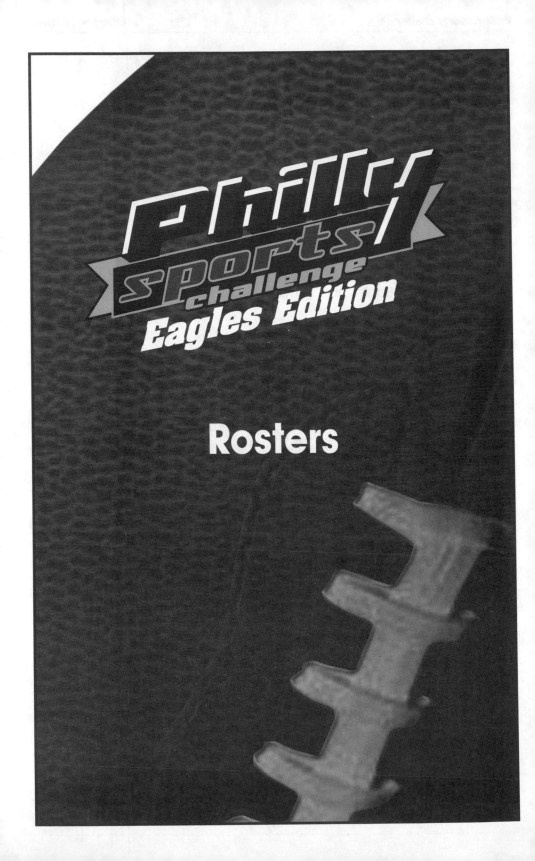

Philly Sports Challenge

Eagles Edition

Rosters

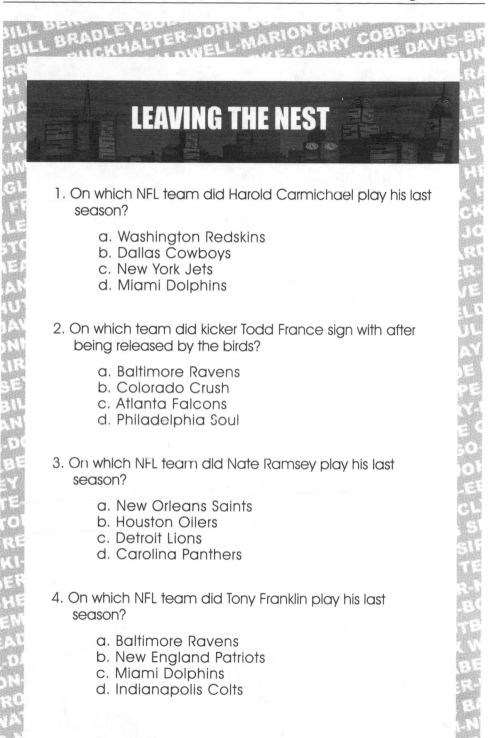

LEAVING THE NEST

1. On which NFL team did Harold Carmichael play his last season?

    a. Washington Redskins
    b. Dallas Cowboys
    c. New York Jets
    d. Miami Dolphins

2. On which team did kicker Todd France sign with after being released by the birds?

    a. Baltimore Ravens
    b. Colorado Crush
    c. Atlanta Falcons
    d. Philadelphia Soul

3. On which NFL team did Nate Ramsey play his last season?

    a. New Orleans Saints
    b. Houston Oilers
    c. Detroit Lions
    d. Carolina Panthers

4. On which NFL team did Tony Franklin play his last season?

    a. Baltimore Ravens
    b. New England Patriots
    c. Miami Dolphins
    d. Indianapolis Colts

5. On which NFL team did Ron Jaworski play his last season?

   a. Miami Dolphins
   b. Phoenix Cardinals
   c. Atlanta Falcons
   d. Kansas City Chiefs

6. On which NFL team did Tom Brookshier play his last season?

   a. New York Giants
   b. Cleveland Browns
   c. Buffalo Bills
   d. Philadelphia Eagles

7. Which Eagles player became a probation officer upon ending his football career?

   a. Mike Morgan
   b. Bernard Wilson
   c. Tim Brown
   d. Mel Tom

8. Which former Eagles player joined the FBI after retiring from the team?

   a. Bosh Pritchard
   b. Vic Sears
   c. Tommy Thompson
   d. Davey O'Brien

9. On which NFL team did Bill Bradley play his last season?

   a. Cincinnati Bengals
   b. San Diego Chargers
   c. St. Louis Cardinals
   d. New Orleans Saints

10. On which NFL team did Ed Khayat play his last season?

    a. Chicago Bears
    b. New York Jets
    c. Boston Patriots
    d. Washington Redskins

11. On which NFL team did Maxie Baughan play his last season?

    a. Washington Redskins
    b. Chicago Cardinals
    c. Oakland Raiders
    d. Los Angeles Rams

12. On which NFL team did Tommy McDonald play his last season?

    a. Cleveland Browns
    b. Dallas Cowboys
    c. Atlanta Falcons
    d. Los Angeles Rams

13. On which NFL team did Russ Craft play his last season?

    a. Cleveland Browns
    b. Atlanta Falcons
    c. Pittsburgh Steelers
    d. Philadelphia Eagles

14. On which NFL team did Glenn Campbell play his last season?

    a. Philadelphia Eagles
    b. New York Giants
    c. Pittsburgh Pirates
    d. Boston Yanks

15. On which NFL team did Bosh Pritchard play his last season?

   a. Boston Yanks
   b. New York Giants
   c. Brooklyn Tigers
   d. Cleveland Rams

16. On which NFL team did Herm Edwards play his last season?

   a. Seattle Seahawks
   b. Carolina Panthers
   c. Atlanta Falcons
   d. Los Angeles Rams

17. On which NFL team did Billy Campfield play his last season?

   a. New York Giants
   b. Philadelphia Eagles
   c. Washington Redskins
   d. Atlanta Falcons

18. On which NFL team did Frank LeMaster play his last season?

   a. Washington Redskins
   b. Philadelphia Eagles
   c. Detroit Lions
   d. Oakland Raiders

19. On which NFL team did Brian Mitchell play his last season?

   a. Philadelphia Eagles
   b. Washington Redskins
   c. Baltimore Ravens
   d. New York Giants

20. On which NFL team did Cecil Martin play his last season?

    a. Tampa Bay Buccaneers
    b. Washington Redskins
    c. Baltimore Ravens
    d. New York Jets

21. On which NFL team did Randall Cunningham play his last season?

    a. Baltimore Ravens
    b. Phoenix Cardinals
    c. Dallas Cowboys
    d. Minnesota Vikings

22. On which NFL team did Mike Caldwell play his last season?

    a. Cleveland Browns
    b. Carolina Panthers
    c. Arizona Cardinals
    d. Seattle Seahawks

23. On which NFL team did Keith Byars play his last season?

    a. Miami Dolphins
    b. New England Patriots
    c. New York Jets
    d. Tennessee Titans

24. On which NFL team did Carl Hairston play his last season?

    a. Phoenix Cardinals
    b. Cleveland Browns
    c. Philadelphia Eagles
    d. Miami Dolphins

25. On which NFL team did Eric Allen play his last season?

    a. New Orleans Saints
    b. New York Jets
    c. Oakland Raiders
    d. Miami Dolphins

26. With which NFL team did Reggie White sign after the Eagles?

    a. Tennessee Titans
    b. Green Bay Packers
    c. Washington Redskins
    d. New Orleans Saints

27. On which NFL team did Swede Hanson play his last season?

    a. Pittsburgh Pirates
    b. Boston Yanks
    c. Philadelphia Eagles
    d. Chicago Cardinals

28. On which NFL team did Vic Lindskog play his last season?

    a. Baltimore Colts
    b. New York Giants
    c. Philadelphia Eagles
    d. Cleveland Browns

29. On which NFL team did Dick Bielski play his last season?

    a. New York Titans
    b. Dallas Cowboys
    c. Denver Broncos
    d. Baltimore Colts

30. On which NFL team did Billy Barnes play his last season?

    a. Minnesota Vikings
    b. Green Bay Packers
    c. Washington Redskins
    d. Philadelphia Eagles

31. Former Eagles player Herm Edwards landed his first head coaching job for which NFL team?

    a. New York Jets
    b. Atlanta Falcons
    c. New York Giants
    d. Detroit Lions

32. On which NFL team did John Cappelletti play his last season?

    a. Los Angeles Rams
    b. San Diego Chargers
    c. Denver Broncos
    d. Cincinnati Bengals

33. Quarterback Mike McMahon was released by the Eagles and picked up by which team for the 2006 season?

    a. New Orleans Saints
    b. Chicago Bears
    c. Tampa Bay Buccaneers
    d. Minnesota Vikings

34. On which NFL team did Louie Gammona play his last season?

    a. Dallas Cowboys
    b. New York Jets
    c. Philadelphia Eagles
    d. Phoenix Cardinals

35. Which former Eagles player ended his football career coaching an NFL team, where he only won three games in his two-year tenure?

    a. John Reaves
    b. Jim Ringo
    c. Jim McMahon
    d. John Sciarra

answers on page 377

ARE YOU SURE THAT'S MY NUMBER

1. What was Bill Cowher's uniform number while playing for the Eagles?

    a. 57
    b. 63
    c. 71
    d. 78

2. Which one of the following Eagles players did not wear the number 13 jersey?

    a. Leonard Barnum
    b. Rick Engles
    c. Dan Sandifer
    d. George Kenneally

3. Which of the following Eagles players did not wear uniform number 33?

    a. Russ Craft
    b. Billy Ray Barnes
    c. Ollie Matson
    d. Bosh Pritchard

4. What jersey number was middle linebacker Mark Simoneau wearing for the 2004-05 Eagles season?

    a. 50
    b. 53
    c. 59
    d. 77

5. What was Pete Retzlaff's uniform number while playing for the Eagles?

    a. 34
    b. 39
    c. 44
    d. 47

6. What was Eagles linebacker Ray Farmer's uniform number?

    a. 50
    b. 51
    c. 53
    d. 55

7. What uniform number did Irv Cross wear while playing for the Eagles?

    a. 22
    b. 25
    c. 27
    d. 33

8. What uniform number did Bud Grant wear while playing for the Eagles?

    a. 68
    b. 72
    c. 77
    d. 86

9. What uniform number did Rhett Hall wear while playing for the Eagles?

   a. 91
   b. 93
   c. 97
   d. 98

10. What uniform number did Frank LeMaster wear while playing for the Eagles?

   a. 50
   b. 55
   c. 62
   d. 67

11. What uniform number did Jim Weatherall wear while playing for the Eagles?

   a. 69
   b. 73
   c. 77
   d. 84

12. What uniform number did kicker Luis Zendejas wear while playing for the Eagles?

   a. 3
   b. 8
   c. 11
   d. 14

13. What uniform number did Cecil Martin wear while playing for the Eagles?

   a. 38
   b. 42
   c. 47
   d. 53

14. What uniform number did James Willis wear while playing for the Eagles?

     a. 50
     b. 55
     c. 57
     d. 59

15. What uniform number did quarterback Rick Arrington wear while playing for the Eagles?

     a. 5
     b. 9
     c. 11
     d. 16

16. Who is the Eagle wearing jersey number 55 pictured above?

     a. Frank LeMaster
     b. Mike Reichenbach
     c. Ray Farmer
     d. Maxie Baughan   answers on page 378

BEFORE THE BIRDS

1. Which team did Dirk Johnson play for before joining the Eagles?

    a. New York Giants
    b. New England Patriots
    c. New York Jets
    d. New Orleans Saints

2. Which team did Jim Ringo play for before becoming an Eagle?

    a. Green Bay Packers
    b. St. Louis Cardinals
    c. Pittsburgh Steelers
    d. Cleveland Browns

3. Which team did Via Sikahema play for before becoming an Eagle?

    a. Los Angeles Rams
    b. Phoenix Cardinals
    c. Green Bay Packers
    d. Washington Redskins

4. Which team did Kevin Turner play for before becoming an Eagle?

    a. San Diego Chargers
    b. Buffalo Bills
    c. Denver Broncos
    d. New England Patriots

5. Which team did Ricky Watters play for before becoming an Eagle?

    a. San Francisco 49ers
    b. Indianapolis Colts
    c. Seattle Seahawks
    d. Jacksonville Jaguars

6. Which team did Jeff Feagles play for before becoming an Eagle?

    a. New York Giants
    b. Seattle Seahawks
    c. New England Patriots
    d. Kansas City Chiefs

7. Which team did William Frizzell play for before becoming an Eagle?

    a. Detroit Lions
    b. Pittsburgh Steelers
    c. Miami Dolphins
    d. Carolina Panthers

8. Which team did Ron Heller play for before becoming an Eagle?

    a. Miami Dolphins
    b. Was a free agent
    c. Tampa Bay Buccaneers
    d. Atlanta Falcons

9. Which team did Nick Mike-Mayer play for before becoming an Eagle?

    a. Cleveland Browns
    b. Atlanta Falcons
    c. St. Louis Rams
    d. Buffalo Bills

10. Which team did horst Muhlmann play for before becoming an Eagle?

   a. Dallas Cowboys
   b. Washington Redskins
   c. Cincinnati Bengals
   d. Kansas City Chiefs

11. Which team did Manny Sistrunk play for before becoming an Eagle?

   a. New England Patriots
   b. Washington Redskins
   c. New York Jets
   d. Buffalo Bills

12. Which team did Stan Walters play for before becoming an Eagle?

   a. Was a free agent
   b. Washington Redskins
   c. Minnesota Vikings
   d. Cincinnati Reds

13. Which team did Ty Detmer play for before becoming an Eagles player?

   a. Miami Dolphins
   b. Green Bay Packers
   c. San Francisco 49ers
   d. Cleveland Browns

14. Which team did Carlos Emmons play for before becoming an Eagle?

   a. Houston Texans
   b. Carolina Panthers
   c. Pittsburgh Steelers
   d. New York Giants

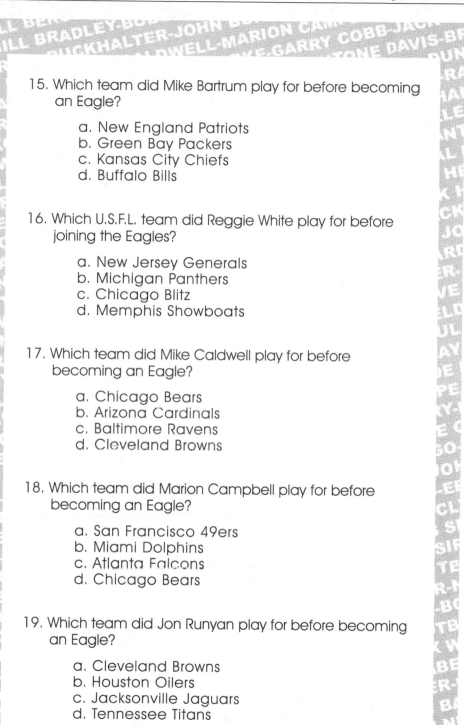

15. Which team did Mike Bartrum play for before becoming an Eagle?

    a. New England Patriots
    b. Green Bay Packers
    c. Kansas City Chiefs
    d. Buffalo Bills

16. Which U.S.F.L. team did Reggie White play for before joining the Eagles?

    a. New Jersey Generals
    b. Michigan Panthers
    c. Chicago Blitz
    d. Memphis Showboats

17. Which team did Mike Caldwell play for before becoming an Eagle?

    a. Chicago Bears
    b. Arizona Cardinals
    c. Baltimore Ravens
    d. Cleveland Browns

18. Which team did Marion Campbell play for before becoming an Eagle?

    a. San Francisco 49ers
    b. Miami Dolphins
    c. Atlanta Falcons
    d. Chicago Bears

19. Which team did Jon Runyan play for before becoming an Eagle?

    a. Cleveland Browns
    b. Houston Oilers
    c. Jacksonville Jaguars
    d. Tennessee Titans

20. Which team did Sean Landeta play for before becoming an Eagle?

    a. Green Bay Packers
    b. New York Giants
    c. New York Jets
    d. St. Louis Rams

21. Which team did Dhani Jones play for before becoming an Eagle?

    a. San Francisco 49ers
    b. Carolina Panthers
    c. New York Giants
    d. Tampa Bay Buccaneers

22. Which team did Steve Everitt play for before becoming an Eagle?

    a. Baltimore Ravens
    b. Cleveland Browns
    c. St. Louis Rams
    d. Washington Redskins

23. Which team did Irving Fryar play for before becoming an Eagle?

    a. New England Patriots
    b. Jacksonville Jaguars
    c. Washington Redskins
    d. Miami Dolphins

24. Which team did Louie Gammona play for before becoming an Eagle?

    a. Dallas Cowboys
    b. Cincinnati Bengals
    c. New York Jets
    d. New Orleans Saints

25. Which team did Tom Dempsey play for before becoming an Eagle?

    a. Los Angeles Rams
    b. New Orleans Saints
    c. Houston Oilers
    d. Buffalo Bills

26. Which team did Mike Ditka play for before becoming an Eagle?

    a. Pittsburgh Steelers
    b. Chicago Bears
    c. Dallas Cowboys
    d. Cincinnati Bengals

27. Which team did Juqua Thomas play for before becoming an Eagle?

    a. New York Giants
    b. Baltimore Ravens
    c. Arizona Cardinals
    d. Tennessee Titans

28. Which team did Ty Detmer play for before becoming an Eagle?

    a. Detroit Lions
    b. Cleveland Browns
    c. Green Bay Packers
    d. Arizona Cardinals

29. Which team did Rodney Peete play for before becoming an Eagle?

    a. Detroit Lions
    b. Dallas Cowboys
    c. Washington Redskins
    d. Carolina Panthers

answers on page 379

BIRDS OF A DIFFERENT FEATHER

1. Former Eagle Marion Campbell flapped his wings coaching which team?

   a. Baltimore Ravens
   b. Atlanta Falcons
   c. Seattle Seahawks
   d. Arizona Cardinals

2. Former Eagle Bobby Walston ended his football career on which birds' team?

   a. Seattle Seahawks
   b. St. Louis Cardinals
   c. Atlanta Falcons
   d. Philadelphia Eagles

3. Former Eagle Norm Van Brocklin soared like an eagle coaching this NFL team until he retired from football?

   a. Seattle Seahawks
   b. Chicago Cardinals
   c. St. Louis Cardinals
   d. Atlanta Falcons

4. Former Eagle Don Owens ended his football career on which birds' team?

   a. St. Louis Cardinals
   b. Chicago Cardinals
   c. Phoenix Cardinals
   d. Atlanta Falcons

5. Former Eagle quarterback King Hill ended his career perched on which NFL team?

    a. Seattle Seahawks
    b. Philadelphia Eagles
    c. St. Louis Cardinals
    d. Atlanta Falcons

6. Former Eagle Tom Woodeshick ended his football career with which birds' team?

    a. St. Louis Cardinals
    b. Atlanta Falcons
    c. Philadelphia Eagles
    d. Seattle Seahawks

7. Before coaching the Eagles, Joe Kuharich started his coaching career with which team?

    a. Chicago Cardinals
    b. Baltimore Ravens
    c. Seattle Seahawks
    d. Atlanta Falcons

8. Former Eagle Bill Bradley ended his football career on which birds' team?

    a. Atlanta Falcons
    b. Seattle Seahawks
    c. Philadelphia Eagles
    d. St. Louis Cardinals

9. Former Eagle Harold Jackson flew over to which team to finish his football career?

    a. Seattle Seahawks
    b. Phoenix Cardinals
    c. Atlanta Falcons
    d. St. Louis Cardinals

10. Mike McCormack started coaching with the Philadelphia Eagles and ended his coaching career with which team?

    a. Arizona Cardinals
    b. Seattle Seahawks
    c. Atlanta Falcons
    d. Baltimore Ravens

11. Charlie Young started his football career playing on the Eagles and ended it on which other birds team?

    a. Seattle Seahawks
    b. Atlanta Falcons
    c. Arizona Cardinals
    d. St. Louis Cardinals

12. Former Eagle Keith Krepfle ended his flying career with which team?

    a. Phoenix Cardinals
    b. Baltimore Ravens
    c. Atlanta Falcons
    d. Philadelphia Eagles

13. Prior to playing for the Eagles, on which feathery team did Art Malone start his pro football career?

    a. Atlanta Falcons
    b. Seattle Seahawks
    c. Chicago Cardinals
    d. St. Louis Cardinals

14. Carl Hairston started his pro football career with the Eagles and ended flying with which birds team?

    a. Baltimore Ravens
    b. Phoenix Cardinals
    c. Atlanta Falcons
    d. Seattle Seahawks

15. Herm Edwards started soaring with the Eagles and ended his football days flying with which team?

    a. Baltimore Ravens
    b. Seattle Seahawks
    c. Atlanta Falcons
    d. Phoenix Cardinals

answers on page 380

BROTHERS

1. Several Eagles players had brothers that played in the NFL. Name Randall Cunningham's brother.

    a. Sam
    b. Tony
    c. Reggie
    d. Charley

2. Eagle Mike Golic had one brother who played in the NFL. What was his name?

    a. Matt
    b. James
    c. Bob
    d. Frank

3. Name Eagle Nick Mike-Mayer's brother.

    a. William
    b. Steve
    c. James
    d. Colin

4. Eagle Jerome McDougle had one brother who played in the NFL. What was his name?

    a. Reggie
    b. James
    c. Elwyn
    d. Stockar

5. Name former Eagle Tim Hasselback's brother.

    a. Don
    b. Scott
    c. Bill
    d. Jim

6. Eagle Antwuan Wyatt had one brother who played in the NFL. What was his name?

    a. Charley
    b. Richard
    c. Alvin
    d. Wayne

7. Name former Eagle Matt Bahr's brother.

    a. Eric
    b. Stan
    c. Ken
    d. Chris

8. Eagle Ed Khayat had one brother who played in the NFL. What was his name?

    a. Jim
    b. Bob
    c. Nick
    d. Dan

9. Name former Eagle Steve Van Buren's brother.

    a. Ebert
    b. Mark
    c. Michael
    d. Henry

10. Eagle Leo Stasica had one brother who played in the NFL. What was his name?

    a. Benny
    b. Eddie
    c. Stan
    d. David   answers on page 380

COWBOYS WHO LEARNED TO FLY

1. Which of the following football players once played for the Dallas Cowboys and then became an Eagle?

    a. Frank Clarke
    b. Keith Adams
    c. Ed Husmann
    d. Garry Cobb

2. Which of the following football players once played for the Dallas Cowboys and then became an Eagle?

    a. Jimmie Jones
    b. Don Heinrich
    c. Bob Bercich
    d. Lynn Howton

3. Which of the following football players once played for the Dallas Cowboys and then became an Eagle?

a. Chuck Howley
b. Broderick Thompson
c. Don Bishop
d. John Wilbur

4. Which of the following football players once played for the Dallas Cowboys and then became an Eagle?

a. David McDaniels
b. Mike Clark
c. Jerry Norton
d. George Hegamin

5. Which of the following football players once played for the Dallas Cowboys and then became an Eagle?

a. Dick Bielski
b. Obert Logan
c. Roger Ruzek
d. Bryan Barker

6. Which of the following football players once played for the Dallas Cowboys and then became an Eagle?

a. George Andrie
b. Jethro Pugh
c. Brian Baldinger
d. Dave Edwards

7. Which of the following football players once played for the Dallas Cowboys and then became an Eagle?

a. Walt Garrison
b. Dave Manders
c. Don Perkins
d. Rodney Peete

8. Which of the following football players once played for the Dallas Cowboys and then became an Eagle?

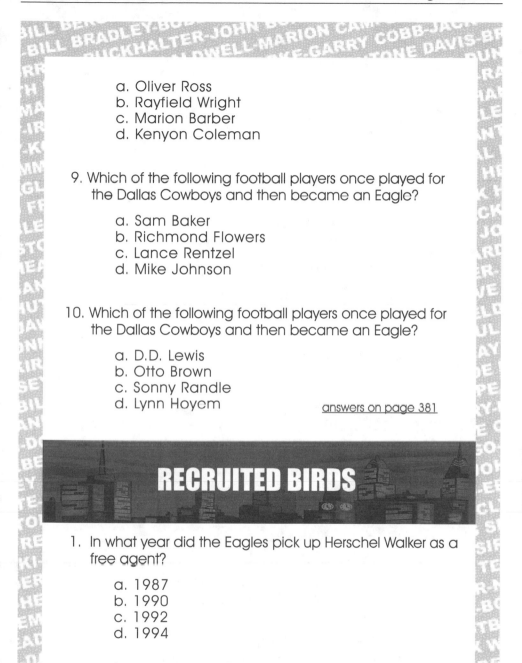

a. Oliver Ross
b. Rayfield Wright
c. Marion Barber
d. Kenyon Coleman

9. Which of the following football players once played for the Dallas Cowboys and then became an Eagle?

a. Sam Baker
b. Richmond Flowers
c. Lance Rentzel
d. Mike Johnson

10. Which of the following football players once played for the Dallas Cowboys and then became an Eagle?

a. D.D. Lewis
b. Otto Brown
c. Sonny Randle
d. Lynn Hoyem

answers on page 381

RECRUITED BIRDS

1. In what year did the Eagles pick up Herschel Walker as a free agent?

a. 1987
b. 1990
c. 1992
d. 1994

2. In 1993 the Eagles signed rookie free agent Vaughn Hebron. He played his college football at which college?

   a. Grambling
   b. Virginia Tech
   c. Indiana
   d. Nebraska

3. For the 2000 season, which one of the following Eagles was not picked up as a free agent?

   a. Mike Bartrum
   b. Paul Grasmanis
   c. Hank Fraley
   d. Jon Runyan

4. Which one of these Eagle players was acquired off waivers?

   a. L.J. Smith
   b. Mark Simoneau
   c. Roderick Hood
   d. Keith Adams

5. In 2003, which one of the following players was not originally signed by the Eagles as a rookie free agent?

   a. L.J. Smith
   b. Roderick Hood
   c. Reno Mahe
   d. Sam Rayburn

6. Which NFL team cut Joe Scarpati, allowing the Eagles to sign him as an undrafted free agent?

   a. Dallas Cowboys
   b. Green Bay Packers
   c. Washington Redskins
   d. Los Angeles Rams

7. In 2001 the Eagles signed rookie free agent Josh Parry. He played his college football at which college?

    a. Tulsa
    b. Clemson
    c. San Jose State
    d. Iowa

8. Quarterback Jay Fiedler was signed by the Eagles as a rookie free agent after attending which college?

    a. Clemson
    b. Dartmouth
    c. Princeton
    d. Illinois

9. Hollis Thomas was signed as a rookie free agent by the Eagles after playing his college football where?

    a. Syracuse
    b. Memphis
    c. North Illinois
    d. Tennessee

10. In 2004 the Eagles signed rookie free agent Mike Labinjo. He played his college football at which college?

    a. Michigan State
    b. UCLA
    c. Eastern Kentucky
    d. Georgia Tech

answers on page 381

FIRST ROUND PICKS

```
F I K A P R A H S P I K S M K Y
R N E D R O W L I E N E W R M C
O W R T R B A R T J O N E S S A
E O A E E M H A R R Y G R A N T
S R J E R L O P R Z J N D G J S
S B O B P E L L E G R I N I N N
A E H M I R R A I T N Y A W L A
M M N C E E T Q M O E L N O E R
F O Y O A S N R T S U C W E B I
R R O E J H I R A M E G A A A S
A E N B C Y U S A T E I H S Z A
N J A I B B R M Y Y H C S M E L
C C K T N Y E R E R E O H S V H
I M E O R K A S A O R R M R E R
S P R M I I F J I H J E H A T J
E M L M I K E Q U I C K J E S H
```

ArtJones	BobPellegrini	HarryGrant	HarryJones
JeromeBrown	JerrySisemore	JessieSmall	JoeMuha
JohnYonaker	MikeMamula	MikeQuick	NeilWorden
PeteCase	RonBurton	SamFrancis	ShawnAndrews
SiranStacy	SkipSharp	SteveZabel	TraThomas

<u>answers on page 429</u>

EAGLES FIRST ROUND

1. Prior to Mike Patterson, who was the last defensive lineman that the Eagles drafted in the first round?

    a. Derrick Burgress
    b. Jerome Brown
    c. Mike Mamula
    d. Jerome McDougle

2. Who was the Eagles' first ever first round draft selection?

    a. Dave Smukler
    b. Thomas Hanson
    c. Jay Berwanger
    d. Jack Hinkle

3. Who was the Eagles' first round draft pick in the 1957 draft?

    a. Clarence Peaks
    b. Dick Bielski
    c. Art baker
    d. J.D. Smith

4. Who did the Eagles select ahead of Randall Cunningham in the 1985 draft?

    a. Seth Joyner
    b. Kevin Allen
    c. Stan Walters
    d. Mike Golic

5. Who was the Eagles' first round draft selection in 1996?

    a. Jason Dunn
    b. Bobby Hoying

     c. Brian Dawkins
     d. Jermane Mayberry

6.   In what year was Jerome Brown drafted as the Eagles'
      number one pick?

     a. 1985
     b. 1986
     c. 1987
     d. 1988

7.   Which All-American defensive end did the Eagles draft
      in the first round, only to move him to the offensive line
      (where he failed)?

     a. Pete Pihos
     b. Stan Walters
     c. Antone Davis
     d. Leonard Mitchell

8.   Who is the first round draft selection pictured with Eagles
      trainer Otho Davis?

     a. Leonard Mitchell
     b. Roynell Young
     c. Jerry Robinson
     d. Michael Haddix

9. Which of the following Eagles players was not a first round draft selection?

    a. Jermane Mayberry
    b. Tra Thomas
    c. Corey Simon
    d. Brian Dawkins

10. Who was the Eagles' first round draft pick in the 1992 draft?

    a. Lester Holmes
    b. Siran Stacy
    c. Didn't have one
    d. Antone Davis

11. In what year was John Yonaker the Eagles' first round draft pick?

    a. 1941
    b. 1945
    c. 1948
    d. 1955

12. Which of the following Eagles quarterbacks was not drafted in the first round?

    a. Davey O'Brien
    b. Frank Tripucka
    c. John Reaves
    d. Norm Snead

13. Who was the Eagles' first round draft pick in the 1990 draft?

    a. Ben Smith
    b. John Welbourn
    c. Harper Lebel
    d. Jeff Kemp

14. Since 1936 through 2005 how many years did the Eagles not have a first round draft selection?

       a. 6
       b. 9
       c. 11
       d. 14

15. Who was the Eagles' first round draft pick in the 1997 draft?

       a. Tra Thomas
       b. Jermane Mayberry
       c. Corey Simon
       d. Jon Harris   answers on page 382

EUROPEAN BIRDS

1. In 1999, David Akers played on which NFL Europe team?

       a. Cologne Centurions
       b. Amsterdam Admirals
       c. Hamburg Sea Devils
       d. Berlin Thunder

2. On which NFL Europe team did Eagle Jason Short play?

       a. Barcelona Dragons
       b. Berlin Thunder
       c. Cologne Centurions
       d. Hamburg Sea Devils

3. Which NFL Europe team kept Eagle Andy Hall on the club's practice squad for an entire season?

    a. Frankfurt Galaxy
    b. Berlin Thunder
    c. Rhein Fire
    d. Amsterdam Admirals

4. Which one of the following Eagles players did not play for the Berlin Thunder?

    a. Keith Adams
    b. Eric McCoo
    c. Robert Redd
    d. Josh Parry

5. Kicker Dirk Johnson played on which NFL Europe team?

    a. Hamburg Sea Devils
    b. Rhein Fire
    c. Cologne Centurions
    d. Barcelona Dragons

6. In 2004, which one of the following players did not play on an NFL Europe team?

    a. Howard Clark
    b. Kori Dickerson
    c. Eric McCoo
    d. Dante Ellington

7. Against which NFL team did the Eagles not play a preseason game in Europe?

    a. New Orleans Saints
    b. Cleveland Browns
    c. Buffalo Bills
    d. Detroit Lions

8. Before signing with the Eagles, Todd France scored the most points in the 2005 season playing in Europe. How many points did he score?

a. 87
b. 91
c. 104
d. 108

9. Which one of the following former Eagles first round draft selections ended up playing in Europe?

a. Ben Smith
b. Jessie Small
c. Siran Stacy
d. Lester Holmes

10. While playing for Hamburg (NFL Europe) what was Todd France's longest field goal?

a. 49 yards
b. 51 yards
c. 54 yards
d. 56 yards

answers on page 3820

EAGLES TRAINING CAMPS

1. Where was the Eagles' first training camp located?

a. Atlantic City
b. West Chester
c. Reading
d. Swenksville

2. For the 1970 season, where was the Eagles' training camp located?

a. West Chester
b. Reading
c. Wilmington
d. Glassboro

3. Which college campus held the first Eagles preseason training camp?

    a. Temple University
    b. West Chester State
    c. Albright College
    d. Cheyney University

4. When did Saint Joseph's college first host the Eagles' training camp?

    a. 1936
    b. 1939
    c. 1941
    d. 1943

5. In what year did the Eagles move their training camp to Lehigh University?

    a. 1990
    b. 1992
    c. 1996
    d. 1998

6. How many consecutive years did the Eagles hold their training camp at West Chester University?

    a. 8
    b. 10
    c. 12
    d. 15

7. Which one of the following states has never hosted an Eagles training camp over the years?

    a. Wisconsin
    b. New York
    c. Minnesota
    d. Delaware

8. For two weeks in 1964, which local hotel hosted the Eagles' training camp?

    a. Holiday Inn
    b. Cherry Hill Inn
    c. Best Western Concordville
    d. Ramada Inn

9. Prior to moving the Eagles' training camp to West Chester University, where was camp held?

    a. Widener College
    b. Ursinus College
    c. Swarthmore College
    d. Cheyney University

answers on page 383

NUMBERED EAGLES

1. While playing for the Eagles, which two uniform numbers did quarterback Roman Gabriel wear?

    a. 3, 12
    b. 5, 18
    c. 7, 9
    d. 11, 14

2. Which Eagle was wearing the number 53 jersey when Hugh Douglas returned to the Eagles for the start of the 2004-05 season?

    a. Jerome McDougle
    b. Mark Simoneau
    c. Jason Short
    d. Derrick Burgess

3. What jersey number did quarterback Doug Pederson wear while playing for the Eagles?

    a. 9
    b. 12
    c. 14
    d. 17

4. After Ron Jaworski was traded from the Eagles, who was the next player to wear jersey number 7?

    a. Roger Ruzek
    b. Bobby Hoying
    c. Sean Landeta
    d. John Huarte

5. What was Garry Cobb's uniform number as an Eagles player?

    a. 50
    b. 52
    c. 57
    d. 63

6. When newly-acquired Eagle Terrell Owens joined the birds, who was wearing jersey number 81?

    a. Dameane Douglas
    b. Billy McMullen
    c. L.J. Smith
    d. Sean Morey

7. While playing for the Eagles, what was Stan Walters's uniform number?

    a. 58
    b. 62
    c. 70
    d. 75

8. Which of the following Eagles players did not wear uniform number 33?

    a. Russ Craft
    b. Billy Ray Barnes
    c. Ollie Matson
    d. Bosh Pritchard

9. What jersey number did Eagles end/kicker Bobby Walston wear?

    a. 00
    b. 68
    c. 72
    d. 83

10. What was Bill Cowher's uniform number while playing for the Eagles?

    a. 57
    b. 63
    c. 71
    d. 78

11. Which one of the following Eagles players did not wear the number 13 jersey?

    a. Leonard Barnum
    b. Rick Engles
    c. Dan Sandifer
    d. George Kenneally

12. Which one of the following Eagles players is not shown in the above photo?

    a. Leo Sugar
    b. Irv Cross
    c. Bob Pellegrini
    d. Al Davis

13. Besides Norm Van Brocklin, who on the Eagles wore uniform number 11?

    a. Tommy Thompson
    b. Adrian Burk
    c. Timmy Brown
    d. Nate Ramsey

14. What was Marion Campbell's uniform number while playing for the Eagles?

    a. 53
    b. 62
    c. 78
    d. 86

COWBOYS WHO BECAME EAGLES

```
I  G I  H L  E A N T  E O R Y O Z T  B
L  L V  N N R  S D O O R  S L R G R  L
G  E M N I  R N R A H I  O E R L O  H
V  L L E T  M T  N O C G E Y J I  G E
T  H Y B R I  A N B A L  D I  N G E R
L  S R R A R T  G C E O J  O R T  R S
I  L S A M L I  R E M L  B U T R R  C
B  E L E N N I  L T  H S R E H E U H
R  R S J I  N I  R L I  E V I  E E Z E
N  A N O V R N O R D A G H A T  E L
R  Z O H L O A H S L O M R G G K W
L  B I  N E K C M T  E H U S O H S A
A  O R R K N H R H I  V Z G L E A L
N  G R O D N E Y P E E T  E L P G K
G  O P P S B B U T  S L E I  N A D E
T  E A E O V R R O D H A R R I  S R
R  H T  R I  G Y E I  N E A H M D R P
```

BrianBaldinger	ChrisBoniol	DanielStubbs
GeorgeHegamin	HerschelWalker	JohnRoper
KelvinMartin	MerrillDouglas	RobertLavette
RodHarris	RodneyPeete	RogerRuzek

answers on page 425

15. Roger Kirkman, Mark Moseley and Eddie Murray all wore Eagles jersey number 3. Which Eagles quarterback wore that number?

    a. Benjy Dial
    b. Jack Concannon
    c. Al Dorow
    d. Jeff Christensen

16. Before Randall Cunningham wore jersey number 12, who was the last Eagles quarterback to wear that number?

    a. Bill Troup
    b. Rick Arrington
    c. Jeff Christensen
    d. Bob Holly

answers on page 383

EAGLES WHO BECAME COWBOYS

1. Which one of the following Eagles players ended up playing for the Dallas Cowboys?

    a. Bill Striegel
    b. Garry Cobb
    c. Max Runager
    d. Ray Romero

2. Which one of the following Eagles players ended up playing for the Dallas Cowboys?

    a. Harry Dowda
    b. Tony Brooks
    c. Mike Hogan
    d. Randall Cunningham

3. Which one of the following Eagles players ended up playing for the Dallas Cowboys?

   a. Mike Ditka
   b. Adrian Young
   c. Michael Williams
   d. Chris Johnson

4. Which one of the following Eagles players ended up playing for the Dallas Cowboys?

   a. Mike Hogan
   b. Walt Kowalczyk
   c. Mark McMillan
   d. Harold Jackson

5. Which one of the following Eagles players ended up playing for the Dallas Cowboys?

   a. Junior Tautalatasi
   b. Dick Chapura
   c. Carl Hairston
   d. Kent Lawrence

6. Which one of the following Eagles players ended up playing for the Dallas Cowboys?

   a. Ted Laux
   b. Chuck Allen
   c. Dick Bielski
   d. Dave Archer

7. Which one of the following Eagles players ended up playing for the Dallas Cowboys?

   a. Tommy McDonald
   b. John Niland
   c. Mark Moseley
   d. Joe Panos

8. Which one of the following Eagles players ended up playing for the Dallas Cowboys?

    a. James Thrash
    b. Jerry Norton
    c. Corey Walker
    d. John Sciarra

9. Which one of the following Eagles players ended up playing for the Dallas Cowboys?

    a. Trey Darliek
    b. Milton Leathers
    c. Jim Thrower
    d. Terrell Owens

answers on page 384

JERSEY NUMBERS HISTORY

1. Which uniform number has been worn by the fewest Eagles players?

    a. 3
    b. 13
    c. 92
    d. 99

2. Who was the first Eagles player to wear jersey number 1?

    a. Happy Feller
    b. Nick Mike-Mayer
    c. Tony Franklin
    d. Gary Anderson

3. Who was the first Eagles player to wear jersey number 5?

     a. Tom Skladany
     b. Dean May
     c. Roman Gabriel
     d. Joe Kresky

4. Who was the first Eagles quarterback to wear jersey number 7?

     a. John Huarte
     b. Roy Zimmerman
     c. Jim Ward
     d. John Reaves

5. Who was the first Eagles quarterback to wear jersey number 10?

     a. Adrian Burk
     b. Al Dorow
     c. Tommy Thompson
     d. Frank Tripucka

6. Fifteen different quarterbacks wore jersey number 11, but who was the first Eagles player to wear that jersey number?

     a. Lee Woodruff
     b. Ed Manske
     c. John Ferko
     d. Bernie Lee

7. Brian Dawkins currently wears jersey number 20, but who was the first Eagles player to wear jersey that number?

     a. Clyde Williams
     b. Pete Stevens
     c. John Lipski
     d. Henry Reese

8. Hall of Famer Tommy McDonald wore jersey number 25, but who was the first Eagles player to wear that jersey number?

    a. Osborne Willson
    b. Pete Retzlaff
    c. Leonard Gudd
    d. Henry Reese

9. Wilbert Montgomery, Al Harris and Dexter Wynn all wore jersey number 31, but who was the first Eagles player to wear that jersey number?

    a. Dan Sandifer
    b. William Brian
    c. Jerry Ginney
    d. Joe Carter

10. Brian Westbrook, Stanley Pritchett and Michael Zordich all wore jersey number 36, but who was the first Eagles player to wear that jersey number?

    a. Carl Kane
    b. Ed Manske
    c. Joe Bukant
    d. Norm Bulaich

11. Herm Edwards wore jersey number 46, but who was the first Eagles player to wear that jersey number?

    a. Don Miller
    b. Glen Amerson
    c. Lee Bouggess
    d. Chris Gerhard

12. Garry Cobb, James Willis and Mark Simoneau are just a few players that wore jersey number 50, but who was the first Eagles player to wear that jersey number?

a. Don Johnson
b. Bob Kelley
c. Al Wukits
d. Alabama Pitts

13. Jeremiah Trotter, Kurt Gouveia and Jim Ringo are just some of the players that wore jersey number 54, but who was the first Eagles player to wear that jersey number?

a. Bill Lapham
b. Gene Ceppetelli
c. Gerry Huth
d. Chuck Allen

14. Ray Farmer, Frank LeMaster and Dhani Jones all wore jersey number 55, but who was the first Eagles player to wear that jersey number?

a. Maxie Baughan
b. Frank Bausch
c. Fred Brown
d. Basilio Marchi

15. Who was the first Eagles player to wear jersey number 56?

a. Bill Hewitt
b. Bill Hobbs
c. Bill Overmeyer
d. Fred Whittingham

16. Seth Joyner, Derrick Burgess and Mike Mamula all wore jersey number 59, but who was the first Eagles player to wear that jersey number?

a. Tom Ehlers
b. Al Chesley
c. Joseph Wendlick
d. Mike Evans

17. Bill Bergey wore jersey number 66, but who was the first Eagles player to wear that jersey number?

    a. Ed Sharkey
    b. John Wyhonic
    c. Joe Robb
    d. Baptiste Manzini

18. Jon Runyan has worn jersey number 69 the longest, but who was the first Eagles player to wear that jersey number?

    a. Joe Tyrell
    b. Rich Glover
    c. Dave DiFilippo
    d. Carl Gersbach

19. Former head coach and player Ed Khayat wore jersey number 73, but who was the first Eagles player to wear that jersey number?

    a. Rocco Canale
    b. Henry Gude
    c. Fred Hartman
    d. Ed Kasky

20. Stan Walters wore jersey number 75, but who was the first Eagles player to wear that jersey number?

    a. Bill Halverson
    b. Bob Suffridge
    c. George Savitsky
    d. Walt Stickel

21. Wide receivers Irving Fryar, Don Zimmerman and James Lofton all wore jersey number 80, but who was the first Eagles player to wear that jersey number?

    a. Granville Harrison
    b. Kirk Hershey

c. Leonard Supulski
d. Fred Meyer

22. Terrell Owens wore jersey number 81, but who was the first Eagles player to wear that jersey number?

    a. Ray Reutt
    b. Walt Nowak
    c. Dick Humbert
    d. Willie Irvin

23. Keith Jackson, John Spagnola and Mike Bartrum all wore jersey number 88, but who was the first Eagles player to wear that jersey number?

    a. Bill Larson
    b. Herschel Ramsey
    c. John Durko
    d. Jay MacDowell

24. Clyde Simmons wore jersey number 96, but who was the first Eagles player to wear that jersey number?

    a. Mike Flores
    b. John Sodaski
    c. Harvey Armstrong
    d. Marvin Ayers

25. Who was the first Eagles player to wear jersey number 98?

    a. Tommy Jeter
    b. Mike Ditka
    c. Greg Brown
    d. Jimmy Jones

answers on page 384

REVERSE UNIFORMS 2004 SEASON

1. On the Eagles' 2004 roster, which player's jersey number is the reverse of Darwin Walker's 97?

    a. Alonzo Ephraim
    b. Artis Hicks
    c. Steve Sciullo
    d. Ian Allen

2. On the Eagles' 2004 roster, which player's jersey number is the reverse of Ike Reese's 58?

    a. Dominic Furio
    b. Jeff Thomason
    c. Mike Bartrum
    d. Jerome McDougle

3. On the Eagles' 2004 roster, which player's jersey number is the reverse of L.J. Smith's 82?

    a. Bruce Perry
    b. Jon Ritchie
    c. Eric McCoo
    d. Correll Buckhalter

4. On the Eagles' 2004 roster, which player's jersey number is the reverse of Jason Short's 52?

    a. Dorsey Levens
    b. Lito Sheppard
    c. Eric McCoo
    d. Roderick Hood

5. On the Eagles' 2004 roster, which player's jersey number is the reverse of Jon Runyan's 69?

    a. Sam Rayburn
    b. Paul Grasmanis
    c. Darwin Walker
    d. Jerome McDougle

6. On the Eagles' 2004 roster, which player's jersey number is the reverse of Jamaal Jackson's 67?

    a. Dominic Furio
    b. Trey Darilek
    c. Alonzo Ephraim
    d. Jamaal Green

7. On the Eagles' 2004 roster, which player's jersey number is the reverse of Brian Westbrook's 36?

    a. Jamaal Green
    b. Adrien Clarke
    c. Hank Fraley
    d. Jermane Mayberry

8. On the Eagles' 2004 roster, which player's jersey number is the reverse of N.D. Kalu's 94?

    a. Jon Ritchie
    b. Thomas Tapeh
    c. Josh Parry
    d. Quintin Mikell

answers on page 385

REVERSE UNIFORMS 2005 SEASON

1. If you reverse Keith Adams's number 57, which player would you get from the Eagles' 2005 roster?

   a. Todd Herremans
   b. Juqua Thomas
   c. Artis Hicks
   d. Sam Rayburn

2. If you reverse Hollis Thomas's number 78, which player would you get from the Eagles' 2005 roster?

   a. Mike Patterson
   b. Mike Bartrum
   c. Tra Thomas
   d. Todd Pinkston

3. If you reverse Jerome McDougle's number 95, which player would you get from the Eagles' 2005 roster?

   a. Mark Simoneau
   b. Mike Labinjo
   c. Josh Parry
   d. Roderick Hood

4. If you reverse Correll Buckhalter's number 28, which player would you get from the Eagles' 2005 roster?

   a. L.J. Smith
   b. Greg Lewis
   c. Billy McMullen
   d. Todd Pinkston

5. If you reverse Shawn Andrews's number 73, which player would you get from the Eagles' 2005 roster?

    a. Matt Ware
    b. Reno Mahe
    c. Artis Hicks
    d. Sean Considine

6. If you reverse Hank Fraley's number 63, which player would you get from the Eagles' 2005 roster?

    a. Michael Lewis
    b. Reno Mahe
    c. Brian Westbrook
    d. Bruce Perry

7. If you reverse Jeremiah Trotter's number 54, which player would you get from the Eagles' 2005 roster?

    a. Andy Thorn
    b. Thomas Tapeh
    c. Jeremy Thornburg
    d. Stephen Spach

8. If you reverse Darnerien McCants's number 85, which player would you get from the Eagles' 2005 roster?

    a. Trent Cole
    b. Matt McCoy
    c. Keith Adams
    d. Mike Labinjo

9. If you reverse Darwin Walker's number 97, which player would you get from the Eagles' 2005 roster?

    a. Artis Hicks
    b. Juqua Thomas
    c. Todd Herremans
    d. Hollis Thomas

10. If you reverse Michael Lewis's number 32, which player would you get from the Eagles' 2005 roster?

    a. Ryan Moats
    b. Lito Sheppard
    c. Robert Redd
    d. Lamar Gordon

11. If you reverse Tra Thomas's number 72, which player would you get from the Eagles' 2005 roster?

    a. Sean Considine
    b. Jamaal Jackson
    c. Robert Redd
    d. Quintin Mikell

12. If you reverse Paul Grasmanis's number 96, which player would you get from the Eagles' 2005 roster?

    a. Keyonta Marshall
    b. Alonzo Jackson
    c. Jon Runyan
    d. Adrien Clarke

answers on page 385

ROOKIE SEASONS

1. Which one of the following player became the first rookie in NFL history to lead a conference in sacks?

    a. Jevon Kearse
    b. Reggie White
    c. Jerome Brown
    d. Bill Dunstan

2. As a rookie, which Eagles running back had the most yards gained in a single game?

    a. Steve Van Buren
    b. Correll Buckhalter
    c. Keith Byars
    d. Charlie Garner

3. Who was the only rookie to start every game for the 1960 Eagles championship team?

    a. Ron Burton
    b. Dick Lucas
    c. Bobby Walston
    d. Maxie Baughan

4. Name the Eagles player who joined the birds in '76 as the NFL's oldest rookie for that season?

    a. Woody Peoples
    b. Frank LeMaster
    c. Vince Papale
    d. Art Malone

5. Which Eagles player has caught the most touchdowns in his rookie season?

    a. Freddie Mitchell
    b. Fred Barnett
    c. Tommy McDonald
    d. Calvin Williams

6. Which Eagles rookie receiver caught 10 passes for 156 yards and scored one touchdown?

    a. Mike Quick
    b. Tommy McDonald
    c. Harold Carmichael
    d. Charles Smith

7. Which Eagles rookie broke Steve Van Buren's 1944 rookie record of 129 rushing yards in a single game?

    a. Keith Byars
    b. Charlie Garner
    c. Wilbert Montgomery
    d. Correll Buckhalter

8. As a rookie wide receiver, how many passes did Victor Bailey catch?

    a. 37
    b. 41
    c. 46
    d. 52

9. Which player caught more touchdown passes than any other rookie in team's history?

    a. Calvin Williams
    b. Victor Bailey
    c. Pete Retzlaff
    d. Mike Quick

10. How many interceptions did Eagle Tom Brookshier have in his rookie season?

    a. 5 interceptions
    b. 8 interceptions
    c. 11 interceptions
    d. 14 interceptions

11. What jersey number was Eagle Duce Staley originally assigned as a rookie?

    a. 24
    b. 27
    c. 36
    d. 41

12. Which Eagles player was the only rookie to finish the 1999 season as a defensive starter?

    a. Barry Gardner
    b. Damon Moore
    c. Doug Brzezinski
    d. Jon Welbourn

answers on page 386

BIRDS THAT FLEW THE COOP

1. The Eagles traded Jon Welbourn to which team?

    a. Kansas City Chiefs
    b. Washington Redskins
    c. Denver Broncos
    d. Arizona Cardinals

2. The Eagles acquired Hugh Douglas from which team?

    a. St. Louis Rams
    b. Jacksonville Jaguars
    c. Carolina Panthers
    d. New York Jets

3. Eagles quarterback Rodney Peete was traded to which team?

    a. Tennessee Titans
    b. New Orleans Saints
    c. Washington Redskins
    d. Seattle Seahawks

4. What player did the Eagles receive when they traded Wilbert Montgomery?

    a. Garry Cobb
    b. Nate Ramsey
    c. Wes Hopkins
    d. A second round draft choice

5. The Eagles acquired Bill Bergey in a trade deal with what team?

    a. Houston Oilers
    b. New York Giants
    c. Cincinnati Bengals
    d. Miami Dolphins

6. The Eagles traded a pair of picks for Matt Cavanaugh in a 1986 draft day trade with what team?

    a. San Francisco 49ers
    b. Pittsburgh Steelers
    c. Houston Oilers
    d. L.A. Rams

7. The Eagles traded running back Clarence Peaks to which team?

    a. Washington Redskins
    b. Pittsburgh Steelers
    c. St. Louis Cardinals
    d. Cleveland Browns

8. The Eagles traded quarterback Sonny Jurgensen to what team?

    a. Los Angeles Rams
    b. Washington Redskins
    c. New York Giants
    d. New Orleans Saints

9. Which Eagles player was traded to the San Francisco
   49ers as part of the Terrell Owens deal?

   a. Trey Darilek
   b. Clinton Hart
   c. Freddie Milons
   d. Brandon Whiting

10. Which player did the Eagles trade for Ron Jaworski?

    a. Charlie Young
    b. Bob Brown
    c. Mike Boryla
    d. Mike Hogan

11. Who did the Eagles receive when they traded Don
    McPherson?

    a. Mike Pitts
    b. Lester Holmes
    c. Andy Harmon
    d. Ron Solt

12. When the Eagles traded A.J. Feeley to the Dolphins, who
    did they receive?

    a. Trent Cole
    b. Reggie Brown
    c. Ryan Moats
    d. Michael Lewis

13. The Eagles traded Allen Rossum to which team?

    a. Cleveland Browns
    b. New York Jets
    c. Kansas City Chiefs
    d. Green Bay Packers

14. The Eagles acquired John Spagnola from which team?

    a. New England Patriots
    b. New York Giants
    c. Oakland Raiders
    d. Atlanta Falcons

15. Who did the Eagles receive when they traded Ben Hawkins?

    a. Tom Roussel
    b. Mike Boryla
    c. Joe Jones
    d. Art Malone

16. In what year was Ron Jaworski waived by the Eagles?

    a. 1983
    b. 1985
    c. 1987
    d. 1989

17. In 2000, from which team did the Eagles claim Hank Fraley off waivers?

    a. New York Giants
    b. Pittsburgh Steelers
    c. Tampa Bay Buccaneers
    d. Baltimore Ravens   answers on page 386

UNUSUAL BIRTHPLACES

1. Where were Eagles brothers Steve and Ebert Van Buren born?

    a. Honduras
    b. Mexico
    c. Spain
    d. Venezuela

2. Which one of the following Eagles players was born in Russia?

   a. Gerald Nichols
   b. George Mrkonic
   c. Max Padlow
   d. Chuck Gorecki

3. Where was Eagle Via Sikahema born?

   a. Gabon
   b. Tonga
   c. Trinidad
   d. Congo

4. Eagles kicker Gary Anderson was born in what country?

   a. Grenada
   b. Samoa
   c. Estonia
   d. South Africa

5. Where was Eagle Luis Zendejas born?

   a. Mexico
   b. Peru
   c. El Salvador
   d. Chile

6. Where was Eagle Thomas Tapeh born?

   a. Ecuador
   b. Chad
   c. Liberia
   d. Paraguay

7. Eagles kicker Nick Mike-Mayer was born in what country?

   a. England
   b. Italy
   c. France
   d. Germany

answers on page 387

PUZZLES

UNUSUAL NAMES

```
Y E E I T S B O Y R N E H C B B
A R L T A U S U A O U H I I C R
G N L T D E H E D L A V T O P C
A N T E U C B R B W O U N R A E
D A B L N Y M R C T U E O C D L
N T O O O O E G E B A V C L N I
E H D P H H R M K W E G O A U W
L E S P T S K B O R R U I U A O
B R A U A E R A B N M Y N D U U
R O L C T B H J H O P T E E Y R
S N N E R R A W T I S U B C A E
D S P E I C Y L O F T R O R B P
J A I R O P E N A R A N D A P P
J P P B E M L R A L D B W B G V
A P S F R A N K W Y D O P B E R
P A N P E P B E E I B W U N S N
```

BlendaGay	BreeCuppoletti	BusitWarren
ClaudeCrabb	DonChuy	EnioConti
FrankWydo	GuyTurnbow	HenryObst
JairoPenaranda	LutherBlue	MelTom
PeteKmetovic	ProverbJacobs	TheronSapp

answers on page 434

On The Field

BIG FOOT

1. Eagles field goal kicker Norm Johnson entered the '99 season with an NFL record of how many consecutive extra-point conversions?

   a. 257
   b. 276
   c. 283
   d. 291

2. Which Eagles kicker holds the record for the longest successful field goal?

   a. Tom Dempsey
   b. Paul McFadden
   c. David Akers
   d. Tony Franklin

3. What was Eagles kicker David Akers's longest game-winning overtime field goal?

   a. 45 yards
   b. 48 yards
   c. 50 yards
   d. 53 yards

4. Which Eagles kicker made all 48 points-after-touchdowns in a single season?

   a. Gary Anderson
   b. Roger Ruzek
   c. David Akers
   d. Tony Franklin

5. How many 50-yard-plus field goals did kicker Tony Franklin make while playing with the Eagles?

    a. 5
    b. 7
    c. 9
    d. 11

6. Against which team did Eagle David Akers successfully kick a 57-yard field goal?

    a. New England Patriots
    b. Miami Dolphins
    c. Baltimore Ravens
    d. Washington Redskins

7. Who holds the record for the longest punt made in Eagles history?

    a. Sean Landeta
    b. Randall Cunningham
    c. Jason Baker
    d. Tom Hutton

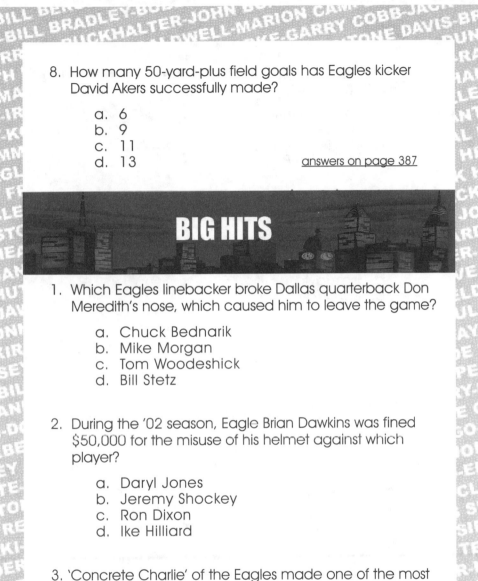

8. How many 50-yard-plus field goals has Eagles kicker David Akers successfully made?

    a. 6
    b. 9
    c. 11
    d. 13   <u>answers on page 387</u>

BIG HITS

1. Which Eagles linebacker broke Dallas quarterback Don Meredith's nose, which caused him to leave the game?

    a. Chuck Bednarik
    b. Mike Morgan
    c. Tom Woodeshick
    d. Bill Stetz

2. During the '02 season, Eagle Brian Dawkins was fined $50,000 for the misuse of his helmet against which player?

    a. Daryl Jones
    b. Jeremy Shockey
    c. Ron Dixon
    d. Ike Hilliard

3. 'Concrete Charlie' of the Eagles made one of the most famous tackles in NFL history when he crushed which future NFL announcer?

    a. Don Meredith
    b. Roger Staubach
    c. Frank Gifford
    d. Terry Bradshaw

4. Which Eagle is credited with knocking out two Pittsburgh Steelers quarterbacks in a single game?

    a. Reggie White
    b. Andre Waters
    c. Clyde Simmons
    d. Bill Bergey

5. Who did Eagle Chuck Bednarik tackle and pin for the last play of the 1960 championship game?

    a. Paul Hornung
    b. Lew Carpenter
    c. Jim Taylor
    d. Bart Starr

6. Former Eagle Bill Cowher once broke the leg of a Chicago Bear's player during a punt return. Who was the player?

    a. Jeff Fisher
    b. Willie Gault
    c. Dave Duerson
    d. Al Harris

7. Eagle Bill Bergey back in the '70s made a big hit on which Dallas Cowboy's player, causing a fumble in which Eagle Joe Lavender returned the ball for a 96-yard touchdown?

    a. Calvin Hill
    b. Walt Garrison
    c. Doug Dennison
    d. Robert Newhouse

answers on page 388

BIRDS ON THE FIELD

1. Jerry Sisemore played what position for the Eagles?

    a. Guard
    b. Defensive back
    c. Linebacker
    d. Tackle

2. Steve Van Buren played what position for the Eagles?

    a. Quarterback
    b. Fullback
    c. Halfback
    d. Wide receiver

3. Tom Woodeshick played which position for the Eagles?

    a. Safety
    b. Running back
    c. Cornerback
    d. Linebacker

4. Before becoming an NFL coach, Marion Campbell played what position for the Eagles?

    a. Tackle
    b. Safety
    c. Linebacker
    d. Guard

5. What position did Bill Bradley for the Eagles?

    a. Safety
    b. Cornerback
    c. Linebacker
    d. Defensive back

6. What position did Lum Snyder play for the Eagles?

   a. Guard
   b. Center
   c. Linebacker
   d. Tackle

7. What position did Maxie Baughan play for the Eagles?

   a. Tight end
   b. Linebacker
   c. Tackle
   d. Safety

8. Before becoming an NFL coach, Bill Cowher played what position for the Eagles?

   a. Tackle
   b. Safety
   c. Linebacker
   d. Defensive end

9. What position did Woody Peoples play for the Eagles?

   a. Guard
   b. Tight end
   c. Linebacker
   d. Tackle

10. What position did Tom Brookshier play for the Eagles?

   a. Safety
   b. Cornerback
   c. Defensive back
   d. Strong safety

11. What position did Walter Barnes play for the Eagles?

    a. Guard
    b. Center
    c. Linebacker
    d. Tackle

12. What position did Ty Allert play for the Eagles?

    a. Guard
    b. Center
    c. Linebacker
    d. Tackle

13. Before becoming an NFL coach, Mike Ditka played what position for the Eagles?

    a. Tackle
    b. Safety
    c. Linebacker
    d. End

14. Who replaced Pete Retzlaff after he retired as the Eagles' tight end?

    a. Mike Ditka
    b. Tom Brookshier
    c. Jim Palmer
    d. Marion Campbell

15. What position did former Eagle Keith Krepfle play?

    a. Tight end
    b. Linebacker
    c. Guard
    d. Punter

answers on page 388

BROKEN EAGLES

1. Against which team did Eagle Clarence Peaks break his leg?

    a. St. Louis Rams
    b. New York Giants
    c. Washington Redskins
    d. Cleveland Browns

2. During the '62 season Eagle Don Burroughs suffered what injury that sidelined him?

    a. Broken leg
    b. Cracked ribs
    c. Separated shoulder
    d. Broken arm

3. During the '62 season, Pete Retzlaff, Dick Lucas and Bobby Walston all suffered with the same injury. What was it?

    a. Concussion
    b. Fractured leg
    c. Fractured ribs
    d. Broken arm

4. Who were the Eagles playing when center Hank Fraley got injured?

    a. Dallas Cowboys
    b. Kansas City Chiefs
    c. Washington Redskins
    d. Denver Broncos

5. Against which team did Donovan McNabb play in his last game of the 2005 season before being benched due to his sports hernia injury?

    a. San Diego Chargers
    b. Dallas Cowboys
    c. New York Giants
    d. Oakland Raiders

6. In 1979 who were the Eagles playing when Bill Bergey suffered a season-ending knee injury?

    a. Green Bay Packers
    b. Cincinnati Bengals
    c. New Orleans Saints
    d. Pittsburgh Steelers

7. In 1984 against which team did Eagles quarterback Ron Jaworski break his leg ended his streak of 116 consecutive starts?

    a. Miami Dolphins
    b. St. Louis Cardinals
    c. San Francisco 49ers
    d. New England Patriots

8. In 1981 against which team did Eagle Scott Fitzkee break his foot missing the balance of the post season games?

    a. Dallas Cowboys
    b. Oakland Raiders
    c. Minnesota Vikings
    d. Atlanta Falcons

9. Name this Eagles player pictured who is carried off the field by the training staff?

    a. Rodney Parker
    b. Kevin Bowman
    c. Michael Young
    d. Don Hultz

answers on page 389

EAGLES CELEBRATIONS

1. Which Eagle was know for 'chopping down a tree' as part of his celebration after a good play?

    a. Corey Simon
    b. Jeremiah Trotter
    c. Hugh Douglas
    d. Darwin Walker

2. Which Eagle celebrates a sack by playing an air guitar?

    a. Dhani Jones
    b. Jerome McDougle
    c. Jevon Kearse
    d. Ike Reese

3. Which Eagle celebrates a sack or a great stop by flying like a bird?

    a. Hollis Thomas
    b. Dexter Wynn
    c. Jevon Kearse
    d. Sam Rayburn

4. Which Eagle was known for celebrating after a touchdown by stretching out his arms to form the letter 't'?

    a. Thomas Tapeh
    b. Kevin Turner
    c. James Thrash
    d. Jeff Thomason

5. Which Eagle was the first in the NFL to kneel in prayer in the end zone as part of his touchdown celebration?

   a. Herb Lusk
   b. Tony Baker
   c. Keith Krepfle
   d. Po James

6. Which Eagles player celebrates a great play by pulling the cord on a diesel truck horn?

   a. Ike Reese
   b. Sam Rayburn
   c. Brandon Whiting
   d. Darwin Walker

7. Which Eagle would celebrate after a touchdown by rolling the ball and snapping his fingers like a guy shooting craps?

   a. Todd Pinkston
   b. Mike Quick
   c. Charlie Smith
   d. Harold Carmichael

8. Which Eagles player was known for his 'whip-cracking' gesture after making a big play?

   a. Corey Simon
   b. Freddie Mitchell
   c. Koy Detmer
   d. Jeremiah Trotter

9. Who was the first Eagle to celebrate his touchdown by boxing with the goal post?

   a. Duce Staley
   b. Via Sikahema
   c. Joe Scarpati
   d. Terrell Owens

answers on page 389

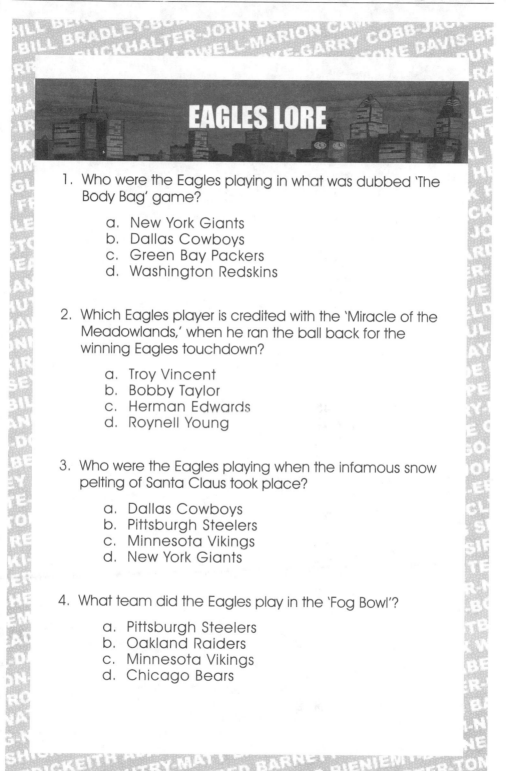

EAGLES LORE

1. Who were the Eagles playing in what was dubbed 'The Body Bag' game?

    a. New York Giants
    b. Dallas Cowboys
    c. Green Bay Packers
    d. Washington Redskins

2. Which Eagles player is credited with the 'Miracle of the Meadowlands,' when he ran the ball back for the winning Eagles touchdown?

    a. Troy Vincent
    b. Bobby Taylor
    c. Herman Edwards
    d. Roynell Young

3. Who were the Eagles playing when the infamous snow pelting of Santa Claus took place?

    a. Dallas Cowboys
    b. Pittsburgh Steelers
    c. Minnesota Vikings
    d. New York Giants

4. What team did the Eagles play in the 'Fog Bowl'?

    a. Pittsburgh Steelers
    b. Oakland Raiders
    c. Minnesota Vikings
    d. Chicago Bears

5. The Eagles defeated the Chicago Cardinals 7-0 for the 1948 NFL Championship. What was this game nicknamed?

    a. Fog Bowl
    b. Snow Game
    c. Birds Championship
    d. Wind Bowl

6. Who were the Eagles playing in what was dubbed the 'House of Pain' game?

    a. New York Giants
    b. Dallas Cowboys
    c. Houston Oilers
    d. St. Louis Cardinals

7. In which years were the Eagles nicknamed 'The Duffel-Bag Dynasty'?

    a. 1936-38
    b. 1942-45
    c. 1947-49
    d. 1951-54

8. What play was called when Eagles quarterback Donovan McNabb hit Freddie Mitchell on the 4th down with 26 yards to go?

    a. 86 split right
    b. 74 double go
    c. 55 slant right
    d. Hail Mary

9. Which player did Eagle Chuck Bednarik make the game ending tackle against in the 1960 championship game?

    a. Tom Moore
    b. Jim Taylor
    c. Paul Hornung
    d. Lew Carpenter

answers on page 390

EAGLES RUNNING BACKS

1. Prior to 2003, when was the last time the Eagles' running backs scored three touchdowns against Dallas in a single game?

    a. 1989
    b. 1992
    c. 1995
    d. 2001

2. In 1992-93 season, Herschel Walker rushed for over 1,000 yards for the Eagles. How many rushing touchdowns did he have?

    a. 6 touchdowns
    b. 8 touchdowns
    c. 10 touchdowns
    d. 12 touchdowns

3. Which of the following Eagles running backs did not have a total of 17 rushing touchdowns in his career?

    a. Tom Sullivan
    b. Keith Byars
    c. Charlie Garner
    d. Heath Sherman

4. Which of the following Eagles running backs did not have at least 30 rushing touchdowns as an Eagle?

    a. Wilbert Montgomery
    b. Timmy Brown
    c. Steve Van Buren
    d. Ricky Watters

5. During the 2003-04 season, the Eagles trio of running backs combined for how many total yards gained?

    a. 1,072 yards
    b. 1,278 yards
    c. 1,463 yards
    d. 1,618 yards

6. Which former Eagles running back is the only player in NFL history to lead the league in rushing yards for four consecutive seasons?

    a. Steve Van Buren
    b. Duce Staley
    c. Ollie Matson
    d. Wilbert Montgomery

7. Which Eagle holds the record for most rushing attempts in a single season?

    a. Ricky Watters
    b. Duce Staley
    c. Wilbert Montgomery
    d. Tom Sullivan

8. In what year did Eagles quarterback Ron Jaworski rush for five touchdowns?

    a. 1977
    b. 1979
    c. 1980
    d. 1982

9. How many touchdowns did Eagle Steve Van Buren score from 1944 through 1951?

    a. 58
    b. 62
    c. 69
    d. 74

10. In 1980, everyone remembers Wilbert Montgomery as the Eagles leading rusher, but who was the team's second leading rusher?

     a. Leroy Harris
     b. Perry Harrington
     c. Louie Gammona
     d. Billy Campfield

11. Who was the last Eagles player to rush for three touchdowns in a single game?

     a. Duce Staley
     b. Charlie Garner
     c. James Joseph
     d. Kevin Turner

12. Who was the last Eagle to gain over 1,000 rushing yards prior to Wilbert Montgomery?

     a. Steve Van Buren
     b. Timmy Brown
     c. Tom Sullivan
     d. Herschel Walker

13. Who is the only Eagles player to rush for more than 1,000 yards in three consecutive seasons?

    a. Duce Staley
    b. Ricky Watters
    c. Timmy Brown
    d. Wilbert Montgomery

14. How many times has Eagles quarterback Donovan McNabb rushed for over 100 yards?

    a. 3 games
    b. 4 games
    c. 5 games
    d. 6 games

15. In 1949, who were the Eagles playing when Steve Van Buren rushed for 205 yards?

    a. New York Bulldogs
    b. Los Angeles Rams
    c. Pittsburgh Steelers
    d. Chicago Cardinals

16. Only three Eagles players have had back-to-back 1,000 yard rushing seasons. Which of the following was not one of them?

    a. Herschel Walker
    b. Duce Staley
    c. Wilbert Montgomery
    d. Ricky Watters

answers on page 390

PUZZLES

RUNNING BACKS

```
Y D A L M H T R Z E E N I  T H E T
S J U A N I  S I  A S K Y N S K G K
R O R C J E K R M D S O C E T O H
D H K I  E A O E D B P O N T O T E
R N A R C S M A H O R K H R N O R
U H I  E R K T E J O E O B I  A M S
E U H O A N Y A S L G T W I  E S C
S Z I  L A A M W L J S A N N T U H
R V E A M E H E A E O P N K B L E
A A R E S E R A W T Y S S A J L L
Y R E M O G T N O M T R E B L I  W
B I  L L Y B A R N E S E A P R V A
H E L K N I  H K C A J R R B H A L
T C L A R E N C E P E A K S W N K
I  B R B N O S N A H E D E W S W E
E R B D B M D A V E S M U K L E R
K E C E A H E N N V A R O E T P A
```

BillyBarnes	BrianWestbrook	ClarencePeaks
DaveSmukler	DuceStaley	HerschelWalker
JackHinkle	JamesJoseph	JohnHuzvar
KeithByars	KenKeller	MikeHogan
PoJames	RickyWatters	SwedeHanson
TimBrown	TomSullivan	WilbertMontgomery

answers on page 433

EAGLES STARTS

1. Against which team did Eagle L.J. Smith make his first NFL start?

   a. New England Patriots
   b. Dallas Cowboys
   c. Chicago Bears
   d. Baltimore Ravens

2. What was the Eagles' first play from scrimmage to start the 2004-05 regular season?

   a. Run by Westbrook
   b. Pass to Owens
   c. Run by Tapeh
   d. Pass to Lewis

3. Against which team did Brandon Whiting of the Eagles make his first Monday Night Football start?

   a. Dallas Cowboys
   b. Washington Redskins
   c. Miami Dolphins
   d. Baltimore Ravens

4. When was the last time prior to the 2004 season that the Eagles started 3-0?

   a. 1980
   b. 1983
   c. 1989
   d. 1993

5. In 2005 against the Packers, which one of the following Eagles played in his first ever NFL game?

    a. Todd Herremans
    b. Trent Cole
    c. Ryan Moats
    d. Jamaal Jackson

6. In what year did Tom Brookshier begin his playing career with the Eagles?

    a. 1948
    b. 1951
    c. 1953
    d. 1956

7. Against which team did Eagles quarterback Jack Concannon get his first NFL start?

    a. Dallas Cowboys
    b. Cleveland Browns
    c. Pittsburgh Steelers
    d. Chicago Bears

8. Eagles quarterback Koy Detmer started his first NFL game against which team?

    a. Washington Redskins
    b. Dallas Cowboys
    c. Green Bay Packers
    d. St. Louis Rams   answers on page 391

EAGLES DEBUT

1. At what position did Artis Hicks make his Eagles debut?

    a. Left tackle
    b. Left guard
    c. Right guard
    d. Right tackle

2. Who were the Eagles playing when Pete Pihos made his Eagles debut?

     a. New York Giants
     b. Chicago Bears
     c. Washington Redskins
     d. Pittsburgh Steelers

3. Who were the Eagles playing when Steve Van Buren made his Eagles debut?

     a. Boston Yanks
     b. Cleveland Rams
     c. Brooklyn Tigers
     d. Washington Redskins

4. Against which team did Ron Jaworski debut as the Eagles' quarterback?

     a. Dallas Cowboys
     b. New York Jets
     c. Detroit Lions
     d. Tampa Bay Buccaneers

5. Against which team did Ty Detmer make his first start as the Eagles quarterback?

     a. Miami Dolphins
     b. New York Giants
     c. Dallas Cowboys
     d. Carolina Panthers

6. Which Eagles receiver did Todd Pinkston replace when he made his debut on the team?

     a. James Thrash
     b. Charles Johnson
     c. Torrance Small
     d. Irving Fryar

7. In 2005, who were the Eagles playing when safety Jack Brewer made his Eagles debut?

    a. Washington Redskins
    b. New York Giants
    c. Green Bay Packers
    d. Oakland Raiders

8. The Eagles played against what team in Charlie Garner's first pro start?

    a. San Francisco 49ers
    b. St. Louis Cardinals
    c. Miami Dolphins
    d. Detroit Lions

9. Against which team did Terrell Owens make his first regular season start for the Eagles?

    a. Dallas Cowboys
    b. Atlanta Falcons
    c. New York Giants
    d. Washington Redskins

10. Against which team did Tommy McDonald make his Eagles debut?

    a. Cleveland Browns
    b. Los Angeles Rams
    c. Washington Redskins
    d. Detroit Lions

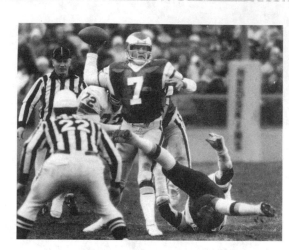

11. Which team were the Eagles playing when quarterback Ron Jaworski made his debut?

    a. New York Giants
    b. New Orleans Saints
    c. Tampa Bay Buccaneers
    d. Los Angeles Rams

12. Against which team were the Eagles playing when running back Wilbert Montgomery made his first NFL start?

    a. New York Jets
    b. Dallas Cowboys
    c. New England Patriots
    d. St. Louis Cardinals

answers on page 391

EAGLES QBs

1. Which of the following quarterbacks did not pass for 10,000 yards in his Eagles career?

    a. Norm Van Brocklin
    b. Randall Cunningham
    c. Tommy Thompson
    d. Ron Jaworski

2. Which Eagles quarterback was the last to win a game before Donovan McNabb became the starter?

   a. A.J. Feeley
   b. Doug Pederson
   c. Koy Detmer
   d. Bobby Hoying

3. Which Eagles quarterback holds the NFL single season record for being sacked the most times?

   a. Ron Jaworski
   b. Randall Cunningham
   c. Donovan McNabb
   d. Mike Boryla

4. Which Eagles player caught Koy Detmer's first touchdown completion?

   a. Kevin Turner
   b. Jeff Graham
   c. Irving Fryar
   d. Jason Dunn

5. Which Eagles quarterback passed for 32 touchdowns in a single season?

   a. Randall Cunningham
   b. Sonny Jurgensen
   c. Ron Jaworski
   d. Norman Snead

6. How many touchdowns did Eagles quarterback Koy Detmer throw in his first NFL start?

   a. 1 touchdown
   b. 2 touchdowns
   c. 3 touchdowns
   d. None

7. Who holds the Eagles' team record for most pass attempts by a quarterback in a single game?

    a. Davey O'Brien
    b. Sonny Jurgensen
    c. Donovan McNabb
    d. Randall Cunningham

8. Who was the first Eagles quarterback to pass for over 400 yards in a single game?

    a. Bobby Thomason
    b. Sonny Jurgensen
    c. Ron Jaworski
    d. Norm Snead

9. Which Eagles quarterback threw the most 300-yard games?

    a. Ron Jaworski
    b. Sonny Jurgensen
    c. Donovan McNabb
    d. Randall Cunningham

10. Prior to the Eagles signing quarterback Doug Pederson, how many regular season passes did he throw in his seven-year career?

    a. 14
    b. 32
    c. 46
    d. 59

11. Which Eagles quarterback holds the record for most pass attempts in a single season?

    a. Sonny Jurgensen
    b. Randall Cunningham
    c. Davey O'Brien
    d. Donovan McNabb

12. Which Eagles quarterback holds the single season record for most touchdowns thrown?

    a. Donovan McNabb
    b. Sonny Jurgensen
    c. Randall Cunningham
    d. Norman Snead

13. Which Eagles quarterback threw for seven touchdowns in a single game?

    a. Norman Snead
    b. Randall Cunningham
    c. Donovan McNabb
    d. Adrian Burk

14. Which Eagles quarterback threw the longest pass completion in team history, gaining 99 yards?

    a. Randall Cunningham
    b. Ron Jaworski
    c. Norm Van Brocklin
    d. Adrian Burk

15. Which Eagles quarterback threw the most interceptions in a single season?

    a. Norman Snead
    b. Ron Jaworski
    c. Sonny Jurgensen
    d. Randall Cunningham

16. To whom did quarterback Mike McMahon throw his first touchdown as an Eagle?

    a. Greg Lewis
    b. Reggie Brown
    c. L.J. Smith
    d. Ryan Moats

17. In 2002, what was Eagles quarterback A.J. Feeley's record when he started for the injured Donovan McNabb?

    a. 1-4
    b. 2-3
    c. 3-2
    d. 4-1

18. Which Eagles quarterback threw 33 completions in a single game and still lost?

    a. Randall Cunningham
    b. Sonny Jurgensen
    c. Koy Detmer
    d. Bobby Hoying

19. During the 2004 season, how many times did Eagles quarterback Donovan McNabb pass for four or more touchdowns in a single game?

    a. 4
    b. 5
    c. 7
    d. 8

20. In 2004, who was the other player (besides Donovan McNabb) that threw a touchdown pass?

    a. Jeff Blake
    b. Koy Detmer
    c. Mike Bartrum
    d. Freddie Mitchell

21. To whom did Eagle quarterback Roman Gabriel throw his last completion?

    a. Keith Krepfle
    b. Vince Papale
    c. Wally Henry
    d. Charlie Smith

22. In what year did Eagles quarterback Sonny Jurgensen throw 32 touchdowns?

    a. 1961
    b. 1964
    c. 1966
    d. 1967

23. In what season did former Eagles quarterback Matt Cavanaugh win the national title while at the University of Pittsburgh?

    a. 1973-74
    b. 1974-75
    c. 1976-77
    d. 1978-79

24. Who was the Eagles quarterback before Ron Jaworski?

    a. Roman Gabriel
    b. Pete Liske
    c. John Reeves
    d. Mike Boryla

25. Besides Donovan McNabb, which one of the following past Eagles quarterbacks also played his college football at Syracuse?

    a. Jay Fiedler
    b. Don McPherson
    c. Bobby Hoying
    d. Brad Goebel

26. During the 1998 season, how many touchdown passes did Eagles quarterback Bobby Hoying throw?

    a. 0
    b. 2
    c. 5
    d. 9

27. In what year did Eagles quarterback Randall Cunningham only throw one touchdown?

    a. 1985
    b. 1986
    c. 1991
    d. 1993

28. Against which team did Eagles quarterback Mike Boryla win his first NFL start?

    a. Washington Redskins
    b. Green Bay Packers
    c. Detroit Lions
    d. New York Giants

29. How many touchdowns did backup quarterback Matt Cavanaugh throw in his four years with the Eagles?

    a. 0
    b. 4
    c. 7
    d. 12

30. Which Eagles quarterback was the first to defeat the Bears?

    a. Tommy Thompson
    b. Sonny Jurgensen
    c. Bill Mackrides
    d. Adrian Burk

31. Against which NFL team did Eagles quarterback Donovan McNabb score his first rushing touchdown?

    a. Washington Redskins
    b. Dallas Cowboys
    c. Pittsburgh Steelers
    d. New York Giants

answers on page 392

EAGLES QUARTERBACKS

```
C C M D R J I  M M C M A H O N A B
J O H N R E A V E S D R A M R L B
A D N G O N M N B R B D L I E B K
E A N E U R Y T I  M A M Y L T L I
L V T D S A M A E N N J R J S E N
B E A O U N N S P D R O O A I  B G
O Y I  R M B E A N J Y S B C R E H
B O O R U M S G V E A O E K B O I
B B I  R B T Y S R A A U K C Y G L
Y R K I  O A R T M U C D I  O D D L
H E R R R B G Z H I  J T M N D A W
O I  I  N N N A N B O A Y T C U R L
Y N R D O N O V A N M C N A B B B
I  S R M B A O N T M L P N N M O R
N A M R E M M I  Z Y O R S N O A M
G I  K S R O W A J N O R A O M S I
R A J O E P I  S A R C I  K N N R E
```

AdrianBurk	BobbyHoying	BradGoebel
BuddyBrister	DanPastorini	DaveyOBrein
DonovanMcNabb	JackConcannon	JimMcMahon
JoePisarcik	JohnReaves	KingHill
KoyDetmer	MattCavanaugh	MikeBoryla
NormSnead	RomanGabriel	RonJaworski
RoyZimmerman	SonnyJurgensen	TommyThompson

<u>answers on page 428</u>

EAGLES RECEPTIONS

1. Which receiver set an Eagles record with 88 pass receptions in a single season?

   a. Fred Barnett
   b. Mike Quick
   c. Terrell Owens
   d. Irving Fryar

2. Which Eagle caught Donovan McNabb's first pass of the 2005 regular season?

   a. L.J. Smith
   b. Terrell Owens
   c. Brian Westbrook
   d. Reggie Brown

3. What is Eagle Chad Lewis's longest reception of his career?

   a. 36 yards
   b. 42 yards
   c. 49 yards
   d. 52 yards

4. Prior to the 2004-05 season, which Eagles wide receiver was the last to record a 150-plus yard receiving game?

   a. Cris Carter
   b. James Thrash
   c. Todd Pinkston
   d. Fred Barnett

5. Who caught the Eagles first NFL touchdown pass from quarterback Red Kirkman?

    a. Jodie Whire
    b. Swede Hansen
    c. Les Woodruff
    d. Porter Lainhart

6. How many touchdowns did Harold Carmichael catch while playing for the Eagles?

    a. 72
    b. 79
    c. 83
    d. 87

7. Which former Eagles player had a career average of 19.2 yards per reception?

    a. Tommy McDonald
    b. Mike Quick
    c. Harold Carmichael
    d. Irving Fryar

8. Which Eagles player made his first career reception on Donovan McNabb's 1,000th career completion?

    a. Freddie Mitchell
    b. L.J. Smith
    c. Billy McMullen
    d. Greg Lewis

9. Against which team did Eagle Todd Pinkston have the first 100-yard receiving game of his career?

    a. New York Giants
    b. Dallas Cowboys
    c. Washington Redskins
    d. San Francisco 49ers

10. Which Eagles wide receiver has the most 100-yard games?

    a. Terrell Owens
    b. Harold Carmichael
    c. Mike Quick
    d. Pete Retzlaff

11. Which rookie wide receiver has had the most receiving yards for the Eagles?

    a. Reggie Brown
    b. Todd Pinkston
    c. L.J. Smith
    d. Freddie Mitchell

12. Which Eagles receiver has caught the most touchdowns in a single season?

   a. Mike Quick
   b. Tommy McDonald
   c. Terrell Owens
   d. Irving Fryar

13. Which Eagle caught a team high of 10 passes in a single game?

   a. Todd Pinkston
   b. Mike Quick
   c. Terrell Owens
   d. Brian Westbrook

14. In 1999, which Eagle scored on an 84-yard touchdown reception?

   a. Torrance Small
   b. Chad Lewis
   c. James Thrash
   d. Duce Staley

15. Which one of the following Eagles did not have at least 80 receptions in a single season?

   a. Irving Fryar
   b. Keith Jackson
   c. Keith Byars
   d. Fred Barnett

16. Which Eagle caught the longest pass reception from scrimmage?

   a. Mike Quick
   b. Fred Barnett
   c. Ben Hawkins
   d. Tommy McDonald

17. Against which team did Eagle Terrell Owens catch his 100th reception?

    a. Dallas Cowboys
    b. San Diego Chargers
    c. Washington Redskins
    d. Oakland Raiders

18. In what year did Eagle Harold Carmichael catch 11 touchdowns?

    a. 1973
    b. 1975
    c. 1977
    d. 1979

19. During the 1960 championship season, which Eagle led the team in both receiving and receptions total yards?

    a. Pete Retzlaff
    b. Bobby Walston
    c. Tommy McDonald
    d. Billy Barnes

20. Who was the last Eagles receiver to score four touchdowns in a single game?

    a. Mike Quick
    b. Terrell Owens
    c. Irving Fryar
    d. Fred Barnett

21. While playing for the Eagles, what was Todd Pinkston's longest pass reception?

    a. 65 yarder
    b. 72 yarder
    c. 80 yarder
    d. 84 yarder

22. How many 100-yard receiving games did Terrell Owens have in his first season with the Eagles?

    a. 6
    b. 7
    c. 8
    d. 9

23. Which one of the following Eagles players did not have a reception in Super Bowl XXIX?

    a. Josh Parry
    b. L.J. Smith
    c. Todd Pinkston
    d. Chad Lewis

24. Which Eagles player has the longest non-scoring catch?

    a. Herschel Walker
    b. Mike Quick
    c. Harold Carmichael
    d. James Joseph

25. How many 100-yard receiving games did Eagle Pete Retzlaff have?

    a. 19
    b. 24
    c. 28
    d. 32

26. Against which team did Eagle Brian Westbrook have a career high 62-yard reception?

    a. Chicago Bears
    b. Oakland Raiders
    c. Kansas City Chiefs
    d. Green Bay Packers

27. In 2004, what was Eagle Terrell Owens longest pass reception resulting in a touchdown?

     a. 55 yards
     b. 59 yards
     c. 61 yards
     d. 63 yards

28. How many receptions did Terrell Owens end up with in his last season as an Eagle?

     a. 42
     b. 47
     c. 53
     d. 59

29. How many touchdown receptions did the Eagles wide receivers score during the 2005 season after the departure of Terrell Owens?

     a. 4
     b. 6
     c. 8
     d. 11

answers on page 393

EAGLES SACK ATTACK

1. Which Eagles player registered the first sack of the 2004-05 regular season?

     a. Nate Wayne
     b. Dhani Jones
     c. Jevon Kearse
     d. Hugh Douglas

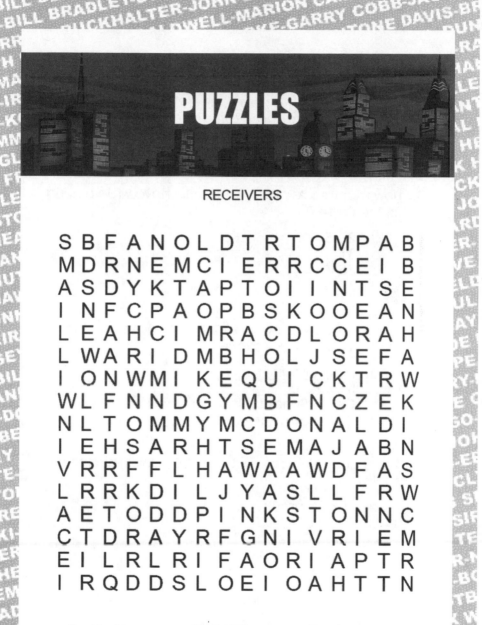

PUZZLES

RECEIVERS

```
S B F A N O L D T R T O M P A B
M D R N E M C I E R R C C E I B
A S D Y K T A P T O I I N T S E
I N F C P A O P B S K O O E A N
L E A H C I M R A C D L O R A H
L W A R I D M B H O L J S E F A
I O N W M I K E Q U I C K T R W
W L F N N D G Y M B F N C Z E K
N L T O M M Y M C D O N A L D I
I E H S A R H T S E M A J A B N
V R R F F L H A W A A W D F A S
L R R K D I L J Y A S L L F R W
A E T O D D P I N K S T O N N C
C T D R A Y R F G N I V R I E M
E I L R L R I F A O R I A P T R
I R Q D D S L O E I O A H T T N
```

BenHawkins	CalvinWilliams	FredBarnett
HaroldCarmichael	HaroldJacksoon	IrvingFryar
JamesThrash	MikeQuick	PeteRetzlaff
TerrellOwens	ToddPinkston	TommyMcDonald

answers on page 431

2. Against which team did Eagles first round draft pick Mike Patterson have his first sack?

   a. Oakland Raiders
   b. San Francisco 49ers
   c. Kansas City Chiefs
   d. Dallas Cowboys

3. How many sacks did Mike Mamula have while playing for the Eagles?

   a. 28.5
   b. 31.5
   c. 35
   d. 37.5

4. In the 2003-04 season, which Eagles player led the team in quarterback sacks?

   a. Mark Simoneau
   b. N.D. Kalu
   c. Corey Simon
   d. Darwin Walker

5. During the '99 season, who led the Eagles with the most sacks?

   a. Mike Mamula
   b. Greg Jefferson
   c. Hugh Douglas
   d. Hollis Thomas

6. In his rookie season, how many sacks did Eagle Corey Simon record?

   a. 6.5 sacks
   b. 9.5 sacks
   c. 11.5 sacks
   d. 14.5 sacks

7. Since 1982, which Eagles player has the most quarterback sacks?

    a. Hugh Douglas
    b. Ike Reese
    c. Clyde Simmons
    d. Reggie White

8. Since the 2000 season, which Eagles player has the most quarterback sacks?

    a. Jevon Kearse
    b. Hugh Douglas
    c. Ike Reese
    d. Derrick Burgess

9. How many quarterback sacks did the Eagles record from 2000 through 2004?

    a. 236
    b. 251
    c. 264
    d. 273

10. How many sacks did Reggie White make in his 121 games playing for the Eagles?

    a. 117
    b. 124
    c. 136
    d. 148

11. Which of the following Eagles sack leaders did not have at least 13 sacks in a single season?

    a. Reggie White
    b. Clyde Simmons
    c. Dennis Harrison
    d. William Fuller

12. How many sacks did the Eagles record in 2004, to finish second in the NFL?

    a. 43
    b. 47
    c. 51
    d. 59

13. In1989, the Eagles set a club record of how many sacks?

    a. 58
    b. 62
    c. 68
    d. 73

14. In what year did Eagle Reggie White record 21 sacks in a single season?

    a. 1986
    b. 1987
    c. 1988
    d. 1991

15. In 2004, Eagle Jevon Kearse recorded three of his team-leading 7.5 sacks in a single game. What team was it against?

    a. Dallas Cowboys
    b. New York Giants
    c. Detroit Lions
    d. Chicago Bears

16. Two Eagles have recorded 4.5 sacks in a single game; Hugh Douglas is one. Name the other.

    a. Jerome Brown
    b. Clyde Simmons
    c. Seth Joyner
    d. Reggie Brown

17. How many seasons did Hugh Douglas lead the Eagles in the sack category?

    a. 3
    b. 4
    c. 5
    d. 6

18. While playing for the Eagles, which quarterback did Reggie White sack the most times?

    a. Mark Rypien
    b. Troy Aikman
    c. Neil Lomax
    d. Phil Simms

19. In the 2004 regular season, against which team did Jevon Kearse record his first sack as an Eagle?

    a. Chicago Bears
    b. New York Giants
    c. Detroit Lions
    d. Minnesota Vikings

20. In 2000, who led the Eagles in total sacks?

    a. Hugh Douglas
    b. Carlos Emmons
    c. Jeremiah Trotter
    d. Mike Mamula

answers on page 394

E-A-G-L-E-S TOUCHDOWNS

1. How many touchdowns did Harold Carmichael score in his seven postseason games with the Eagles?

    a. 3
    b. 6
    c. 9
    d. 12

2. In the Eagles first season, who scored the most touchdowns?

    a. Joe Carter
    b. Swede Hanson
    c. Red Kirkman
    d. Red Davis

3. Tommy McDonald threw his first career touchdown pass to which Eagles player?

    a. Tim Brown
    b. Dick Lucas
    c. Frank Budd
    d. Pete Retzlaff

4. Who scored the Eagles' first touchdown of the 2004-05 regular season?

    a. Brian Westbrook
    b. L.J. Smith
    c. Chad Lewis
    d. Terrell Owens

5. Which one of the following Eagles players has scored a touchdown off of a fake punt?

    a. Koy Detmer
    b. Reggie Brown
    c. Brian Dawkins
    d. Sean Landeta

6. Which Eagle has the longest run from scrimmage to score a touchdown?

    a. Wilbert Montgomery
    b. Via Sikahema
    c. Brian Mitchell
    d. Herschel Walker

7. Which Eagle has rushed for the most yards in a single game?

    a. Duce Staley
    b. Steve Van Buren
    c. Tim Brown
    d. Wilbert Montgomery

8. Name the Eagle who has scored the most touchdowns in a single season.

    a. Brian Westbrook
    b. Terrell Owens
    c. Wilbert Montgomery
    d. Steve Van Buren

9. How many touchdowns did Harold Carmichael catch while playing for the Eagles?

    a. 72
    b. 79
    c. 83
    d. 87

10. During the 2003-04 season, how many touchdowns did Eagle Correll Buckhalter score?

    a. 5
    b. 7
    c. 9
    d. 11

11. Who was the first Eagles player to return a kickoff for a touchdown?

    a. Emmett Mortel
    b. Dave Smukler
    c. John Kusko
    d. Dick Riffle

12. In 1934, which Eagle scored four touchdowns in the Eagles blowout of the Cincinnati Reds by a score of 64-0?

    a. Swede Hanson
    b. Jim Leonard
    c. Joe Carter
    d. John Norby

13. Who was on the receiving end of Eagle Freddie Mitchell's first NFL touchdown pass?

    a. L.J. Smith
    b. Brian Westbrook
    c. Todd Pinkston
    d. Chad Lewis

14. In 2004, who was the only Eagles defensive player to score a touchdown?

    a. Brian Dawkins
    b. Sheldon Brown
    c. J.R. Reed
    d. Lito Sheppard

15. In 1993, which one of the following Eagles caught 10 touchdown passes?

    a. Calvin Williams
    b. Mark Bavaro
    c. Victor Bailey
    d. Fred Barnett

16. Against which team did Eagles wide receiver Freddie Mitchell throw his first NFL touchdown pass?

    a. Baltimore Ravens
    b. Miami Dolphins
    c. Dallas Cowboys
    d. Seattle Seahawks

17. In 2004, against which team did Eagles quarterback Donovan McNabb pass for five touchdowns in a single game?

    a. Dallas Cowboys
    b. Washington Redskins
    c. Cleveland Browns
    d. Green Bay Packers

18. Who scored the Eagles' first touchdown of the 2005-2006 regular season?

    a. L.J. Smith
    b. Brian Westbrook
    c. Terrell Owens
    d. Greg Lewis

19. Which one of the following players did not have at least two punts returned for a touchdown while playing for the Eagles?

    a. Steve Van Buren
    b. Brian Mitchell
    c. Brian Westbrook
    d. Bosh Pritchard

20. Against which team did Eagles tackle Bill Dunstan recover a fumble and run 46 yards for his first NFL touchdown?

   a. Washington Redskins
   b. St. Louis Cardinals
   c. New Orleans Saints
   d. San Diego Chargers

   <u>answers on page ???</u>

EAGLES-COWBOYS INJURIES

1. In 1990, which Eagles player separated Dallas quarterback Troy Aikman's shoulder?

   a. Clyde Simmons
   b. Seth Joyner
   c. Wes Hopkins
   d. Mike Pitts

2. In 1979, which Cowboys player injured Eagle Harold Carmichael, ending his streak of 127 consecutive games with a catch?

   a. Harvey Martin
   b. Randy White
   c. Dennis Thurman
   d. Benny Barnes

3. Which Dallas Cowboys player caused injury to both Terrell Owens in 2004 and Donovan McNabb in 2005?

   a. Terence Newman
   b. Nate Jones
   c. Roy Williams
   d. Tony Dixon

4. In 1999, Dallas Cowboy Michael Irvin received a career-ending injury caused by which Eagles player?

   a. Brian Dawkins
   b. Al Harris
   c. Allen Rossum
   d. Tim Hauck

5. In 1971, which Eagles player hit Dallas Cowboys quarterback Roger Staubach in the back of the head, which knocked him out?

   a. Steve Zabel
   b. Mel Tom
   c. Al Nelson
   d. Jim Skaggs

6. During the so-called 'Bounty Bowl' game between the Cowboys and Eagles, which Eagle laid out Dallas kicker Luis Zendejas?

   a. Seth Joyner
   b. Andre Waters
   c. Izel Jenkins
   d. Jessie Small

7. In September of 1996, which Dallas Cowboy player was the cause of Eagles quarterback Rodney Peete's season-ending injury?

   a. Tony Tolbert
   b. Darren Woodson
   c. Deion Sanders
   d. Mark Tuinei

answers on page 395

INTERCEPTIONS

1. Who was the last Eagles player to have three interceptions in a single game?

   a. Roynell Young
   b. Joe Scarpati
   c. Michael Zordich
   d. Troy Vincent

2. Which Eagles player was the first in NFL history to lead the league in interceptions in consecutive seasons?

   a. Bill Bradley
   b. Tom Brookshier
   c. Eric Allen
   d. Troy Vincent

3. Before cornerback Lito Sheppard did it in 2004, who was the last Eagles player to return two interceptions for touchdowns in a single season?

   a. Brian Dawkins
   b. Troy Vincent
   c. Eric Allen
   d. Bobby Taylor

4. Which Eagles player holds the team's record for yards returned off of an interception?

   a. Troy Vincent
   b. Bill Bradley
   c. Roynell Young
   d. Eric Allen

5. For the first time in his career, against which team did Eagle Bobby Taylor have two interceptions in a single game?

    a. St. Louis Rams
    b. Seattle Seahawks
    c. Washington Redskins
    d. Arizona Cardinals

6. Which Eagle has the most career interceptions?

    a. Troy Vincent
    b. Brian Dawkins
    c. Eric Allen
    d. Herman Edwards

7. Which Eagle has scored the most career touchdowns off of interceptions?

    a. Joe Scarpati
    b. Roynell Young
    c. Eric Allen
    d. Randy Logan

8. Which Eagle picked off four interceptions in a single game?

   a. Nate Ramsey
   b. Russ Craft
   c. Lito Sheppard
   d. Seth Joyner

9. In 2005, the Seahawks scored touchdowns on two interceptions against the Eagles. Who was the last team to perform the same feat?

   a. Washington Redskins
   b. Los Angeles Rams
   c. Detroit Lions
   d. Baltimore Ravens

10. During the 2004 season, how many interceptions did the Eagles' quarterbacks throw?

   a. 9
   b. 11
   c. 14
   d. 17

11. In 2004, how long was Eagles cornerback Lito Sheppard's longest interception return?

   a. 78 yards
   b. 83 yards
   c. 96 yards
   d. 101 yards

12. In 1999, Troy Vincent became the first Eagle to lead the entire NFL in interceptions. Who was the last Eagle to do so?

   a. Michael Zordich
   b. Herm Edwards
   c. Bill Bradley
   d. Jerry Robinson

13. Which one of the following players did not record at least 30 interceptions in his career while playing for the Eagles?

    a. Herman Edwards
    b. Bill Bradley
    c. Troy Vincent
    d. Eric Allen

14. Which Eagle holds the team's record for most interceptions in a season?

    a. Bill Bradley
    b. Don Burroughs
    c. Herman Edwards
    d. Eric Allen

15. In 1995, who led the Eagles' team with the most interceptions?

    a. Bobby Taylor
    b. William Thomas
    c. Mark McMillian
    d. Michael Zordich

16. How many total inceptions did Reggie White have while playing for the Eagles?

    a. 0
    b. 2
    c. 4
    d. 7

17. Against which team did Eagle Hugh Douglas register his first career interception?

    a. Pittsburgh Steelers
    b. Dallas Cowboys
    c. Tennessee Titans
    d. Atlanta Falcons

18. Which Eagle caught the first interception of the 2005 regular season?

    a. Quintin Mikell
    b. Keith Adams
    c. Brian Dawkins
    d. Michael Lewis

19. In 1957, which Eagles player intercepted a pass that bounced off the goal post, then returned it 99 yards for a touchdown?

    a. Eddie Bell
    b. Neil Worden
    c. Jerry Norton
    d. Tom Brookshier

answers on page 395

KICKERS

1. Before becoming an Eagle who was the holder for Tom Dempsey's record 63-yard field goal attempt?

    a. Joe Scarpati
    b. Clark Hoss
    c. Tony Baker
    d. Norm Snead

2. Which Eagles player started the 'Kicks for Kids' charity?

    a. David Akers
    b. Sean Landeta
    c. Paul McFadden
    d. Tony Franklin

3. For the start of the 2004-05 season, whom did the Eagles list as their third string place kicker?

   a. Dirk Johnson
   b. Chad Lewis
   c. Billy McMullen
   d. Dexter Wynn

4. During the '03 season, how many consecutive field goals did Eagle David Akers make before he missed the 42- and 47-yarders against the 49ers?

   a. 11
   b. 13
   c. 15
   d. 17

5. How many Eagles kickers have had perfect seasons, regarding kicking the point after touchdowns?

   a. 5 different kickers
   b. 9 different kickers
   c. 11 different kickers
   d. 15 different kickers

6. Which of the following Eagles kickers did not wear uniform number 1?

   a. David Jacobs
   b. Nick Mike-Mayer
   c. Gary Anderson
   d. Happy Feller

7. Roger Ruzek of the Eagles was the first one in the NFL to do what?

   a. Kick off with the new commissioner's ball
   b. Kick the ball on a tee
   c. Kick off in the wrong direction
   d. Tackle the runner

8. Which Eagles kicker has scored the most career points after a touchdown?

   a. David Akers
   b. Tony Franklin
   c. Bobby Walston
   d. Sam baker

9. Which two barefooted kickers played for the Eagles during the 20th century?

   a. Chris Boniol and Tony Franklin
   b. Horst Muhlmann and Sam Baker
   c. Tony Franklin and Paul McFadden
   d. Tom Dempsey and Roger Ruzek

10. Which kicker has had the most blocked punts while playing for the Eagles?

   a. John Teltschik
   b. Adrian Burk
   c. Tommy Hutton
   d. Sean Landeta

11. How many punts did John Teltschik of the Eagles kick when he set the NFL rookie record in 1986?

   a. 94
   b. 97
   c. 108
   d. 114

12. In 2004, how many touchbacks did Eagles kicker David Akers have off of his kickoffs?

   a. 12
   b. 14
   c. 16
   d. 18

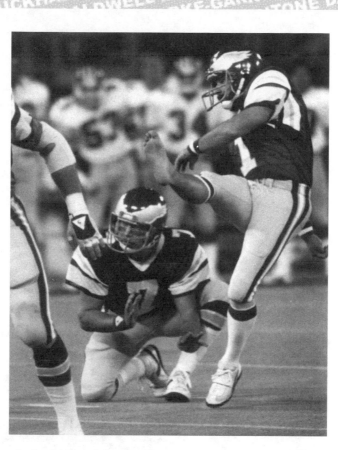

13. Against which team did Tony Franklin kick the Eagles' longest field goal?

     a. Green Bay Packers
     b. Atlanta Falcons
     c. Detroit Lions
     d. Dallas Cowboys

14. Which one of the following Eagles kickers has kicked four field goals of 40 or more yards in a single game?

     a. Gary Anderson
     b. Tony Franklin
     c. David Akers
     d. Luis Zendejas

15. In what year did Eagles kicker David Akers hit 17 consecutive field goals?

    a. 2000
    b. 2001
    c. 2003
    d. 2004

16. Against which team did kicker Tom Dempsey account for all the Eagles points by kicking six field goals in a single game?

    a. Houston Oilers
    b. New Orleans Saints
    c. Chicago Bears
    d. Kansas City Chiefs

17. While playing for the Eagles, how many successful field goals did Tony Franklin make?

    a. 80
    b. 89
    c. 93
    d. 97

18. In 1999, Eagles kicker Norm Johnson finished the season with how many consecutive conversions on extra-point attempts?

    a. 287
    b. 309
    c. 312
    d. 326

19. Which Eagles kicker was the last one to throw a touchdown off of a fake field goal?

    a. Roger Ruzek
    b. Sean Landeta
    c. Paul McFadden
    d. David Akers

20. Against which team did Eagle Tom Dempsey kick his 54-yard field goal at the Vet?

    a. Chicago Bears
    b. Houston Oilers
    c. Detroit Lions
    d. St. Louis Cardinals

answers on page 396

PLAYERS' STRIKE

1. Which one of the following Eagles players did not cross the picket line during the '74 players' strike?

    a. Bill Bergey
    b. Kent Kramer
    c. Roman Gabriel
    d. Jerry Sisemore

2. How many Eagles veterans crossed the picket line during the 1974 players' strike?

    a. 12 players
    b. 17 players
    c. 20 players
    d. 28 players

3. Which one of the following players was not a replacement Eagles player during the '87 players' strike?

   a. Matt Long
   b. Dan McMillan
   c. Troy West
   d. Walter Abercrombie

4. Which one of the following Eagles players did not cross the picket line during the '74 players' strike?

   a. Randy Logan
   b. Johnny Outlaw
   c. Jerry Patton
   d. Don Zimmerman

5. During the '87 NFL players' strike, what was the Eagles team record using replacement players?

   a. 2-1
   b. 1-2
   c. 3-0
   d. 0-3

6. During the '87 NFL players' strike, which one of the following teams did the Eagles not play against with replacement players?

   a. Chicago Bears
   b. New Orleans Saints
   c. Dallas Cowboys
   d. Green Bay Packers

answers on page 397

PUNT RETURNS

1. Who scored on the Eagles' longest punt return?

   a. Duce Staley
   b. Brian Mitchell
   c. Herschel Walker
   d. Vai Sikahema

2. Which Eagle holds the record for the most punt returns in a single game?

   a. J.R. Reed
   b. Vai Sikahema
   c. Larry Marshall
   d. Brian Mitchell

3. Which Eagle has the highest career punt return average?

   a. Brian Westbrook
   b. Brian Mitchell
   c. Bosh Pritchard
   d. Vai Sikahema

4. Who was the first Eagle to score a touchdown off of a punt return?

   a. Ernie Steele
   b. Ed Manske
   c. Steve Van Buren
   d. Neil Worden

5. Which one of the following Eagles never returned a punt return for a touchdown?

    a. Pete Pihos
    b. Allen Rossum
    c. Tommy McDonald
    d. Gregg Garrity

6. Which one of the following Eagles did not score at least two punt return touchdowns?

    a. Brian Westbrook
    b. Steve Van Buren
    c. Larry Marshall
    d. Brian Mitchell

answers on page 397

PUNTERS

1. Who drafted punter Sean Landeta in the 14th round of the first USFL draft?

    a. Philadelphia Stars
    b. New Jersey Generals
    c. Chicago Blitz
    d. Memphis Showboats

2. How many punts did John Teltschik of the Eagles kick when he set the NFL rookie record in 1986?

    a. 94
    b. 97
    c. 108
    d. 114

3. Which Eagles kicker holds the record for 15 punts in a single game?

   a. John Teltschik
   b. Sean Landeta
   c. Jeff Fagles
   d. Tom Hutton

4. Which Eagle holds the team record for the longest punt?

   a. Joe Muha
   b. Randall Cunningham
   c. Sean Landeta
   d. Jeff Feagles

5. Against which team did Randall Cunningham kick a 91-yard punt?

   a. Dallas Cowboys
   b. Los Angeles Raiders
   c. New York Giants
   d. Minnesota Vikings

answers on page 397

SEASON OPENERS

1. Who did the Eagles play in their '34 season opener?

   a. Pittsburgh Steelers
   b. Boston Redskins
   c. Green Bay Packers
   d. Brooklyn Dodgers

2. Who did the Eagles play in their '40 season opener?

    a. Pittsburgh Pirates
    b. Cleveland Rams
    c. Brooklyn Dodgers
    d. Green Bay Packers

3. Who did the Eagles play in their '50 season opener?

    a. Detroit Lions
    b. Cleveland Browns
    c. Los Angeles Rams
    d. Chicago Cardinals

4. Who did the Eagles play in their '60 season opener?

    a. Cleveland Browns
    b. Dallas Cowboys
    c. Pittsburgh Steelers
    d. Washington Redskins

5. Who did the Eagles play in their '70 season opener?

    a. Miami Dolphins
    b. Dallas Cowboys
    c. Chicago Bears
    d. Washington Redskins

6. Who did the Eagles play in their '80 season opener?

    a. Minnesota Vikings
    b. Oakland Raiders
    c. Denver Broncos
    d. San Diego Chargers

7. Who did the Eagles play in their '90 season opener?

    a. Buffalo Bills
    b. New York Giants
    c. Carolina Panthers
    d. Tampa Bay Buccaneers

8. Who did the Eagles play in their '95 season opener?

  a. Tampa Bay Buccaneers
  b. Arizona Cardinals
  c. San Diego Chargers
  d. Oakland Raiders

9. Who did the Eagles play in their 2000 season opener?

  a. Miami Dolphins
  b. Dallas Cowboys
  c. Chicago Bears
  d. Washington Redskins

answers on page 398

SPECIAL TEAMS

1. Against Carolina in 2004, which Eagles player recovered a successful onside kick?

  a. Ike Reese
  b. Sam Rayburn
  c. David Akers
  d. Jeremiah Trotter

2. Who was the last Eagles player to return a blocked punt for a touchdown?

  a. Eric Allen
  b. L.J. Smith
  c. Matt Ware
  d. Ken Rose

3. Prior to Brian Westbrook, who was the last Eagle to return two punts for touchdowns in the same season?

a. Herschel Walker
b. Keith Byars
c. Brian Mitchell
d. Duce Staley

4. Which Eagles player has scored the most touchdowns off of kickoff returns?

a. Timmy Brown
b. Derrick Witherspoon
c. Steve Van Buren
d. Brian Mitchell

5. In 2005, Matt Ware recovered a blocked field goal attempt and ran it in for a touchdown. Did you know that the Eagles only had 10 players on the field? Who was the missing Eagle?

a. Keith Adams
b. Darwin Walker
c. Dhani Jones
d. Mike Patterson

6. In 1947, Bosh Pritchard returned a punt how many yards for a touchdown in the Eagles' Eastern Division playoff game?

a. 58 yards
b. 63 yards
c. 72 yards
d. 79 yards

7. In 2004, who led the Eagles with 33 tackles on special teams?

a. Ike Reese
b. Lito Sheppard
c. Michael Lewis
d. Jeremiah Trotter

8. In 2004, which Eagles player blocked a punt against the Giants?

    a. Derrick Burgess
    b. Sheldon Brown
    c. Jevon Kearse
    d. Mark Simoneau

9. In the sixties, which Eagles player ran for a 100-yard touchdown off of a missed field goal?

    a. Jim Nettles
    b. Nate Ramsey
    c. Maxie Baughan
    d. Al Nelson

answers on page 398

TWO TIMES

1. In 2004, the Eagles defeated the Minnesota Vikings twice. How many points did the Eagles score on each occasion?

    a. 17 points
    b. 23 points
    c. 27 points
    d. 31 points

2. During the 2004 season, which Eagles player intercepted Vikings quarterback Daunte Culpepper in both games they played?

    a. Ike Reese
    b. Brian Dawkins
    c. Sheldon Brown
    d. Michael Lewis

3. In 2004, which Eagles teammates each had a pair of sacks against Green Bay?

     a. Brown/Rayburn
     b. Kearse/Dawkins
     c. Burgess/Green
     d. Simon/Walker

4. Who were the Eagles two first-round picks in the 1973 NFL draft?

     a. John Reaves/Jerry Sisemore
     b. Charles Young/Jerry Sisemore
     c. Mitch Sutton/John Reaves
     d. Richard Harris/Bill Capraun

5. Against which team did Eagle Duce Staley score two rushing touchdowns?

     a. Dallas Cowboys
     b. San Francisco 49ers
     c. Green Bay Packers
     d. Kansas City Chiefs

6. For the first time in his career, Eagle Bobby Taylor had two interceptions in a single game against which team?

     a. St. Louis Rams
     b. Seattle Seahawks
     c. Washington Redskins
     d. Arizona Cardinals

7. Since 2005, in how many games has Eagle Brian
   Westbrook scored two rushing touchdowns?

    a. 0
    b. 2
    c. 4
    d. 6

8. During the '30s, which two years did the Eagles not win
   any home games?

    a. '33/'35
    b. '34/'39
    c. '35/'37
    d. '36/'38

answers on page 399

Honors

EAGLES PRO BOWLERS

1. In what year did Eagle Irv Cross make his first Pro Bowl appearance?

    a. 1959
    b. 1962
    c. 1964
    d. 1969

2. The Eagles sent four defensive players to the 2003 Pro Bowl. Who of the following did not go?

    a. Hugh Douglas
    b. Troy Vincent
    c. Brian Dawkins
    d. Barry Gardner

3. Which of the following Eagles players was not selected to the 1964 Pro Bowl?

    a. Pete Retzlaff
    b. Jim Ringo
    c. Norm Snead
    d. Irv Cross

4. Which of the following Eagles players was not selected for the '96 Pro Bowl?

    a. William Fuller
    b. Ricky Watters
    c. Bobby Taylor
    d. William Thomas

5. Which Eagles player has had the most Pro Bowl appearances?

    a. Pete Pihos
    b. Eric Allen
    c. Reggie White
    d. Chuck Bednarik

6. Prior to the 1998 season, when was the last time the Eagles were not represented in the Pro Bowl game?

    a. 1970
    b. 1971
    c. 1973
    d. 1975

7. In 1954, which Eagle returned an interception for a touchdown and recovered a fumble, which produced a field goal for the East squad?

    a. Chuck Bednarik
    b. Pete Pihos
    c. Al Wistert
    d. John green

8. Which Eagle was named MVP of the '87 Pro Bowl?

    a. Mike Quick
    b. Wes Hopkins
    c. Reggie White
    d. Randall Cunningham

9. Which Eagles player was added to the 2005 Pro Bowl team after another selected player was injured?

    a. Brian Dawkins
    b. Tra Thomas
    c. David Akers
    d. Reggie Brown

10. Who is the only Eagles player to appear in seven consecutive Pro Bowls?

    a. Chuck Bednarik
    b. Pete Pihos
    c. Tommy McDonald
    d. Reggie White

11. In which year was Eagle Marion Campbell selected to the Pro Bowl?

    a. 1956
    b. 1959
    c. 1962
    d. 1967

answers on page 399

EAGLES HONORS

1. In what year was the Eagles Honor Roll started?

    a. 1985
    b. 1987
    c. 1989
    d. 1991

2. Who was selected as the Eagles' special teams MVP in 2003?

    a. Sean Morey
    b. Brian Westbrook
    c. David Akers
    d. Keith Adams

3. In 2000, which Eagle was named to Howie Long's 'Tough Guy' team?

    a. Hugh Douglas
    b. Duce Staley
    c. Jon Runyan
    d. Brian Dawkins

4. When did the Eagles become the first team in 16 years to lead the NFL in total defense, run defense, and pass defense?

    a. 1987
    b. 1989
    c. 1991
    d. 1993

5. In 2003, which Eagles player was named by the Sporting News as the magazine's 'Good Guy in Sports'?

    a. Hugh Douglas
    b. Troy Vincent
    c. Bobby Taylor
    d. Brian Dawkins

6. Which one of the following Eagles players never won the Maxwell Club's Bert Bell Award?

    a. Norm Van Brocklin
    b. Pete Retzlaff
    c. Donovan McNabb
    d. Ron Jaworski

7. Which one of the following Eagles players never won the Ed Block Courage Award?

    a. Chad Lewis
    b. Derrick Burgess
    c. Shawn Barber
    d. Ron Heller

8. Bill Hewitt was the first NFL player to earn all-league honors with the Eagles and which other team?

    a. Chicago Bears
    b. Detroit Lions
    c. Pittsburgh Pirates
    d. St. Louis Gunners

9. Who was the only Eagles player to win the Associated Press NFL Most Valuable Player Award?

    a. Chuck Bednarik
    b. Pete Retzlaff
    c. Norm Van Brocklin
    d. Alex Wojciechowicz

answers on page 400

EAGLES PRO BOWLS

1. Former Eagle Reggie White appeared in how many consecutive Pro Bowl games while with the Eagles?

    a. 5 games
    b. 6 games
    c. 7 games
    d. 8 games

2. Who was the only Eagle selected to play in the '84 Pro Bowl?

    a. Wilbert Montgomery
    b. Randall Cunningham
    c. Jerry Robinson
    d. Mike Quick

3. How many Eagles players were selected for the '98 Pro Bowl team?

     a. 1 player
     b. 3 players
     c. 5 players
     d. None

4. In what year did the Eagles send the most players to the NFL Pro Bowl?

     a. 1960
     b. 1978
     c. 1980
     d. 2003

5. Prior to the 1998 season, when was the last time the Eagles were not represented in the Pro Bowl game?

     a. 1970
     b. 1971
     c. 1973
     d. 1975

6. Which one of the following Eagles linebackers did not have at least four Pro Bowl appearances?

     a. Jeremiah Trotter
     b. Maxie Baughan
     c. Bill Bergey
     d. Frank LeMaster

7. Who was the only Eagles player selected to start on the 2005 NFC Pro Bowl?

     a. Brian Dawkins
     b. Jeremiah Trotter
     c. Brian Westbrook
     d. L.J. Smith

8. Who was the lone Eagle selected to the 1998 NFC Pro Bowl squad?

    a. William Fuller
    b. Ricky Watters
    c. William Thomas
    d. Irving Fryar

9. Which one of the following Eagle Pro Bowlers was not selected as the Bowl's MVP?

    a. Floyd Peters
    b. Tommy McDonald
    c. Randall Cunningham
    d. Chuck Bednarik

10. Which one of the following players that was drafted by the Eagles did not make a Pro Bowl appearance?

    a. Bobby Taylor
    b. Lito Sheppard
    c. Michael Lewis
    d. Brian Westbrook

11. Which one of the following Eagles did not participate in the 1951 Pro Bowl?

    a. Chuck Bednarik
    b. Al Wistert
    c. John Green
    d. Russ Craft

12. In 1967, which Eagles player was selected MVP of the Pro Bowl?

    a. Bob Brown
    b. Jim Ringo
    c. Floyd Peters
    d. Maxie Baughan

13. In what year did the Eagles have two players selected with All-Pro Honors for the first time?

     a. 1936
     b. 1938
     c. 1940
     d. 1942

14. Name the Eagle who earned five Pro Bowl appearances in six seasons from 1989–1994.

     a. Mike Quick
     b. Randall Cunningham
     c. Eric Allen
     d. Keith Jackson

15. In what year did Eagle Lito Sheppard make his first Pro Bowl appearance?

     a. 2001
     b. 2003
     c. 2004
     d. 2005

16. In what year was Eagles quarterback Randall Cunningham selected as the Pro Bowl's Most Valuable Player?

     a. 1987
     b. 1989
     c. 1991
     d. 1993

17. Which one of the following Eagles safety was never selected to the Pro Bowl?

     a. Wes Hopkins
     b. Brian Dawkins
     c. Bill Bradley
     d. Brenard Wilson

answers on page 400

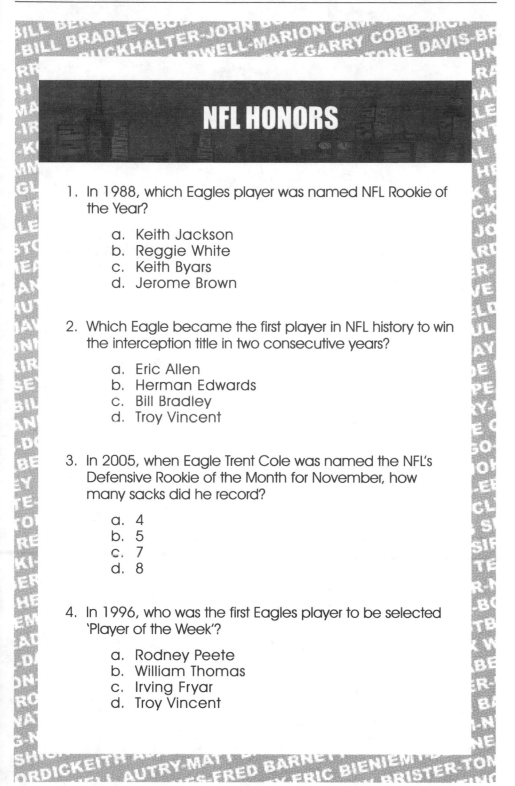

NFL HONORS

1. In 1988, which Eagles player was named NFL Rookie of the Year?

    a. Keith Jackson
    b. Reggie White
    c. Keith Byars
    d. Jerome Brown

2. Which Eagle became the first player in NFL history to win the interception title in two consecutive years?

    a. Eric Allen
    b. Herman Edwards
    c. Bill Bradley
    d. Troy Vincent

3. In 2005, when Eagle Trent Cole was named the NFL's Defensive Rookie of the Month for November, how many sacks did he record?

    a. 4
    b. 5
    c. 7
    d. 8

4. In 1996, who was the first Eagles player to be selected 'Player of the Week'?

    a. Rodney Peete
    b. William Thomas
    c. Irving Fryar
    d. Troy Vincent

5. Against which team did Brian Mitchell of the Eagles become the NFL's all-time career kickoff return yardage leader?

    a. Houston Oilers
    b. New Orleans Saints
    c. Pittsburgh Steelers
    d. Detroit Lions

6. Which one of the following Eagles Head Coaches was not a recipient of the NFL's Coach of the Year Award?

    a. Greasy Neale
    b. Ray Rhodes
    c. Andy Reid
    d. Ed Khayat

7. During the 2003 season, when was Eagles quarterback Donovan McNabb named the NFC's Offensive Player of the Month?

    a. October
    b. November
    c. December
    d. He never was selected

8. In 1973, which Eagles player won the NFL's Comeback Player Award?

    a. Norm Bulaich
    b. Charlie Young
    c. Po James
    d. Roman Gabriel

9. Which Eagles player was named the 1980 Walter Payton NFL Man of the Year?

    a. Ron Jaworski
    b. Harold Carmichael
    c. Mike Quick
    d. Randy Logan

10. Which Eagles player was inducted into the NFL Hall of Fame in 1971?

    a. Pete Pihos
    b. Chuck Bednarik
    c. Ollie Matson
    d. Norm Van Brocklin

11. Which of the following Eagles players has been a 'Rookie of the Year'?

    a. Paul McFadden
    b. Reggie White
    c. Ron Jaworski
    d. Steve Van Buren

12. In November 2005, which Eagles rookie received a monthly honor?

    a. Ryan Moats
    b. Reggie Brown
    c. Trent Cole
    d. Mike Patterson

13. Which of the following Eagles players was named to an all-rookie team in his career?

    a. L.J. Smith
    b. Hollis Thomas
    c. Brian Westbrook
    d. Brian Dawkins

14. In 1971, which Eagle was named to the Associated Press All-Pro Team?

    a. Tom Woodeshick
    b. Pete Retzlaff
    c. Bill Bradley
    d. Tom Dempsey

15. Which player was the first Eagle to be honored as the NFL's Most Valuable Player?

    a. Norm Van Brocklin
    b. Pete Retzlaff
    c. Bucko Kilroy
    d. Chuck Bednarik

16. Which Eagles player is the shortest player to have been inducted into the Pro Football Hall of Fame?

    a. Sonny Jurgensen
    b. Ollie Matson
    c. Bill Hewitt
    d. Tommy McDonald

17. In which year did Eagles Head Coach Dick Vermeil win Coach of the Year?

    a. 1976
    b. 1978
    c. 1979
    d. 1980

18. Which Eagle was named Rookie of the Year in 1988?

    a. Mike Quick
    b. Randall Cunningham
    c. Keith Jackson
    d. Matt Cavanaugh

19. Which of the following Eagles players never won the NFL's Comeback Player of the Year Award?

    a. Ron Jaworski
    b. Randall Cunningham
    c. Roman Gabriel
    d. Jim McMahon

20. Who was Eagle Chuck Bednarik's presenter when he was inducted into the Pro Football Hall of Fame?

    a. Maxie Baughan
    b. Pete Retzlaff
    c. Greasy Neale
    d. Steve Van Buren

answers on page 401

RETIRED JERSEYS

1. Chuck Bednarik had his Eagles jersey number 60 retired, but who was the first player to wear this jersey number?

   a.   Don Weedon
   b.   Bob Suffridge
   c.   Alvin Thacker
   d.   Ed Michaels

answers on page 401

RETIRED JERSEYS

2. Jerome Brown had his Eagles jersey number 99 retired, but who was the first player to wear this jersey number?

    a. Joe Drake
    b. Skip Hamilton
    c. Greg Liter
    d. Mel Tom

answers on page 401

RETIRED JERSEYS

3. Steve Van Buren had his Eagles jersey number 15 retired,
   but who was the first player to wear this jersey number?

   a. Dick Lackman
   b. Laf Russell
   c. Stumpy Thomason
   d. Osborne Willson

answers on page 401

RETIRED JERSEYS

4. Al Wistert had his Eagles jersey number 70 retired, but who was the last player to wear this jersey number before him?

   a.   Don Owens
   b.   Leo Brennan
   c.   Jim Skaggs
   d.   Joseph Frank

answers on page 401

RETIRED JERSEYS

5. Pete Retzlaff had his Eagles jersey number 44 retired, but who was the first player to wear this jersey number?

    a. Harry Dowda
    b. Albert Johnson
    c. Norm Willey
    d. Frank Emmons

answers on page 401

RETIRED JERSEYS

6. Tom Brookshier had his Eagles jersey number 40 retired, but who was the first player to wear this jersey number?

   a. Charles Newton
   b. Sonny Karnofsky
   c. Frank Reagan
   d. Elliott Ormsbe

answers on page 401

RETIRED JERSEYS

7. Reggie White had his Eagles jersey number 92 retired, but who was the first player to wear this jersey number?

   a. Greg Mark
   b. Steve Martin
   c. Smiley Creswell
   d. he was

answers on page 401

PUZZLES

RETIRED JERSEYS

```
A T E A J K N E B N O L R
A O T E E W E H T I R R E
B M I O R E R I I O R N J
S B H E O N U B G N N L O
E R W E M E B U E I T N F
G O E E E Z N O G N S S A
I O I N B N A T I T K J E
B K G A R R V R E U U C C
G S G A O R E O H W O A G
E H E T W E V E E R T E C
K I R A N D E B K C U H C
P E T E R E T Z L A F F R
R R A L W I S T E R T N A
```

AlWistert   ChuckBednarik   JeromeBrown
PeteRetzlaff   ReggieWhite   SteveVanBuren
TomBrookshier

answers on page 432

PERCHED IN THE HALL

CHUCK BEDNARIK
CENTER-LINEBACKER
PLAYED WITH THE EAGLES 1949-62
CLASS OF 1967

BERT BELL
OWNER- HEAD COACH
YEARS WITH EAGLES 1933-40
CLASS OF 1963

BOB BROWN
OFFENSIVE TACKLE
PLAYED WITH THE EAGLES 1964-68
CLASS OF 2004

PERCHED IN THE HALL

MIKE DITKA
TIGHT END
PLAYED WITH THE EAGLES 1967-68
CLASS OF 1988

SID GILLMAN
COACH
YEARS WITH EAGLES 1979-80
CLASS OF 1983

BILL HEWITT
END
PLAYED WITH THE EAGLES 1937-39
CLASS OF 1971

PERCHED IN THE HALL

SONNY JURGENSEN
QUARTERBACK
PLAYED WITH THE EAGLES 1957-63
CLASS OF 1983

MARV LEVY
COACH
YEARS WITH EAGLES 1969
CLASS OF 2001

JAMES LOFTON
WIDE RECEIVER
PLAYED WITH THE EAGLES 1993
CLASS OF 2003

PERCHED IN THE HALL

OLLIE MATSON
HALFBACK
PLAYED WITH THE EAGLES 1964-66
CLASS OF 1972

TOMMY MCDONALD
WIDE RECEIVER
PLAYED WITH THE EAGLES 1957-63
CLASS OF 1998

EARLE (GREASY) NEALE
COACH
YEARS WITH EAGLES 1941-50
CLASS OF 1969

PERCHED IN THE HALL

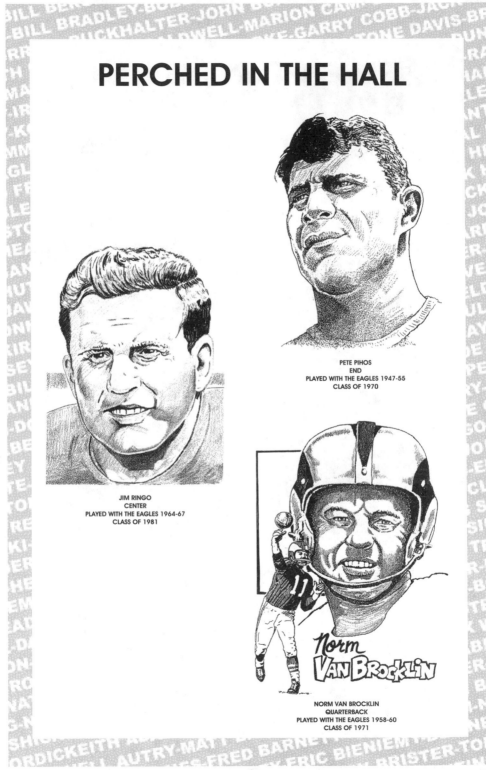

PETE PIHOS
END
PLAYED WITH THE EAGLES 1947-55
CLASS OF 1970

JIM RINGO
CENTER
PLAYED WITH THE EAGLES 1964-67
CLASS OF 1981

NORM VAN BROCKLIN
QUARTERBACK
PLAYED WITH THE EAGLES 1958-60
CLASS OF 1971

PERCHED IN THE HALL

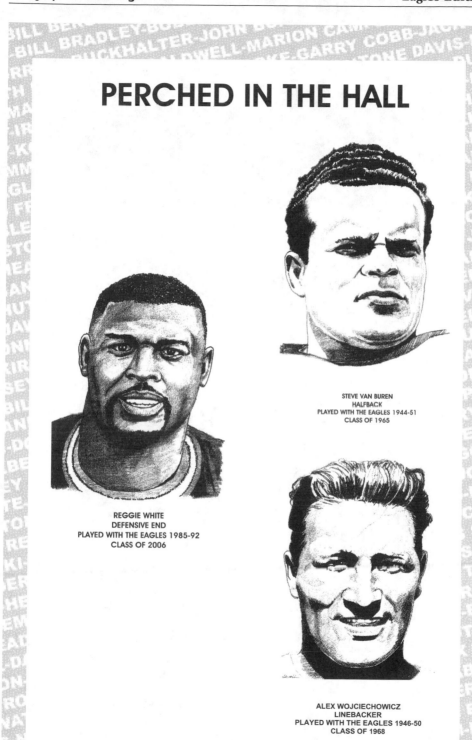

STEVE VAN BUREN
HALFBACK
PLAYED WITH THE EAGLES 1944-51
CLASS OF 1965

REGGIE WHITE
DEFENSIVE END
PLAYED WITH THE EAGLES 1985-92
CLASS OF 2006

ALEX WOJCIECHOWICZ
LINEBACKER
PLAYED WITH THE EAGLES 1946-50
CLASS OF 1968

PUZZLES

HALL OF FAMERS

```
P N I S J I M R I N G O S O A
N O B O E E N R I A L Z U A L
I S N H N B R E G L B N I N E
L N D R R S O H I P E T E P X
K E N I E O E E B B A R M E W
C G U T B E M V R T U O J E O
O R K I R A N D E B K C U H C
R U E E T O E L N R S N V L I
B J G S G R E A S Y N E A L E
N Y O I E O V N N N L O I E C
A N Y N E E T J E M U B V B H
V N H E V U E O B K L U Y T O
M N B E E A G N J T W S E R W
R O T T I W E H L L I B A E I
O S M N A C A E O V A N X B C
N T O M M Y M C D O N A L D Z
```

AlexWociechowicz   BertBell   BillHewitt
ChuckBednarik   GreasyNeale   JimRingo
NormVanBrocklin   OllieMatson   PetePihos
SonnnyJurgenson   SteveVanBuren   TommyMcDonald

answers on page 430

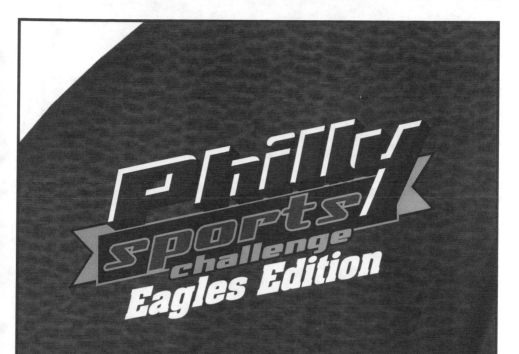

Postseasons

EAGLES POSTSEASONS

1. Who did the Eagles play in the team's first ever playoff game?

   a. Pittsburgh Steelers
   b. Chicago Bears
   c. Los Angeles Rams
   d. Green Bay Packers

2. Who did the Eagles defeat to win their first NFL Championship?

   a. Boston Yanks
   b. Detroit Lions
   c. Washington Redskins
   d. Chicago Cardinals

3. Against which team did Eagles quarterback Ron Jaworski throw three touchdowns in a postseason game?

   a. Minnesota Vikings
   b. Chicago Bears
   c. Tampa Bay Buccaneers
   d. Dallas Cowboys

4. Which Eagles quarterback is the only one to pass for over 400 yards in a playoff game?

   a. Norm Van Brocklin
   b. Randall Cunningham
   c. Donovan McNabb
   d. Ron Jaworski

5. How many Eagle post season games were played at the Vet?

    a. 8
    b. 11
    c. 13
    d. 15

6. Which team did the Eagles score the most points against in a playoff game?

    a. Detroit Lions
    b. St. Louis Rams
    c. Chicago Bears
    d. Arizona Cardinals

7. Who holds the Eagles' postseason record for the longest run from scrimmage?

    a. Duce Staley
    b. RIcky Watters
    c. Brian Westbrook
    d. Wilbert Montgomery

8. Who scored the Eagles first touchdown in the '60 NFL Championship game?

    a. Billy Barnes
    b. Timmy Brown
    c. Clarence Peaks
    d. Tommy McDonald

9. Who scored the Eagles winning touchdown in the '60 NFL Championship game?

    a. Pete Retzlaff
    b. Bobby Walston
    c. Ted Dean
    d. Norm Van Brocklin

10. To whom did Eagles quarterback Randall Cunningham throw the Eagles' longest pass in postseason history?

    a. Calvin Williams
    b. Keith Jackson
    c. Fred Barnett
    d. Keith Byars

11. In the 1978 playoff game against Atlanta, which kicker missed his field goal attempt, costing the Eagles the game?

    a. Tony Franklin
    b. Nick Mike-Mayer
    c. Horst Muhlmann
    d. Mike Michel

12. Who did the Eagles defeat in the 1979 NFC Wild Card playoff game?

    a. Tampa Bay Buccaneers
    b. Chicago Bears
    c. Atlanta Falcons
    d. Minnesota Vikings

13. During the '81 Wild Card playoff game against the Giants which Eagles player fumbled two kick-off returns?

    a. Larry Marshall
    b. Billy Campfield
    c. Wally Henry
    d. Louie Gammona

14. In the '81 NFC title game against the Cowboys, how many yards did Wilbert Montgomery gain on the ground?

    a. 187 yards
    b. 194 yards
    c. 201 yards
    d. 219 yards

15. During the '89 Wild Card playoff game against the Los Angeles Rams who was the only Eagle to score a touchdown?

    a. Heath Sherman
    b. Cris Carter
    c. Anthony Toney
    d. Keith Byars

16. During the '91 Wild Card playoff game against the Redskins who replaced Eagles quarterback Randall Cunningham for one series of downs?

    a. Jeff Kemp
    b. Pat Ryan
    c. Keith Byars
    d. Jim McMahon

17. During the '95 season, the Eagles set an NFL playoff record for the most combined points in a game when they defeated which team?

    a. Tampa Bay Buccaneers
    b. Detroit Lions
    c. Atlanta Falcons
    d. Chicago Bears

18. Against which team did Eagles quarterback Rodney Peete throw three touchdowns in a postseason game?

    a. Detroit Lions
    b. San Francisco 49ers
    c. Arizona Cardinals
    d. New Orleans Saints

19. Against which team did Eagle Donovan McNabb complete two touchdown passes and run for another in his first playoff game appearance?

a. Tampa Bay Buccaneers
b. Green Bay Packers
c. Detroit Lions
d. Atlanta Falcons

20. Prior to 2001, when was the last time the Eagles won an NFC East Title?

    a. 1960
    b. 1965
    c. 1974
    d. 1988

21. Which one of the following teams did the Eagles not play in the 2001-2002 NFL playoffs?

    a. Tampa Bay Buccaneers
    b. St. Louis Rams
    c. Green Bay Packers
    d. Chicago Bears

22. In the 2002 NFC Championship game against St. Louis, who was the Eagles' leading rusher?

    a. Donovan McNabb
    b. Duce Staley
    c. Correll Buckhalter
    d. Dorsey Levens

23. Eagles quarterback Donovan McNabb rushed for how many yards against the Packers during the '03 playoff game?

    a. 101 yards
    b. 103 yards
    c. 107 yards
    d. 114 yards

24. During the Eagles /Packers '03 playoff game, how many yards did the Eagles actually gain on the fourth down and 26 yards to go play?

    a. 26 yards
    b. 27 yards
    c. 28 yards
    d. 30 yards

25. Jon Runyan has played in how many postseason games from 1999 through 2005?

    a. 12
    b. 14
    c. 16
    d. 18

26. David Akers kicked the game-winning field goal from which yard line, to win the '03 playoff game against the Packers?

    a. 27 yard line
    b. 31 yard line
    c. 33 yard line
    d. 37 yard line

27. During the Eagles/Packers '03 playoff game, David Akers missed a field goal from how many yards?

    a. 29 yards
    b. 31 yards
    c. 33 yards
    d. 37 yards

28. Against the Minnesota Vikings, which Eagles player recovered L.J. Smith's fumble in the end zone for the Eagles third touchdown of the game?

    a. Freddie Mitchell
    b. Terrell Owens

    c. Reggie Brown
    d. Greg Lewis

29. How many catches did Eagle Freddie Mitchell have in the '03 playoff game against the Packers?

    a. 1 catch
    b. 2 catches
    c. 4 catches
    d. 5 catches

30. Eagles quarterback Donovan McNabb rushed for how many yards against the Packers during the '03 playoff game?

    a. 101 yards
    b. 103 yards
    c. 107 yards
    d. 114 yards

31. Who scored the Eagles' first touchdown in the 2004 NFC Title game?

    a. Brian Westbrook
    b. Chad Lewis
    c. Dorsey Levens
    d. Josh Parry

32. Prior to 2004, how many years had it been since the Eagles last appeared in a Super Bowl?

    a. 18
    b. 24
    c. 27
    d. 32

33. How many postseason wins have the Eagles recorded under head coach Andy Reid, including the victory over the Atlanta Falcons in the 2004 NFC Championship game?

    a. 15
    b. 17
    c. 19
    d. 21

34. In the 2004 NFC Championship game, which Eagles player scored two touchdowns in the win over Atlanta?

    a. Brian Westbrook
    b. Terrell Owens
    c. J.R. Reed
    d. Chad Lewis

35. Prior to the 2005 season, in how many NFC Wild Card games had the Eagles played?

    a. 8 games
    b. 10 games
    c. 12 games
    d. 14 games

36. By the end of the 2005 season, the Eagles have played in 32 postseason games. How many of them were played in Philadelphia?

    a. 9
    b. 15
    c. 18
    d. 23

answers on page 402

SUPER BOWL

1. Which Eagles player wore two different brands of shoes, one on each foot, in Super Bowl XV?

    a. Leroy Harris
    b. Ron Jaworski
    c. Randy Logan
    d. Wilbert Montgomery

2. In their 1980 Super Bowl, which Eagles player led the team in receiving yards?

    a. Wally Henry
    b. Harold Carmichael
    c. Wilbert Montgomery
    d. Charlie Smith

3. In Super Bowl XV, name the tight end who scored the only Eagles touchdown, in their 27-10 loss to the Oakland Raiders.

    a. John Spagnola
    b. David Little
    c. Mickey Shuler
    d. Keith Krepfle

4. In 2005, what was the final score of the Eagles' Super Bowl loss to the New England Patriots?

    a. 17-14
    b. 24-21
    c. 19-17
    d. 27-24

5. Which Eagles player caught the first touchdown pass against the Patriots in Super Bowl XXXIX?

    a. Chad Lewis
    b. Terrell Owens
    c. Brian Westbrook
    d. L.J. Smith

6. What was Eagle quarterback Donovan McNabb's longest completion in Super Bowl XXXIX?

    a. 40 yards
    b. 48 yards
    c. 53 yards
    d. 61 yards

7. Which one of the following Eagles players never won a Super Bowl with another team?

    a. Sean Landeta
    b. Mike Bartrum
    c. Jeff Thomason
    d. Brian Mitchell

8. In Super Bowl XXXIX, which Eagles player caught the last touchdown pass from Donovan McNabb?

   a. L.J. Smith
   b. Chad Lewis
   c. Greg Lewis
   d. Thomas Tapeh

9. How many receptions did Eagle Terrell Owens have in Super Bowl XXXIX?

   a. 7
   b. 9
   c. 10
   d. 12

10. When Chad Lewis got injured prior to Super Bowl XXXIX, whom did the Eagles sign to replace him?

   a. Stephen Spach
   b. Dorsey Levens
   c. Jeff Thomason
   d. Chauncey Stovell

11. Who did the Eagles defeat in the 1980 NFC Championship game to advance to Super Bowl XV?

    a. St. Louis Cardinals
    b. Dallas Cowboys
    c. Minnesota Vikings
    d. Oakland Raiders

12. The Eagles had two sacks in Super Bowl XXXIX. One was credited as a team sack; who was credited with the other?

    a. Jeremiah Trotter
    b. Brian Dawkins
    c. Derrick Burgess
    d. Sam Rayburn

13. What was the game-day point spread for the Eagles Super Bowl appearance in 1981?

    a. Eagles by 3
    b. Raiders by 4
    c. Eagles by 6
    d. Raiders by 7.5

answers on page 403

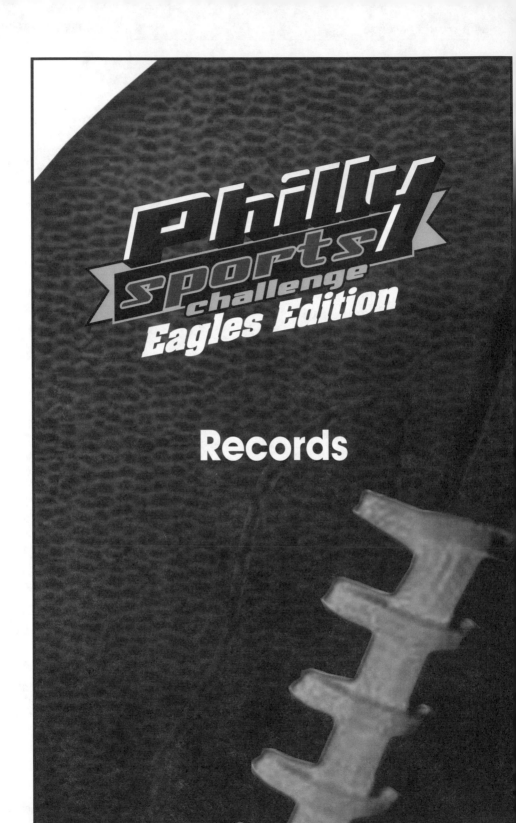

Records

EAGLES HIGHS AND LOWS

1. During the 2000 season, the Eagles ran up the score to 41 points against which team?

   a. Dallas Cowboys
   b. Atlanta Falcons
   c. Cleveland Browns
   d. Arizona Cardinals

2. Against which NFL team did the Eagles score 64 points?

   a. Chicago Cardinals
   b. New York Bulldogs
   c. Los Angeles Rams
   d. Cincinnati Reds

3. The Eagles once ended a game in a 0-0 tie. Who were they playing?

   a. Brooklyn Dodgers
   b. Cincinnati Reds
   c. New York Bulldogs
   d. Chicago Cardinals

4. In 2005, the Seattle Seahawks shut out the Eagles 42-0 in Seattle. Who was the last team to shut out the Eagles at the Linc?

   a. Tampa Bay Buccaneers
   b. New England Patriots
   c. Green Bay Packers
   d. Tennessee Titans

5. Which team defeated the Eagles by the score 49-0?

    a. Seattle Seahawks
    b. New York Giants
    c. Green Bay Packers
    d. Chicago Bears

6. The Eagles started the 2002 season with a team-record three game scoring total. How many points did they score?

    a. 98 points
    b. 105 points
    c. 109 points
    d. 114 points

7. When was the first time the Eagles had four shutouts in a single season?

    a. 1934
    b. 1936
    c. 1939
    d. 1942

8. In 1972, which NFL team scored 62 points in a single game against the Eagles?

    a. St. Louis Rams
    b. Kansas City Chiefs
    c. Los Angeles Rams
    d. New York Giants

9. In 2004, who were the Eagles playing when they scored a season-high 49 points in a single game?

    a. Baltimore Ravens
    b. Dallas Cowboys
    c. Washington Redskins
    d. New York Giants

10. Who were the Eagles playing when they fell behind 24-0 at halftime and came back in the second half to win the game 28-24?

    a. Oakland Raiders
    b. Washington Redskins
    c. New York Jets
    d. Tennessee Titans

11. In 1996, which team did the Eagles shut out by the score 24-0?

    a. New York Giants
    b. Indianapolis Colts
    c. Carolina Panthers
    d. Atlanta Falcons

12. In which year did the Eagles have their highest scoring team?

    a. 1948
    b. 1960
    c. 1980
    d. 2004

13. Which NFL team was the only one to shut out the Eagles during the 2003 season?

    a. Tampa Bay Buccaneers
    b. New England Patriots
    c. New York Jets
    d. Buffalo Bills

14. In 1942, how many points did the Eagles score for the entire season?

    a. 87 points
    b. 96 points
    c. 105 points
    d. 123 points   <u>answers on page 403</u>

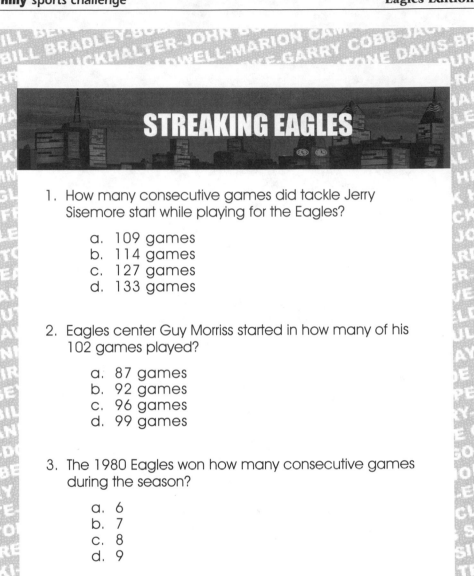

STREAKING EAGLES

1. How many consecutive games did tackle Jerry Sisemore start while playing for the Eagles?

    a. 109 games
    b. 114 games
    c. 127 games
    d. 133 games

2. Eagles center Guy Morriss started in how many of his 102 games played?

    a. 87 games
    b. 92 games
    c. 96 games
    d. 99 games

3. The 1980 Eagles won how many consecutive games during the season?

    a. 6
    b. 7
    c. 8
    d. 9

4. Eagles' Harold Carmichael set an NFL record when he caught a pass in 105 consecutive games. Whose record did he break?

    a. Dan Abramowicz
    b. Jack Snow
    c. Chris Collinsworth
    d. Lynn Swann

5. What has been the Eagles' longest consecutive winning streak?

     a. 8 games
     b. 9 games
     c. 12 games
     d. 14 games

6. By the end of the 2005 season, Eagle Jon Runyan had started in how many consecutive games?

     a. 140
     b. 141
     c. 144
     d. 145

7. Former Eagles receiver Irving Fryar had how many consecutive 50-reception seasons?

     a. 3 seasons
     b. 5 seasons
     c. 8 seasons
     d. 10 seasons

8. Which Eagle holds the record for the most consecutive games with rushing touchdowns?

     a. Randall Cunningham
     b. Ricky Watters
     c. Steve Van Buren
     d. Duce Staley

9. The Eagles under Head Coach Greasy Neale set a franchise record by scoring at least one touchdown in how many consecutive games?

     a. 67
     b. 73
     c. 88
     d. 92

10. Who were the Eagles playing when Harold Carmichael's streak of 127 consecutive games with a reception was broken?

     a. Chicago Bears
     b. New York Giants
     c. Dallas Cowboys
     d. Washington Redskins

11. When Eagles' Harold Carmichael set a team record by playing in 162 consecutive games, at the same time another Eagle moved into second place with 159 consecutive games. Name him.

     a. Randy Logan
     b. Tommy McDonald
     c. Wilbert Montgomery
     d. Charles Young

12. In 2004, how many consecutive games did the Eagles win?

     a. 6
     b. 7
     c. 8
     d. 9

13. The Eagles set a franchise record by winning how many consecutive home games from 1947 through 1949?

     a. 12
     b. 14
     c. 15
     d. 17

14. The 2004 Eagles were the first team ever to host how many consecutive conference championships?

     a. 2
     b. 3
     c. 4
     d. 6

15. During the 2004 season, the Eagles won four consecutive games by at least 20 points. In what year was this first achieved?

    a. 1946
    b. 1949
    c. 1951
    d. 1957

16. The Eagles have won nine consecutive games twice, in 1960 and in what other year?

    a. 1976
    b. 1999
    c. 2001
    d. 2003

17. During the 1947 season, how many consecutive games did Eagle Steve Van Buren score a rushing touchdown in?

    a. 6
    b. 8
    c. 9
    d. 11

18. Harold Carmichael set an Eagles record by playing in how many consecutive games?

    a. 153
    b. 162
    c. 174
    d. 187

19. When Eagles quarterback Ron Jaworski broke his leg during the '84 season, it ended his streak of how many consecutive starts?

    a. 97 games
    b. 110 games
    c. 116 games
    d. 127 games

answers on page 404

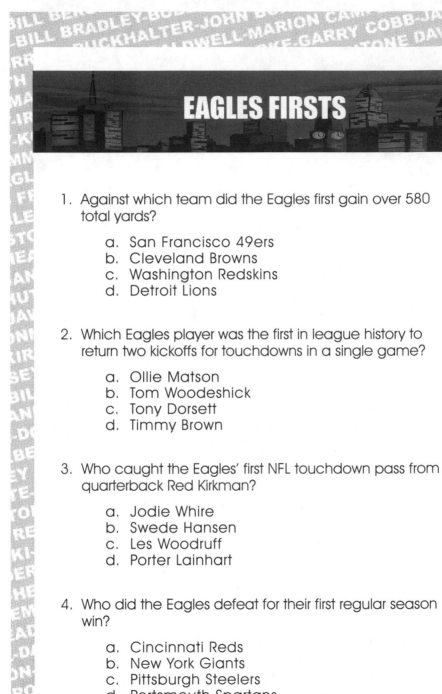

EAGLES FIRSTS

1. Against which team did the Eagles first gain over 580 total yards?

     a. San Francisco 49ers
     b. Cleveland Browns
     c. Washington Redskins
     d. Detroit Lions

2. Which Eagles player was the first in league history to return two kickoffs for touchdowns in a single game?

     a. Ollie Matson
     b. Tom Woodeshick
     c. Tony Dorsett
     d. Timmy Brown

3. Who caught the Eagles' first NFL touchdown pass from quarterback Red Kirkman?

     a. Jodie Whire
     b. Swede Hansen
     c. Les Woodruff
     d. Porter Lainhart

4. Who did the Eagles defeat for their first regular season win?

     a. Cincinnati Reds
     b. New York Giants
     c. Pittsburgh Steelers
     d. Portsmouth Spartans

5. Who were the Eagles playing when they first used the new football bearing NFL Commissioner Paul Tagliabue's name on it?

    a. St. Louis Rams
    b. Green Bay Packers
    c. Washington Redskins
    d. New York Giants

6. When the Eagles lost their first home game, what was the score?

    a. 24-21
    b. 25-0
    c. 33-17
    d. 56-19

7. Who scored the Eagles' first safety?

    a. George Kenneally
    b. Ray Keeling
    c. Albert Weiner
    d. Joe Pivarnick

8. Who did the Eagles defeat 6-0 for the team's first shutout?

    a. New York Giants
    b. Cincinnati Reds
    c. Pittsburgh Pirates
    d. Cleveland Browns

9. How many games did it take the 1933 Eagles to win their first game?

    a. 2
    b. 4
    c. 6
    d. 8

10. Against which team did Eagle Reggie Brown score his first NFL touchdown?

    a. Dallas Cowboys
    b. Green Bay Packers
    c. Oakland Raiders
    d. Washington Redskins

11. Who was the first Eagles player to gain 200 receiving yards in a single game?

    a. Pete Pihos
    b. Bobby Walston
    c. Ben Hawkins
    d. Bud Grant

12. Who did the Eagles play in their first overtime game?

    a. New Orleans Saints
    b. Detroit Lions
    c. Atlanta Falcons
    d. Washington Redskins

13. Who was the first Eagles player to rush for 100 yards in a single game?

    a. Steve Van Buren
    b. Joe Carter
    c. Dave Smukler
    d. Swede Hanson

14. In 1933, which Eagle kicked the first successful field goal?

    a. Roger Kirkman
    b. Dave Smukler
    c. Guy Turnbow
    d. Bob Gonya

15. Which Eagles quarterback was the first to attempt 60 or
more passes in a single game?

    a. Roman Gabriel
    b. Randall Cunningham
    c. Davey O'Brien
    d. Sonny Jurgensen

16. Against which team did Brian Westbrook record his first
career 100-yard rushing game?

    a. Chicago Bears
    b. Detroit Lions
    c. Buffalo Bills
    d. New York Giants

17. Which Eagles player caught Donovan McNabb's first
touchdown pass?

    a. Duce Staley
    b. Cecil Martin
    c. James Thrash
    d. Chad Lewis

18. Which quarterback threw the first interception that Eagle
Brian Dawkins caught?

    a. Vinny Testaverde
    b. Troy Aikman
    c. Jake Plummer
    d. Bobby Herbert

19. Which team did quarterback Bobby Hoying defeat to
earn his first win as an Eagles starter?

    a. Pittsburgh Steelers
    b. Green Bay Packers
    c. Baltimore Ravens
    d. Detroit Lions

20. Against which team did Eagle Brian Westbrook score his first career touchdown?

    a. New York Giants
    b. Buffalo Bills
    c. Kansas City Chiefs
    d. Baltimore Ravens

21. Against which team did Eagles running back Brian Westbrook notch the first 100-yard rushing game of his career?

    a. Minnesota Vikings
    b. New York Giants
    c. Baltimore Ravens
    d. Miami Dolphins

22. In his first game as an Eagle, how many touchdowns did Terrell Owens score?

    a. 1
    b. 2
    c. 3
    d. 4

23. In his first year as Head Coach, what was Andy Reid's record?

    a. 4-12
    b. 5-11
    c. 7-9
    d. 8-8

24. In 1997, against which NFL quarterback did Eagle Jon Harris record his first career sack?

    a. Danny Kanell
    b. Jake Plummer
    c. Mark Brunell
    d. Troy Aikman

25. In 1999, against which team did Eagles quarterback Donovan McNabb win his first NFL start?

    a. Washington Redskins
    b. Dallas Cowboys
    c. Buffalo Bills
    d. Carolina Panthers

26. Against which team did Eagle Ryan Moats score his first touchdown?

    a. New York Giants
    b. Seattle Seahawks
    c. Dallas Cowboys
    d. Green Bay Packers

27. Who were the Eagles playing in the first televised NFL football game?

    a. Pittsburgh Pirates
    b. Cleveland Rams
    c. Brooklyn dodgers
    d. Chicago Bears

28. Against which team did the Eagles play their very first home game?

    a. New York Giants
    b. Portsmouth Spartans
    c. Green Bay Packers
    d. Cincinnati Reds

29. In what year did the Eagles win more than 10 games for the first time in team history?

    a. 1938
    b. 1941
    c. 1946
    a. 1949

answers on page 405

EAGLES TEAM RECORDS

1. In 2005, how many completions did Eagles quarterback Donovan McNabb have against the Chargers, to set a new team record?

   a. 32
   b. 35
   c. 37
   d. 39

2. What is the longest field goal made by an Eagles kicker?

   a. 54 yards
   b. 57 yards
   c. 59 yards
   d. 63 yards

3. Which Eagles kicker holds the team's record for the most field goals in a single game?

   a. David Akers
   b. Gary Anderson
   c. Tom Dempsey
   d. Roger Ruzek

4. Which NFL team have the Eagles defeated the most times?

   a. Pittsburgh Steelers
   b. St. Louis Cardinals
   c. New York Giants
   d. Washington Redskins

5. Which Eagles kicker holds the team's record for the most punts?

    a. Tommy Hutton
    b. John Teltschik
    c. Adrian Burk
    d. Sean Landeta

6. Which Eagles player holds the team's record for the most punt returns?

    a. Brian Mitchell
    b. Larry Marshall
    c. John Sciarra
    d. Wally Henry

7. Which Eagles quarterback set a club record by throwing six interceptions in a single game?

    a. Randall Cunningham
    b. Ron Jaworski
    c. Bobby Thomason
    d. Bobby Hoying

8. Against which team did the Eagles set a club record of 582 total yards in a single game (and still lost)?

    a. New York Giants
    b. Cleveland Browns
    c. Washington Redskins
    d. Detroit Lions

9. In 1944, which team did the Eagles shut out and only allow 29 total yards, for a club record?

    a. Brooklyn Dodgers
    b. Cleveland Rams
    c. Boston Yanks
    d. New York Giants

10. Who holds the Eagles record for most games played?

    a. Chuck Bednarik
    b. Tommy McDonald
    c. Harold Carmichael
    d. Jon Runyan

11. In 1954, who scored a club record 25 points in a 49-21 Eagles victory over the Redskins?

    a. Pete Pihos
    b. Hal Giancanelli
    c. Don Luft
    d. Bobby Walston

12. In the 2000-01 season, how many passes did Donovan McNabb attempt, to set an Eagles team record?

    a. 487
    b. 493
    c. 521
    d. 569

13. At the end of the 2005 season, in which category did Eagle Reno Mahe lead the NFL?

    a. Fumbles
    b. Punt-return average
    c. Special teams tackles
    d. Dropped balls

14. In 2005, whose record did Eagle wide receiver Reggie Brown break when he caught 43 receptions?

    a. Ben Hawkins
    b. Mike Quick
    c. Victor Bailey
    d. Harold Jackson

15. Which Eagles defensive tackle holds the team's record for most sacks in a single season?

    a. Antone Davis
    b. Andy Harmon
    c. Sam Rayburn
    d. Jerome Brown

16. Against which team did Eagle Sam Rayburn set a career high record for quarterback sacks?

    a. Pittsburgh Steelers
    b. New York Giants
    c. Green Bay Packers
    d. Minnesota Vikings

17. Which one of the following players returned a fumble for a 96-yard touchdown and an Eagles record?

    a. Troy Vincent
    b. Eric Allen
    c. Joe Lavender
    d. Roynell Young

18. Who holds the Eagles' single season rushing record?

    a. Ricky Watters
    b. Wilbert Montgomery
    c. Duce Staley
    d. Steve Van Buren

19. Which Eagles quarterback has the lowest percentage for interception?

    a. Koy Detmer
    b. Adrian Burk
    c. Norm Snead
    d. Bubby Brister

20. Which Eagles player holds the record for most catches in a single game?

     a. Tommy McDonald
     b. Terrell Owens
     c. Don Looney
     d. Mike Quick

21. Which Eagles player holds the record for total receiving yards in a single game?

     a. Pete Retzlaff
     b. Terrell Owens
     c. Harold Jackson
     d. Tommy McDonald

22. Who was the last non-kicker to lead the Eagles in scoring for a single season?

     a. Calvin Williams
     b. Terrell Owens
     c. Tommy McDonald
     d. Harold Carmichael

23. Which Eagles player caught more passes than any other rookie wide receiver in team history?

     a. Keith Jackson
     b. Freddie Mitchell
     c. Victor Bailey
     d. Cris Carter

24. Who was the last Eagles running back to lead the team in receiving?

     a. Duce Staley
     b. Cecil Martin
     c. Brian Westbrook
     d. Ricky Watters

25. Which Eagles player has returned more kickoffs for more yards than any other Eagles player?

    a. Billy Campfield
    b. Wally Henry
    c. Marvin Hargrove
    d. Timmy Brown

26. Against which team did Eagles quarterback Randall Cunningham have a record 62 pass attempts in a single game?

    a. Dallas Cowboys
    b. Baltimore Ravens
    c. Chicago Bears
    d. St. Louis Cardinals

27. In 2005, Eagles quarterback Donovan McNabb threw how many consecutive passes when playing against the Chargers?

    a. 19
    b. 22
    c. 25
    d. 29

28. Against which team did Eagles quarterback Donovan McNabb set a team record of 35 completions?

    a. Baltimore Ravens
    b. Green Bay Packers
    c. New York Giants
    d. San Diego Chargers

29. Who were the Eagles playing when Brian Dawkins became the first NFL player to sack the quarterback, intercept a pass, recover a fumble, and catch a TD pass, all in a single game?

a. Tennessee Titans
b. Houston Texans
c. Jacksonville Jaguars
d. Tampa Bay Buccaneers

30. Against which team did Eagle Terrell Owens score his 100th career touchdown?

    a. Kansas City Chiefs
    b. Dallas Cowboys
    c. Washington Redskins
    d. Oakland Raiders

31. Kicker David Akers holds the Eagles club record with how many consecutive points-after-touchdown made?

    a. 124
    b. 137
    c. 153
    d. 168

32. In 2000, how many points did Eagles kicker David Akers score to set a new team record?

    a. 121
    b. 128
    c. 134
    d. 139

33. Against which team did the Eagles allow only 29 total yards, in what is the stingiest defensive effort in club history?

    a. Boston Yanks
    b. Chicago Cardinals
    c. Brooklyn Dodgers
    d. Cleveland Rams

answers on page 406

FIRST TIME OPPONENTS

1. When did the Eagles play against the Atlanta Falcons for the very first time?

    a. 1953
    b. 1957
    c. 1966
    d. 1969

2. When did the Eagles play against the Cleveland Rams for the very first time?

    a. 1934
    b. 1937
    c. 1941
    d. 1944

3. When did the Eagles play against the Baltimore Ravens for the very first time?

    a. 1978
    b. 1983
    c. 1994
    d. 1997

4. When did the Eagles play against the New York Jets for the very first time?

    a. 1961
    b. 1968
    c. 1970
    d. 1973

5. When did the Eagles play against the Baltimore Colts for the very first time?

   a. 1943
   b. 1945
   c. 1950
   d. 1957

6. When did the Eagles play against the Buffalo Bills for the very first time?

   a. 1973
   b. 1975
   c. 1977
   d. 1979

7. When did the Eagles play against the New England Patriots for the very first time?

   a. 1964
   b. 1969
   c. 1973
   d. 1977

8. When did the Eagles play against the Cincinnati Bengals for the very first time?

   a. 1968
   b. 1971
   c. 1975
   d. 1983

9. When did the Eagles play against the Kansas City Chiefs for the very first time?

   a. 1972
   b. 1974
   c. 1977
   d. 1981

10. When did the Eagles play against the Cleveland Browns for the very first time?

    a. 1934
    b. 1942
    c. 1950
    d. 1955

11. When did the Eagles play against the Jacksonville Jaguars for the very first time?

    a. 1995
    b. 1997
    c. 1999
    d. 2001

12. When did the Eagles play against the Denver Broncos for the very first time?

    a. 1957
    b. 1963
    c. 1968
    d. 1971

13. When did the Eagles play against the Houston Texans for the very first time?

    a. 1995
    b. 1997
    c. 1999
    d. 2002

answers on page 407

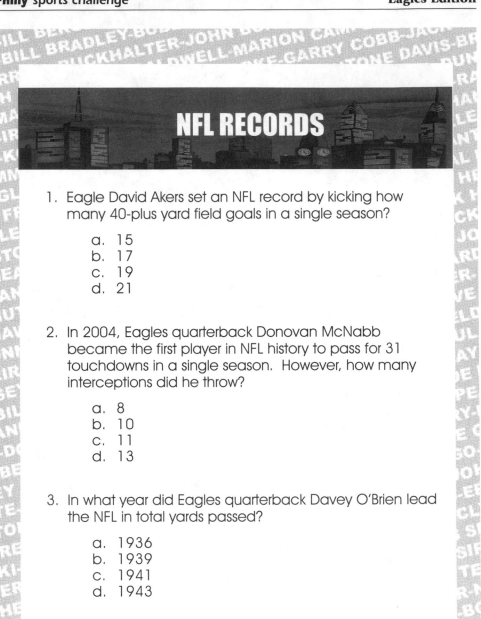

NFL RECORDS

1. Eagle David Akers set an NFL record by kicking how many 40-plus yard field goals in a single season?

    a. 15
    b. 17
    c. 19
    d. 21

2. In 2004, Eagles quarterback Donovan McNabb became the first player in NFL history to pass for 31 touchdowns in a single season. However, how many interceptions did he throw?

    a. 8
    b. 10
    c. 11
    d. 13

3. In what year did Eagles quarterback Davey O'Brien lead the NFL in total yards passed?

    a. 1936
    b. 1939
    c. 1941
    d. 1943

4. To whom did Eagles quarterback Ron Jaworski throw a touchdown pass of 99-2/3 yards, for an NFL record?

    a. Harold Carmichael
    b. Mike Quick
    c. Wilbert Montgomery
    d. Keith Byars

5. As an Eagle, Bobby Hoying holds the NFL record for most passes without a touchdown. How many did he throw?

    a. 177 passes
    b. 197 passes
    c. 227 passes
    d. 257 passes

6. As an Eagle, how many years did Reggie White lead the NFL in sacks?

    a. 1
    b. 2
    c. 3
    d. 5

7. How many times was Eagles quarterback Randall Cunningham sacked, to set a NFL single season record for most sacks?

    a. 68
    b. 72
    c. 76
    d. 81

8. Who were the Eagles playing when Al Nelson scored an NFL record 101-yard touchdown after catching a missed field goal in the opposite end zone?

    a. St. Louis Cardinals
    b. Oakland Raiders
    c. Minnesota Vikings
    d. Dallas Cowboys

answers on page 407

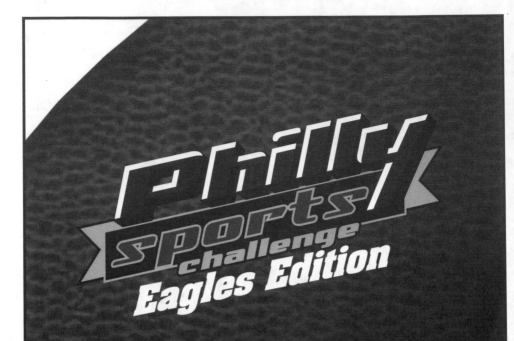

College Facts

PUZZLES

DRAFT SELECTIONS

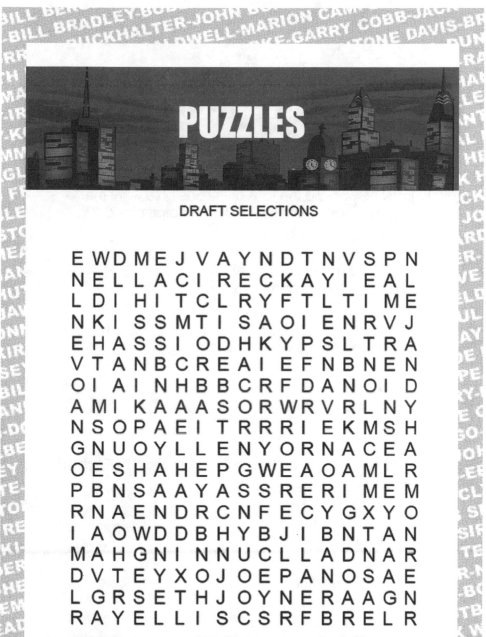

```
E W D M E J V A Y N D T N V S P N
N E L L A C I R E C K A Y I E A L
L D I H I T C L R Y F T L T I M E
N K I S S M T I S A O I E N R V J
E H A S S I O D H K Y P S L T R A
V T A N B C R E A I E F N B N E N
O I A I N H B B C R F D A N O I D
A M I K A A A S O R W R V R L N Y
N S O P A E I T R R R I E K M S H
G N U O Y L L E N Y O R N A C E A
O E S H A H E P G W E A O A M L R
P B N S A A Y A S S R E R I M E M
R N A E N D R C N F E C Y G X Y O
I A O W D D B H Y B J I B N T A N
M A H G N I N N U C L L A D N A R
D V T E Y X O J O E P A N O S A E
L G R S E T H J O Y N E R A A G N
R A Y E L L I S C S R F B R E L R
```

AndyHarmon	BarryGardner	BenSmith
ByronEvans	EricAllen	JoePanos
MattDarwin	MichaelHaddix	PetePerot
RandallCunningham	RayEllis	RayFarmer
RoynellYoung	SethJoyner	TonyFranklin
VictorBailey	VytoKab	WesHopkins

answers on page 426

DRAFT SELECTIONS

1. In 1999, who did the fans of Philadelphia want the Eagles to select with their first round draft pick?

   a. Donovan McNabb
   b. Ricky Williams
   c. Daunte Culpepper
   d. Edgerrin James

2. From the Eagles 2004 draft, how many of the 10 players drafted actually made the roster?

   a. 3
   b. 5
   c. 7
   d. 9

3. Who was the Eagles' last draft pick in the '97 NFL draft?

   a. Deauntae Brown
   b. Bryon Capers
   c. Edward Jasper
   d. Luther Broughton

4. Who was Rich Kotite's first draft pick for the Eagles?

   a. William Thomas
   b. Andy Harmon
   c. Siran Stacy
   d. Antone Davis

5. In which round did the Eagles draft Hollis Thomas?

    a. Second
    b. Third
    c. Fifth
    d. Never drafted

6. Which of the following Eagles was not drafted from the University of Kentucky?

    a. Tommy Thompson
    b. Frank LeMaster
    c. Steve Campassi
    d. Kelly Kirchbaum

7. Which Eagle was not drafted by the birds but was a starter in 2005?

    a. Mike Patterson
    b. Reno Mahe
    c. Jeremiah Trotter
    d. Hollis Thomas

8. Who did the Eagles select ahead of Randall Cunningham in the 1985 draft?

    a. Seth Joyner
    b. Kevin Allen
    c. Stan Walters
    d. Miko Golic

9. Who did the Eagles select with their first pick in the 2000 NFL draft?

    a. Freddie Mitchell
    b. Corey Simon
    c. Todd Pinkston
    d. Derrick Burgress

10. In 1973, which Eagle was drafted as the third overall selection?

    a. Jerry Sisemore
    b. Bill Dunstan
    c. Randy Logan
    d. Ben Hawkins

11. The Eagles drafted Tony Franklin from which university?

    a. Georgia
    b. Auburn
    c. Texas A&M
    d. Mississippi State

12. In which round did the Eagles draft quarterback Koy Detmer?

    a. First
    b. Second
    c. Fifth
    d. Seventh

13. Which one of the following players that was drafted by the Eagles in 1995 was still on the team's roster in 1999?

    a. Chris T. Jones
    b. Mike Mamula
    c. Bobby Taylor
    d. Greg Jefferson

14. Name this former Eagles water boy who was drafted by the Eagles after completing college as a quarterback?

    a. Bill Mackrides
    b. Johnny Rauch
    c. Bobby Thomason
    d. Bob Gambold

15. In what year did the Eagles draft Izel Jenkins?

    a. 1982
    b. 1985
    c. 1986
    d. 1988

answers on page 408

EAGLES SMARTS

1. What college did Eagle Shawn Andrews attend?

    a. Arkansas
    b. Tennessee
    c. Texas
    d. Ohio State

2. Eagle Greg Lewis played for what college?

    a. Indiana
    b. Penn State
    c. Illinois
    d. UCLA

3. Eagles quarterback Pete Liske played for which college?

    a. Penn State
    b. San Diego State
    c. Alabama
    d. Michigan State

4. Eagle Norm Snead played for which college?

    a. Ohio State
    b. Wake Forest
    c. Stanford
    d. Baylor

5. Jerome Brown played football for what college?

   a. Ohio State
   b. University of Miami
   c. Florida State
   d. Nebraska

6. Where did Eagles field goal kicker David Akers play his college ball?

   a. Louisville
   b. Mississippi State
   c. Tennessee
   d. Ohio State

7. Duce Staley played for which college when the Eagles drafted him?

   a. Virginia
   b. Clemson
   c. South Carolina
   d. Washington State

8. Where did Eagle Keith Byars play football?

   a. Tennessee
   b. Ohio State
   c. Mississippi State
   d. Auburn

9. Where did Eagles quarterback Ron Jaworski play his college football?

   a. Texas
   b. Iowa State
   c. Youngstown State
   d. Georgia

10. On which college team did Eagles 2004 rookie Matt Ware play football?

    a. Boston College
    b. Florida State
    c. Northern Iowa
    d. UCLA

11. Where did Eagles Head Coach Andy Reid play football?

    a. San Francisco State
    b. Brigham Young
    c. Texas El Paso
    d. Northern Arizona

12. What college did Eagles quarterback Koy Detmer play for?

    a. Colorado
    b. Southern Cal
    c. Washington State
    d. Oregon State

13. Reggie White played football for which college?

    a. Ohio State
    b. Texas
    c. Memphis State
    d. University of Tennessee

14. What position did Andy Reid play at BYU?

    a. Tackle/Guard
    b. Tackle
    c. Center
    d. Defensive end

15. Sonny Jurgensen was the quarterback for which college team?

     a. Georgia
     b. Michigan State
     c. Duke
     d. Georgia Tech

16. Where did Eagles quarterback Donovan McNabb play his college football?

     a. Illinois
     b. Ohio State
     c. Syracuse
     d. Boston University

17. Where did Maxie Baughan play his college football?

     a. Ohio State
     b. Georgia State
     c. Penn State
     d. Colorado State

18. Where did Tommy McDonald play his college football?

     a. Kentucky
     b. Alabama State
     c. Louisiana State
     d. Oklahoma

19. Where did Mike Bartrum play his college football?

     a. Eastern Kentucky
     b. Wake Forest
     c. Marshall
     d. Bowling Green

20. Where did Hugh Douglas play his college football?

    a. Central State
    b. Youngstown State
    c. Langston
    d. Clemson

answers on page 408

LOCAL COLLEGES

1. Who was the first Penn football player drafted by the Philadelphia Eagles?

    a. Art Littleton
    b. Chuck Bednarik
    c. John Schwader
    d. George Savitsky

2. Which one of the following Eagles players did not spend his college days playing football at Temple University?

    a. Kevin Reilly
    b. Joe Sutton
    c. Mike Jarmoluk
    d. Chuck Brodnicki

3. Which one of the following Eagles players did not spend his college football days at Villanova?

    a. Joe Restic
    b. Zachary Dixon
    c. Brian Finneran
    d. Nick Basca

4. Which one of the following Eagles players did not spend his college football days at Penn State?

    a. Michael Zordich
    b. Robert Wear
    c. Mickey Shuler
    d. Mike Sebastian

5. Which one of the following Eagles players spent his college football days at West Chester?

    a. Chuck Weber
    b. Mike Curcio
    c. Jack Myers
    d. John Green

6. Back in the '30s, who was the first Eagles player from St. Joseph's University?

    a. John Cole
    b. Al Weiner
    c. Glenn Frey
    d. William Holcomb

7. Eagles players Swede Hanson, Tom Graham, and Leonard Gudd all played their college football at which local college?

    a. West Chester
    b. Villanova
    c. Penn
    d. Temple

8. What jersey number did Brian Westbrook wear while playing football at Villanova University?

    a. 20
    b. 24
    c. 32
    d. 36

9. Who was the only free agent signed by the Eagles who played at Cheyney?

    a. Roynell Young
    b. Andre Waters
    c. Ray Ellis
    d. Ken Clarke

answers on page 409

COLLEGE HONORS

1. Name the Eagles player who was the first in NCAA history to pass for more than 5,000 yards, as well as run for over 3,000 yards.

    a. Ty Detmer
    b. Brian Mitchell
    c. Randall Cunningham
    d. Donovan McNabb

2. In what year was Reggie White named to the College Football Hall of Fame?

    a. 1987
    b. 1991
    c. 1998
    d. 2003

3. Which one of the these former Eagles players never won the Heisman Trophy?

    a. Herschel Walker
    b. John Huarte
    c. Ty Detmer
    d. Chuck Bednarik

4. Which one of the following Eagles players never won the Davey O'Brien Award for best quarterback?

    a. Ty Detmer
    b. Jim McMahon
    c. Bobby Hoying
    d. Don McPherson

5. Which one of the following Eagles players was never an All-American in college?

    a. Amp Lee
    b. Corey Simon
    c. William Perry
    d. Jeremiah Trotter

6. Which Eagle was the first All-American in college?

    a. Dave Smukler
    b. Reb Russell
    c. Alex Wojciechowicz
    d. Carl Jorgenson

answers on page 409

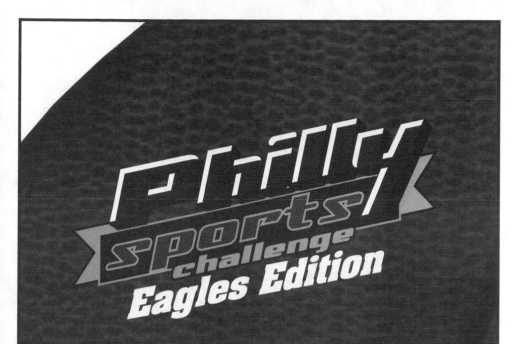

Philly Sports Challenge
Eagles Edition

On The Screen and
In Print

EAGLES IN PRINT

1. What was the name of Eagles broadcaster Merrill Reese's autobiography?

    a. Merrill Reese: *It's Goooooood!*
    b. *The Voice*
    c. *Behind the Voice*
    d. *My Greatest Sports Moments*

2. Which Eagles player had a biography written about him called *They Pay Me To Catch Footballs*?

    a. Cris Carter
    b. Harold Carmichael
    c. Tommy McDonald
    d. Terrell Owens

3. Which Eagle authored the book titled *The Last of the 60 Minute Man*?

    a. Ron Jaworski
    b. Bobby Thomason
    c. Pete Pihos
    d. Chuck Bednarik

4. What was the name of the book that detailed the Eagles team from 1933 to 1993?

    a. *60 Years of Football*
    b. *Sunday's Warriors*
    c. *On the Road to Victory*
    d. *A Look Inside the Eagles*

5. Terrell Owens authored a book called what?

   a. *Give Me the Money*
   b. *Catch This!*
   c. *Just Give Me the Ball!*
   d. *T.O.: The Ultimate Athlete*

6. Which of the following books was not written about the Eagles?

   a. *Tales from the Eagles Sidelines*
   b. *Eagles Pride, More Than a Game*
   c. *Eagles: Where Have They Gone*
   d. *Broken Wing, Broken Promise*

7. Which Eagle authored the book titled *I'm Still Scrambling*?

   a. Ron Jaworski
   b. Jim McMahon
   c. Sonny Jurgensen
   d. Randall Cunningham

8. Which Eagles player is depicted on the front cover of *The History of the Philadelphia Eagles,* a book by Adam Schmalzbauer?

   a. Donovan McNabb
   b. 1980's team photo
   c. Ron Jaworski
   d. Greasy Neale

9. Who co-authored (with Robert Lyons) *The Eagles Encyclopedia*?

   a. Angelo Cataldi
   b. Ray Didinger
   c. Phil Anastasia
   d. Mark Bowden

10. Who wrote the book called *A Sunday Pilgrimage* about his six-day road trip to Jacksonville, Florida to witness the Eagles play in Super Bowl XXXIX?

     a. Michael Barkann
     b. Les Bowen
     c. John Smallwood
     d. Anthony Gargano

answers on page 410

EAGLES IN HOLLYWOOD

1. In which movie did former Eagle Bill Cowher appear as himself?

     a. *Brian's Song*
     b. *The Waterboy*
     c. *The Longest Yard*
     d. *North Dallas Forty*

2. In which one of the following movies did former Eagle Mike Ditka appear?

     a. *Kicking and Screaming*
     b. *Rudy*
     c. *Any Given Sunday*
     d. *Go Tigers*

3. In which movie did former Eagle Jim McMahon appear as himself?

     a. *Necessary Roughness*
     b. *Varsity Blues*
     c. *Johnny Be Good*
     d. *The Replacements*

4. In which one of the following movies did former Eagle Bill Romanowski appear?

    a. *Friday Night Lights*
    b. *The Longest Yard*
    c. *Jerry Maguire*
    d. *Wildcats*

5. In which of the following movies did former Eagle Piggy Barnes not appear?

    a. *Revolt in the Big House*
    b. *The Court of Last Resort*
    c. *Sugarfoot*
    d. *Travelin' On*

6. Which Eagles player was seen in Woody Allen's *Everything You Always Wanted To Know About Sex*?

    a. Stan Walters
    b. Don Chuy
    c. Greg Garrity
    d. Jack Concannon

7. In which football movie did Eagles owner Jeffrey Lurie play himself?

    a. *Jerry Maguire*
    b. *Rudy*
    c. *Any Given Sunday*
    d. *The Longest Yard*

8. Which Eagles player had a speaking role in the movie *The Jersey*?

    a. Greg Jefferson
    b. Ike Reese
    c. Darwin Walker
    d. Bobby Taylor

9. Who was the first Eagles player to appear in a movie?

    a. Piggy Barnes
    b. Reb Russell
    c. Howie Auer
    d. Red Kirkman

10. Which Eagles player was once a roommate of Tom Selleck at USC, and even had a small role in a *Magnum P.I.* episode?

    a. Tim Rossovich
    b. Rodney Peete
    c. Byron Darby
    d. Garry Cobb

11. Which one of the following former Eagles players had a part in the movie *Any Given Sunday*?

    a. Terrell Owens
    b. Irving Fryar
    c. Ricky Watters
    d. Darnell Autry

answers on page 410

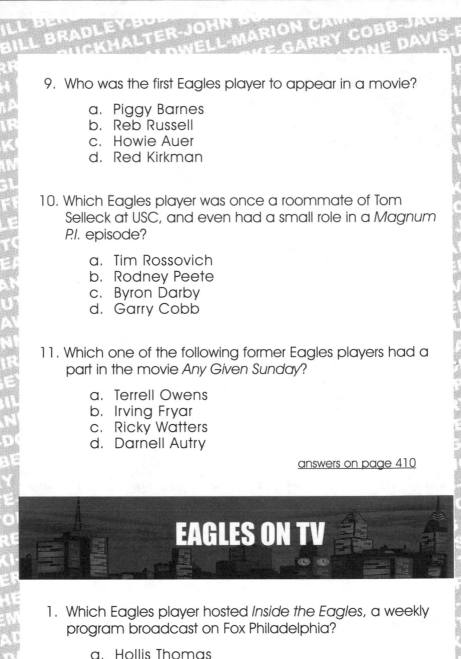

EAGLES ON TV

1. Which Eagles player hosted *Inside the Eagles*, a weekly program broadcast on Fox Philadelphia?

    a. Hollis Thomas
    b. Brian Mitchell
    c. Cecil Martin
    d. Hugh Douglas

2. Which game show was once hosted by former Eagles quarterback Randall Cunningham?

     a. *Scramble*
     b. *Dream League*
     c. *American Gladiators*
     d. *Win, Lose or Draw*

3. Which Eagles player was a celebrity captain on *Extreme Dodgeball*?

     a. Brian Dawkins
     b. Jeremiah Trotter
     c. Dhani Jones
     d. Lito Sheppard

4. Which former Eagles player is one of three regular panelists on Comcast Sportsnet's *Eagles Post Game Live* broadcast?

     a. Mike Quick
     b. Brian Baldinger
     c. Vaughn Hebron
     d. Bill Bergey

5. Which Eagle did Ike Reese team up with to host a segment on WCAU TV called 'Mike and Ike'?

     a. Mike Caldwell
     b. Michael Lewis
     c. Mike Mamula
     d. Mike Bartrum

6. In between NFL teams Randall Cunningham took a job as a football analyst for which network?

     a. CBS
     b. TNT
     c. FOX
     d. ESPN

7. Which Eagles player hosted a TV show on ESPN2 called *Timeless*?

    a. Jevon Kearse
    b. Dhani Jones
    c. Jeremiah Trotter
    d. Jon Ritchie

8. In 2004 which Eagles player represented the Eagles on *Wheel of Fortune*'s NFL players' week?

    a. Donovan McNabb
    b. Lito Sheppard
    c. Shawn Andrews
    d. Jevon Kearse   answers on page 411

MAGAZINES

1. In January 2006, which magazine listed former Eagle Terrell Owens the 'Most Hated Athlete' by his peers?

    a. *Men's Health*
    b. *Philly Magazine*
    c. *Sports Illustrated*
    d. *GQ Magazine*

2. Which Eagles player was on the September 1998 cover of Philadelphia sports magazine *The Fan*?

    a. Charlie Garner
    b. Bobby Hoying
    c. Mike Mamula
    d. Tra Thomas

3. How many times did Eagles quarterback Randall Cunningham appear on the cover of *Sports Illustrated*?

   a. 2
   b. 3
   c. 5
   d. 6

4. Who was the first Eagles player to grace the front cover of *Sports Illustrated*?

   a. Chuck Bednarik
   b. Tommy McDonald
   c. Pete Pihos
   d. Norm Van Brocklin

5. Which of the following Eagles' quarterbacks never made the front cover of *Sports Illustrated*?

   a. Bobby Hoying
   b. Donovan McNabb
   c. Randall Cunningham
   d. Jim McMahon

6. Which Eagles player was on the cover of *Sports Illustrated* with the lead caption 'The Ultimate Weapon'?

   a. Donovan McNabb
   b. Tommy McDonald
   c. Jim McMahon
   d. Randall Cunningham

7. Which Eagles player was on the cover of *Sports Illustrated* with the lead caption 'Party On'?

   a. Brian Dawkins
   b. Jeremiah Trotter
   c. Terrell Owens
   d. Donovan McNabb

8. Which Eagles player is shown on the cover of the December 1982 issue of *Sports Illustrated*?

    a. Harold Carmichael
    b. John Bunting
    c. Leroy Harris
    d. Vyto Kab

9. In 1981, which one of the following magazines featured Eagles quarterback Ron Jaworski on the front cover?

    a. *Sports Illustrated*
    b. *Pro Football Scene*
    c. *Football News*
    d. *Football Digest*

10. *Life Magazine* had a article about dirty football players called 'Savagery on Sunday.' It was about two Eagles players; one was Bucko Kilroy, who was the other?

    a. Bibbles Bawel
    b. Jerry Norton
    c. Lum Snyder
    d. Wayne Robinson

answers on page 411

MONDAY NIGHT FOOTBALL

1. During the 2002 season, which of the following teams did the Eagles not play on Monday night football?

    a. Washington Redskins
    b. New York Giants
    c. Baltimore Ravens
    d. San Francisco 49ers

2. Prior to the '06 season, how many points did Eagles kicker David Akers have in his nine Monday night games?

    a. 57
    b. 59
    c. 61
    d. 63

3. Who did the Eagles play in their last ever Monday night game?

    a. Washington Redskins
    b. Dallas Cowboys
    c. New York Giants
    d. Seattle Seahawks

4. Which team did the Eagles play the most on Monday night football?

    a. New York Giants
    b. Dallas Cowboys
    c. San Francisco 49ers
    d. Washington Redskins

5. Who did the Eagles play in their first Monday night appearance?

    a. Washington Redskins
    b. Dallas Cowboys
    c. New York Giants
    d. Miami Dolphins

6. Prior to the 2005 season, in how many consecutive Monday night football games did Terrell Owens score a touchdown?

    a. 3
    b. 5
    c. 7
    d. 9

7. In 2001, the Eagles had to cancel their Monday night pre-season football game against which NFL team, due to the condition of the Vet's turf?

   a. Arizona Cardinals
   b. Baltimore Ravens
   c. Pittsburgh Steelers
   d. St. Louis Rams

8. Who did the Eagles square off against in the first Monday night football game played at Lincoln Financial field?

   a. New York Giants
   b. Tampa Bay Buccaneers
   c. New Orleans Saints
   d. Baltimore Ravens

9. Who were the Eagles playing on Monday night football when a flare gun was set off inside Veterans Stadium, causing Judge McCaffrey to set up a temporary courtroom at an Eagles games?

   a. Washington Redskins
   b. Dallas Cowboys
   c. Jacksonville Jaguars
   d. San Francisco 49ers

10. In the '70s name the Eagles backup quarterback that threw a touchdown pass against the Dallas Cowboys in a Monday night game?

   a. Rick Engles
   b. John Sciarra
   c. John Walton
   d. Roman Gabriel

11. Which team did the Eagles defeat for their first Monday night football victory played at Veterans Stadium?

   a. Dallas Cowboys
   b. San Diego Chargers
   c. Green Bay Packers
   d. New York Giants

12. Prior to the beginning of the '06 season, how many games have the Eagles won on Monday night football?

   a. 19
   b. 23
   c. 26
   d. 31

13. How many consecutive Monday night games did the Eagles lose from 1995 thru 1998?

   a. 6
   b. 8
   c. 11
   d. 14

answers on page 412

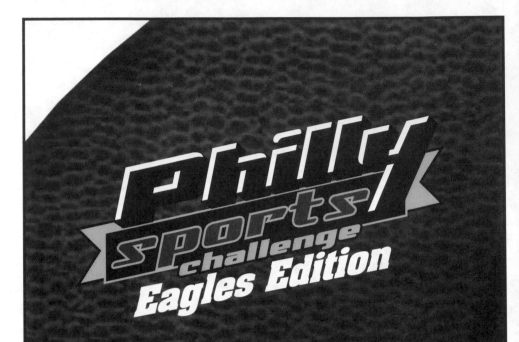

Are You Kiddin' Me?

DATES, DATES AND MORE DATES

1. In what year did the Eagles play their first postseason game?

    a. 1938
    b. 1942
    c. 1945
    d. 1947

2. In what year was the last time the Eagles recorded a shutout against their opponent?

    a. 1992
    b. 1994
    c. 1996
    d. 1998

3. In what year did the Philadelphia Eagles first start using pickle juice to help fight dehydration?

    a. 1998
    b. 1999
    c. 2001
    d. 2002

4. In what year was the first Eagles carnival and auction?

    a. 1992
    b. 1994
    c. 1996
    d. 1997

5. In what year did the Eagles install artificial turf in Franklin Field?

   a. 1963
   b. 1966
   c. 1969
   d. 1971

6. During which season was the infamous Santa Claus snow balling incident?

   a. 1964
   b. 1966
   c. 1968
   d. 1970

7. In what year did the Eagles start holding their preseason camp at West Chester State Teachers College?

   a. 1935
   b. 1937
   c. 1939
   d. 1941

8. When was the first time the Eagles had two players selected to the Pro Football Writers of America All-Pro Team?

   a. 1935
   b. 1938
   c. 1943
   d. 1948

9. In what year did the Eagles fail to sign any of their nine draft picks?

   a. 1934
   b. 1935
   c. 1936
   d. 1939

10. When was the only season that the Eagles merged with the Pittsburgh Steelers?

    a. 1936
    b. 1939
    c. 1943
    d. 1946

11. In what year did the Eagles have their best record in franchise history?

    a. 1949
    b. 1960
    c. 1980
    d. 2004

12. In what year did the Eagles play their first game in Veterans Stadium?

    a. 1968
    b. 1970
    c. 1971
    d. 1973

13. In what year did Randall Cunningham become the first quarterback to lead the Eagles in rushing?

    a. 1985
    b. 1987
    c. 1989
    d. 1991

answers on page 412

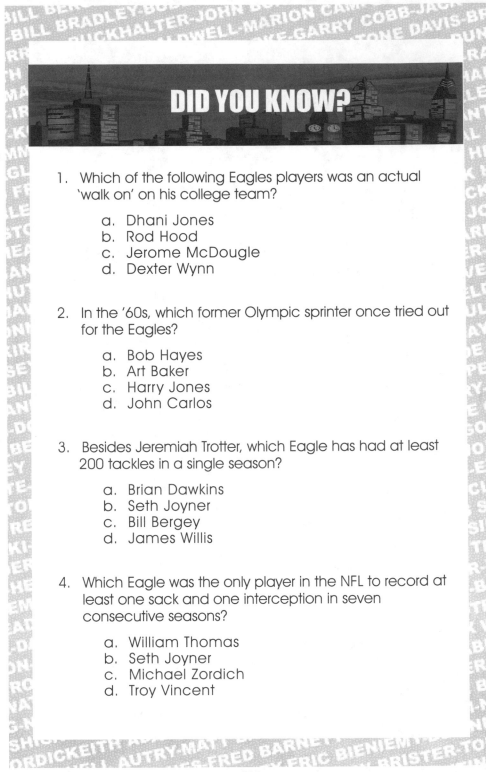

DID YOU KNOW?

1. Which of the following Eagles players was an actual 'walk on' on his college team?

    a. Dhani Jones
    b. Rod Hood
    c. Jerome McDougle
    d. Dexter Wynn

2. In the '60s, which former Olympic sprinter once tried out for the Eagles?

    a. Bob Hayes
    b. Art Baker
    c. Harry Jones
    d. John Carlos

3. Besides Jeremiah Trotter, which Eagle has had at least 200 tackles in a single season?

    a. Brian Dawkins
    b. Seth Joyner
    c. Bill Bergey
    d. James Willis

4. Which Eagle was the only player in the NFL to record at least one sack and one interception in seven consecutive seasons?

    a. William Thomas
    b. Seth Joyner
    c. Michael Zordich
    d. Troy Vincent

5. At the Eagles NovaCare complex, which one of the following players does not have a larger than life portrait in the main auditorium?

    a. Tommy McDonald
    b. Chuck Bednarik
    c. Steve Van Buren
    d. Donovan McNabb

6. During the 2005 season, where did the Eagles sleep before home games?

    a. Hyatt
    b. Sheraton
    c. Brandywine Hilton
    d. Airport Marriot

7. Who were the Eagles playing when the organization honored the life of former all-pro defensive end Reggie White?

    a. Oakland Raiders
    b. Green Bay Packers
    c. Seattle Seahawks
    d. New York Giants

8. In 2005, Matt Ware recovered a blocked field goal attempt and ran it in for a touchdown. Did you know that the Eagles only had 10 players on the field? Who was the missing Eagle?

    a. Keith Adams
    b. Darwin Walker
    c. Dhani Jones
    d. Mike Patterson

9. Which Eagle was the last NFL player not to wear a helmet?

    a. Pete Pihos
    b. Russ Craft
    c. Bill Hewitt
    d. Frank Kilroy

10. Which player did the Eagles sign after his release from Sing Sing Prison?

    a. Ed Strom
    b. Eggs Manske
    c. Burle Robinson
    d. Alabama Pitts

11. When the Eagles drafted Donovan McNabb in the '99 NFL draft, how many quarterbacks did they have on their roster?

    a. 3
    b. 4
    c. 5
    d. 6

12. In 1948, who was the starting quarterback for the Eagles' championship team?

    a. Tommy Thompson
    b. Allie Sherman
    c. Roy Zimmerman
    d. Bill Mackrides

13. In 2000, how many consecutive field goals did Eagles kicker David Akers complete?

    a. 12
    b. 13
    c. 15
    d. 16

14. What was kicker David Akers's longest field goal attempt In his first year as an Eagle?

    a. 36 yds
    b. 42 yds
    c. 49 yds
    d. 53 yds

15. In his brilliant 14-year career with the Eagles, 'Concrete Charlie' played in how many regular season games (out of a possible 172)?

    a. 152 games
    b. 158 games
    c. 163 games
    d. 169 games

16. Which NFL team has defeated the Eagles more than any other opponent?

    a. New York Giants
    b. Arizona Cardinals
    c. Washington Redskins
    d. Dallas Cowboys

17. Since joining the Eagles, which wide receiver has caught the most completed passes from quarterback Donovan McNabb?

    a. James Thrash
    b. Freddie Mitchell
    c. Charles Johnson
    d. Torrance Small

18. For how many consecutive years was Eagles quarterback Randall Cunningham the team's top rusher?

    a. 2
    b. 3

    c. 4
    d. 5

19. In his best season, how many points did Eagles kicker David Akers score?

    a. 122
    b. 133
    c. 139
    d. 146

20. There have been 22 kickoffs returned for touchdowns by an Eagle. How many were scored by Tim Brown?

    a. 2
    b. 3
    c. 5
    d. 6

21. Which Eagle despite having his jersey number retired has not been inducted individually into the Eagles Honor Roll?

    a. Jerome Brown
    b. Al Wistert
    c. Chuck Bednarik
    d. Pete Retzlaff

22. Who was the first team the Eagles defeated by a margin of 38 points?

    a. Houston Oilers
    b. Detroit Lions
    c. Minnesota Vikings
    d. Chicago Bears

23. What is the meaning of Eagle Dhani Jones's first name in the Hindi language?

a. Skilled in writing
b. Intelligence
c. Thinking man
d. Great dreamer

24. Which Eagles Eagles player was fined for an illegal downfield block in his first NFL game?

a. Brandon whiting
b. Paul Grasmanis
c. Hank Fraley
d. Ike Reese

25. Which Eagles player wore this custom-made helmet?

a. Norm Bulaich
b. Harold Carmivhael
c. Tom Sullivan
d. Don Zimmerman

26. Former Eagles quaterbacks Roman Gabriel and Sonny Jurgensen both attended which high school in North Carolina?

    a. Parkland High School
    b. Lexington Senior High School
    c. Riverside High School
    d. New Hanover High School

answers on page 413

DO YOU REMEMBER?

1. Name the infamous Santa Claus that got pelted with snowballs during a 1968 Eagles game.

    a. Fran O'Brien
    b. Steve McCloskey
    c. Chuck Weedon
    d. Frank Olivo

2. The Liberty Belles were sporting new short and splashy uniforms designed by which local women's designer for the Eagles Super Bowl appearance against the Raiders?

    a. Plage Tahiti
    b. Nicole Miller
    c. Nan Duskin
    d. Sophie Curson

3. How long did it take Eagles Safety Brian Dawkins to become a starter?

    a. First game of the season
    b. Second game of the season
    c. Last game of the season
    d. First game, second season

4. In what year did the Eagles defense finish first in all defensive categories: overall, pass and run?

    a. 1989
    b. 1991
    c. 1993
    d. 1995

5. What was the result of the Eagles first play from scrimmage against the Tennessee Titans, in the first game of the 2002 season?

    a. Staley run
    b. McNabb/Levens pass
    c. Levens run
    d. McNabb sacked

6. Against whom did the Eagles play just two days after the assassination of President John F. Kennedy?

    a. Washington Redskins
    b. New York Giants
    c. Chicago Bears
    d. Minnesota Vikings

7. Which Philadelphia Mayor refused to use the Mayor's box at 'The Vet' because he thought it was too extravagant?

    a. Mayor Rizzo
    b. Mayor Tate
    c. Mayor Dilworth
    d. Mayor Green

8. Which Eagles player was featured on the cover for the ESPN NFL 2K5 video game?

    a. Donovan McNabb
    b. Terrell Owens
    c. Brian Westbrook
    d. Correll Buckhalter

9. The 1970 Eagles had a season record of 3-10-1. Which team did they tie that season?

    a. St. Louis Cardinals
    b. Dallas Cowboys
    c. Miami Dolphins
    d. Atlanta Falcons

10. Eagle David Akers kicked the game-winning field goal against Oakland in 2005, after aggravating his hamstring on the opening kickoff. How long was the kick?

    a. 19 yards
    b. 23 yards
    c. 26 yards
    d. 29 yards

11. Who did Eagle Tommy McDonald request to introduce him at his Hall of Fame induction ceremony?

    a. Ray Didinger
    b. Chuck Bednarik
    c. Joe Kuharich
    d. Norm Snead

12. When Hugh Douglas returned to the Eagles in 2004, who was occupying his former locker?

    a. Mark Simoneau
    b. Clinton Hart
    c. Jason Short
    d. Jerome McDougle

13. In what year did brothers Koy and Ty Detmer play together on the same Eagles team?

    a. 1994
    b. 1995
    c. 1997
    d. 1999

14. On which of the following NFL teams did Ron Jaworski not play?

    a. Miami Dolphins
    b. Kansas City Chiefs
    c. Los Angeles Rams
    d. Cleveland Browns

15. Eagles head coach Buddy Ryan gave what reason for cutting wide receiver Cris Carter?

    a. He keeps dropping passes
    b. He's too slow
    c. All he can do is score touchdowns
    d. He doesn't fit my system

16. In 2005 Eagle Brian Westbrook missed most of the season due to injury, but he still made it to the end zone a few times. How many touchdowns was he able to score?

    a. 5
    b. 7
    c. 9
    d. 11

17. When the Eagles suspended Terrell Owens, who was given his locker?

    a. Stephen Spach
    b. Matt Ware
    c. Josh Parry
    d. Jamaal Jackson

18. What is the largest number of tackles in a single season credited to Eagles kicker David Akers?

     a. 4
     b. 5
     c. 7
     d. 8

19. Who was the first Eagles player to return a punt for a touchdown?

     a. Ernie Steele
     b. Swede Hanson
     c. Wes McAfee
     d. Len Barnum

20. Which one of the following Eagle players never played for the Miami Dolphins?

     a. Michael Haddix
     b. Ron Heller
     c. Mike Golic
     d. Keith Jackson

21. Against which team did Eagle John Spagnola catch his first touchdown pass from Ron Jaworski?

     a. Denver Broncos
     b. Minnesota Vikings
     c. New York Giants
     d. Atlanta Falcons

22. How many wins did the Eagles achieve playing in their 50th season in the NFL?

    a. 3
    b. 6
    c. 9   <u>answers on page 414</u>
    d. 12

FUN FACTS

1. At what college did Eagles head coach Rich Kotite win a heavyweight boxing championship?

    a. Texas
    b. University of Miami
    c. Air Force
    d. Fordham

2. What is the name of Donovan McNabb's pet boxer?

    a. Ollie
    b. Sinbad
    c. Zorro
    d. Dexter

3. Which Eagles motorcycle enthusiast owns an NHRA pro stock motorcycle racing team?

    a. Troy Vincent
    b. David Akers
    c. Hank Fraley
    d. Jon Runyan

4. Which Eagles player is known for wearing dapper bow ties?

    a. Mark Simoneau
    b. Brian Westbrook
    c. Clinton Hart
    d. Dhani Jones

5. What is the name of the Eagles' mascot?

    a. Phanatic
    b. Iggle
    c. Swoop
    d. The bird

6. Which one of the following Eagles players celebrates his birthday on Christmas Day?

    a. Shawn Andrews
    b. Ryan Moats
    c. Matt Ware
    d. Rod Hood

7. The Eagles got their nickname in 1933 in honor of what?

    a. Bald Eagle
    b. New Deal's National Recovery Act
    c. Fan contest
    d. Owner's curiosity with birds

8. While former Eagle Freddie Mitchell was in college, he was a baseball teammate of which Phillies player?

    a. Chase Utley
    b. Ryan Howard
    c. Brett Meyers
    d. Ryan Madson

9. Eagles head coach Andy Reid wrote a sports column for which local newspaper while he attended Brigham Young University?

    a. Provo Daily Herald
    b. BYU Gazette
    c. Brigham Young Express
    d. Salt Lake Tribune

10. Eagles' offensive tackle Jon Runyan became part owner of which Arena Two football league team?

    a. Wilkes Barre/Scranton
    b. San Diego
    c. Tennessee Valley
    d. Birmingham

11. Who is the heaviest player ever to play for the Eagles?

    a. Bubba Miller
    b. Tra Thomas
    c. William Perry
    d. Antone Davis

12. In 2005, which Eagles player was selected by People magazine as one of their 50 hottest bachelors?

    a. Dhani Jones
    b. Brian Westbrook
    c. Quintin Mikell
    d. Mike McMahon

13. Which Eagles player was offered a basketball scholarship by Michigan State?

    a. Bobby Morse
    b. Clarence Peaks
    c. Otis Grant
    d. Jon Runyan

14. Who were the Eagles playing when Santa Claus got pelted with snow balls during halftime?

    a. Dallas Cowboys
    b. Minnesota Vikings
    c. Washington Redskins
    d. St. Louis Rams

15. What was the name of the football team when Philadelphia and Pittsburgh merged their two teams?

    a. Steel-gles
    b. Steagles
    c. Ironbirds
    d. Iggles

16. In what year did the ushers picket the Eagles for not recognizing their union?

    a. 1963
    b. 1967
    c. 1970
    d. 1974

17. In the sixties, what were the Eagles' cheerleaders nicknamed?

    a. Birdies
    b. Eaglettes
    c. Swoop-ettes
    d. Eagle dancers

18. When Sylvester Stallone entered the Linc as part of the opening ceremony, what jersey number was he wearing?

    a. 1
    b. 13
    c. 5
    d. 22

19. Who were the Eagles playing when Jeremiah Trotter was tossed from the game during pre-game warm-ups?

    a. Washington Redskins
    b. Atlanta Falcons
    c. Baltimore Ravens
    d. Dallas Cowboys

20. How many touchdowns did Terrell Owens need to score during the 2004 season for Eagles head coach Andy Reid to wear the infamous black tights?

    a. 10
    b. 13
    c. 15
    d. 20

21. Which local radio station did former Eagle Tom Brookshier once co-own?

    a. WWDB
    b. WPEN
    c. WIP
    d. WPHT

22. When Turkey Hill dairies was named the official ice cream of the Eagles, what new flavor did they create to honor the team?

    a. Touchdown Sundae
    b. McNabb's Paradise
    c. Touchdown Paradise
    d. Touchdown Commotion

23. In 1995, Andy Reid coached in Green Bay together with which current Eagles coach?

     a. Bill Shuey
     b. Ted Williams
     c. Ron Rivera
     d. Marty Mornhinweg

24. What jersey number does 'Swoop,' the Eagles' mascot, wear?

     a. 1
     b. 99
     c. 00
     d. Does not have a number

25. Which member of the 1999 Eagles squad played in Super Bowl XXIX with the 1994 San Diego Chargers?

     a. Eric Bieniemy
     b. James Darling
     c. Steve Everitt
     d. Tim Hauck

26. Which Eagle holds Florida State University's weight lifting record for bench pressing 550 pounds?

     a. Tom Bailey
     b. Tra Thomas
     c. Hollis Thomas
     d. Woody Peoples

27. How much money was Duce Staley fined for being a holdout during the 2003 Eagles Training camp?

     a. $75,000
     b. $100,000
     c. $130,000
     d. $145,000

28. During the summer of 2005, which NBA basketball team wanted Eagle Terrell Owens to play on their summer league?

   a. Chicago Bulls
   b. Charlotte Bobcats
   c. Sacramento Kings
   d. Atlanta Hawks

29. What is the minimum number of players the Eagles must dress for every football game?

   a. 39 players
   b. 42 players
   c. 45 players
   d. 48 players

answers on page 415

REMEMBER THIS?

1. Eagle Ricky Watters stated after a game, 'I'm not gonna jump up there and get knocked out. For who? For what?' Who did the Eagles play?

   a. Tampa Bay Buccaneers
   b. Baltimore Ravens
   c. Pittsburgh Steelers
   d. Detroit Lions

2. During the 2004 off-season, Eagle Reno Mahe worked as a guest host in which local Philly restaurant?

   a. Dave and Buster's
   b. Casey's Dugout Saloon
   c. Manny Brown's
   d. Chickie's and Pete's

3. What did the Eagles trainer give the players to help fight dehydration?

    a. Gatorade
    b. Pickle juice
    c. Caffeinated water
    d. Cream Soda

4. Who were the Eagles playing when NFL commissioner Bert Bell suffered a fatal heart attack?

    a. St. Louis Cardinals
    b. Buffalo Bills
    c. Pittsburgh Steelers
    d. Miami Dolphins

5. How many days of the 2003 Eagles training camp did Duce Staley hold out?

    a. 24 days
    b. 26 days
    c. 29 days
    d. 33 days

6. Name the NFL's collective bargaining special master that was appointed to arbitrate whether Terrell Owens could be an Eagle?

    a. Gregory Hunt
    b. Dennis Weiss
    c. Stephen Burbank
    d. Adolpho Birch

7. In 1959, which airplane company was chartered by the Eagles to fly the team to their away games?

    a. Coastal Airline
    b. Frontier Airline
    c. Sky-high Airline
    d. Kingfisher Airline

8. In what year was the Eagles practice bubble moved from JFK Stadium to the Vet?

    a. 1986
    b. 1989
    c. 1992
    d. 1994

9. Which organization established the Philadelphia City All-Star football game along with the Eagles?

    a. Police Athletic League
    b. Department of Recreation
    c. Big Brothers
    d. Daily News Newspaper

10. Which snack company was the first to team up with the Eagles in the fight against leukemia campaign?

    a. Frito-Lay
    b. Herr's Chips
    c. Goldenberg's
    d. Swell Gum Company

11. In its 33 years, how many times was the artificial turf at the Vet replaced?

    a. 3
    b. 6
    c. 9
    d. 12

12. Which one of the following Eagles player was drafted by the Philadelphia Warriors in 1959 for his basketball skills?

    a. Ted Dean
    b. Ken MacAfee
    c. Theron Sapp
    d. Tim Brown

13. In what year were these Eagles soda cans introduced to the fans?

    a. 1972
    b. 1976
    c. 1980
    d. 1993

14. In 2005, which Philadelphia sports announcer provided his voice for 'The Longest Yard' movie trailers?

    a. Bill Campbell
    b. Harry Kalas
    c. Mike Quick
    d. Merrill Reese

15. Which sixties Eagles player's wife was Miss Oklahoma 1955?

    a. Chuck Bednarik
    B. Pete Retzlaff
    c. Tommy McDonald
    d. Bill Bradley

16. In what year did the sack became an official statistic?

    a. 1964
    b. 1971
    c. 1982
    d. 1986

17. Who did the Eagles release to create a roster spot for wide receiver Terrell Owens, who then was deactivated for the rest of the season?

    a. Todd France
    b. Ed Canonico
    c. Andy Hall
    d. Robert Redd

18. Which Eagles player was a teammate of Michael Jordan while playing in a Babe Ruth baseball league in Wilmington, N.C.?

    a. Seth Joyner
    b. Clyde Simmons
    c. Hugh Douglas
    d. Charley Young

answers on page 415

WHAT A STAT!

1. Prior to Lamar Gordon fumbling against Green Bay in 2005, how many games had it been since an Eagles running back lost a fumble?

   a. 37 games
   b. 41 games
   c. 48 games
   d. 56 games

2. How many games did it take the Eagles (including playoff games) to return a blocked field goal for a score?

   a. 873 games
   b. 926 games
   c. 1,018 games
   d. 1,152 games

3. Who was the Eagles' first 300-pound player?

   a. Clyde Simmons
   b. Antone Davis
   c. Frank Giddens
   d. Ron Solt

4. In what year did the Eagles only allow 141 points to be scored against them?

   a. 1947
   b. 1950
   c. 1953
   d. 1957

5. The Eagles scored the biggest season opening total in club history in their first three games of the 2002 season. How many points did they score?

    a. 98 points
    b. 105 points
    c. 109 points
    d. 114 points

6. How many regular season games did the Eagles win from 2000 through 2004?

    a. 54 games
    b. 59 games
    c. 61 games
    d. 63 games

7. In 2004, where did the Eagles rank among NFC teams with a turnover differential of plus six?

    a. First
    b. Second
    c. Third
    d. Fourth

8. The Eagles had 16 third-down attempts against the Patriots in Super Bowl XXXIX. How many did they convert?

    a. 5
    b. 7
    c. 9
    d. 11

9. Eagles quarterback Bobby Thomason passed for 437 yards in one game. His single game passing record stood for how many years before it was broken?

    a. 27
    b. 29
    c. 32
    d. 36

10. In 2004, how many touchdowns did the Eagles score off of their 47 attempts inside their opponent's 20-yard line?

    a. 30
    b. 34
    c. 37
    d. 41

11. In 2005, against which team did Eagle David Akers play in his 100th NFL game?

    a. Oakland Raiders
    b. Dallas Cowboys
    c. Atlanta Falcons
    d. San Francisco 49ers

12. In what year did the Eagles defense record four shutouts and only allow 85 points?

    a. 1934
    b. 1939
    c. 1942
    d. 1947

13. At the start of the 2005 season, what was Donovan McNabb's record as a starting quarterback?

    a. 45-34
    b. 52-27
    c. 56-23
    d. 62-17

14. Against which NFL team did the Eagles never lose a single game in team's history?

    a. Tennessee Titans
    b. Buffalo Bills
    c. Dallas Texans
    d. Boston Yanks

15. During the 2005 season, against which of the following teams did the Eagles not score on their first offensive drive?

    a. New York Giants
    b. Green Bay Packers
    c. San Francisco 49ers
    d. Dallas Cowboys

16. In 1965 the Eagles set a club record for total yards in a game when they compiled 582 yards against which team?

    a. Detroit Lions
    b. Cleveland Browns
    c. New York Giants
    d. Baltimore Colts

17. In '98, Duce Staley became the first Eagle to lead the team in both rushing and receptions since which Eagle?

    a. Charlie Garner
    b. Vaughn Hebron
    c. Herschel Walker
    d. Ricky Watters

18. Eagles quarterback Ron Jaworski passed for how many total yards from 1977 to 1986?

    a. 25,427
    b. 26,963
    c. 27,381
    d. 28,279

19. How many different Eagles players caught a pass in Super Bowl XXXIX?

    a. 5
    b. 7
    c. 9
    d. 11

20. How many times in the 96 regular season games played from 1999 to 2004 did the Eagles limit opposing teams to 17 points or less?

    a. 59
    b. 63
    c. 66
    d. 71

21. Entering the 2005 season, how many successful field goals did Eagles kicker David Akers make out of his 167 attempts?

    a. 139
    b. 143
    c. 148
    d. 150

22. When the Eagles played New England in Super Bowl XXXIX, it marked the first time in Super Bowl history that a tied score ended the third quarter. What was the score?

    a. 10-10
    b. 13-13
    c. 14-14
    d. 17-17

23. During the 2005 season, how many replay challenges did Head Coach Andy Reid win?

    a. 1/6
    b. 2/8
    c. 3/6
    d. 4/8

24. How many games did Eagle Chuck Bednarik miss during his 13-year tenure with the birds?

a. 3
b. 5
c. 7
d. 9

25. For the first time in the 2005 season, against which team did Brian Westbrook get 20 touches?

   a. Washington Redskins
   b. New York Giants
   c. Denver Broncos
   d. San Diego Chargers

26. In which one of the following years did Eagles quarterback Randall Cunningham not score at least five rushing touchdowns?

   a. 1986
   b. 1987
   c. 1990
   d. 1992

27. How many times has Eagle kicker David Akers made at least four field goals in a single game?

   a. 8 Times
   b. 12 Times
   c. 15 Times
   d. 19 Times

28. In 2004, how many different players were credited with at least one sack?

   a. 14
   b. 17
   c. 19
   d. 21

29. How many games did it take Eagles coach Andy Reid to win 50 games?

    a. 74
    b. 81
    c. 89
    d. 93

30. In 1999, Eagle Duce Staley recorded 1,567 yards from scrimmage. This represented what percentage of the team's yards (which was the highest percentage of any player in the NFL)?

    a. 40.9%
    b. 52.4%
    c. 56.8%
    d. 61.1%

31. Who was the first Eagles head coach to post his first NFL victory against the Dallas Cowboys?

    a. Ray Rhodes
    b. Andy Reid
    c. Buck Shaw
    d. Marion Campbell

32. During the 2003-04 season, the Eagles trio of running backs combined for how many total yards gained?

    a. 1,618 yards
    b. 1,783 yards
    c. 1,829 yards
    d. 1,861 yards

33. How many touchdown passes did the '99 Eagles defense give up all season?

    a. 14
    b. 19
    c. 22
    d. 26

34. In 1943, the Steagles defeated the Brooklyn Dodgers in their first game. How many total yards did the Dodgers gain running the ball?

    a. 26 yards
    b. 53 yards
    c. 78 yards
    d. -33 yards

35. In what year did the Eagles win eight games for the first time?

    a. 1943
    b. 1945
    c. 1947
    d. 1949

answers on page 416

WHICH EAGLES PLAYER

1. Philadelphia Park named a race 'The Susquehanna Handicap,' in tribute to which former Eagles player?

    a. Steve Van Buren
    b. Sonny Jurgensen
    c. Pete Retzlaff
    d. Norm Van Brocklin

2. Which Eagles player played with an unbuttoned chin strap?

    a. Harold Jackson
    b. Chuck Bednarik
    c. Adrian Burk
    d. Ben Hawkins

3. Who was the Eagles' first African-American player?

    a. Lee Riley
    b. Taft Reed
    c. Al Coleman
    d. Ralph Goldston

4. Which Eagles player is also the CEO and founder of Sore-Loser Athletic Wear?

    a. N.D. Kalu
    b. Hollis Thomas
    c. Ike Reese
    d. Brian Dawkins

5. What is the name of the movie based on the true story of Eagle Vince Papale?

    a. *I Had a Dream*
    b. *E-a-g-l-e-s*
    c. *The Rookie*
    d. *Invincible*

6. Which former Eagle has a son that plays for the Philadelphia Wings?

    a. Ron Jaworski
    b. Bill Bergey
    c. Mike Quick
    d. Chuck Bednarik

7. Which Eagles player was the best man at Corey Simon's wedding?

    a. Jermane Mayberry
    b. Paul Grasmanis
    c. Hank Fraley
    d. Tra Thomas

8. Which major league baseball team drafted Eagle Matt Ware right out of high school?

    a. Oakland Athletics
    b. Texas Rangers
    c. Seattle Mariners
    d. Colorado Rockies

answers on page 417

OTHER PHILLY FOOTBALL TEAMS

1. What was the name of Philadelphia's United States Football League team?

    a. Firebirds
    b. Bells
    c. Stars
    d. Carpenters

2. In what year did the Frankford Yellow Jackets football team start playing in the NFL?

    a. 1922
    b. 1924
    c. 1925
    d. 1926

3. Who was the first coach of the Frankford Yellow Jackets football team?

    a. Punk Berryman
    b. George Sullivan
    c. Guy Chamberlain
    d. Two-Bits Homan

4. When did Guy Chamberlin start coaching the Frankford Yellow Jackets football team?

    a. 1923
    b. 1925
    c. 1927
    d. 1929

5. Who was the head coach of the Philadelphia Stars?

    a. Chuck Fairbanks
    b. Walt Michaels
    c. Jim Mora
    d. Myles Tanenbaum

6. Which USFL Philadelphia Stars player was the league's MVP in 1983?

    a. Sean Landeta
    b. Bryan Thomas
    c. Frank Bruno
    d. Kelvin Bryant

7. The 1926 Frankford Yellow Jackets started their season with a tie against the Akron Indians. Who did they tie 0-0 in their last game?

    a. Detroit Panthers
    b. Pottsville Maroons
    c. Hartford Blues
    d. Canton Bulldogs

8. On January 4, 1983, the USFL held its first draft. Who was the first draft pick for the Philadelphia Stars?

    a. Gary Anderson
    b. Trumaine Johnson
    c. Irv Eatman
    d. Gary Williams

9. How many rushing touchdowns did fullback Two-Bits Homan score in his six years with the Frankford Yellow Jackets?

    a. 2
    b. 4
    c. 9
    d. 12

10. In what division did the Philadelphia Stars of the USFL compete in?

    a. Independence
    b. Liberty
    c. Atlantic
    d. Eastern

11. Whom did the Philadelphia Soul football team play against in its inaugural season opener at the Wachovia Center?

    a. Dallas Desperados
    b. Carolina Cobras
    c. Georgia Force
    d. New Orleans Voodoo

12. Whom did the Philadelphia Stars lose to in the first USFL Championship Game?

    a. Denver Gold
    b. Michigan Panthers
    c. Jacksonville Bulls
    d. Pittsburgh Maulers

answers on page 417

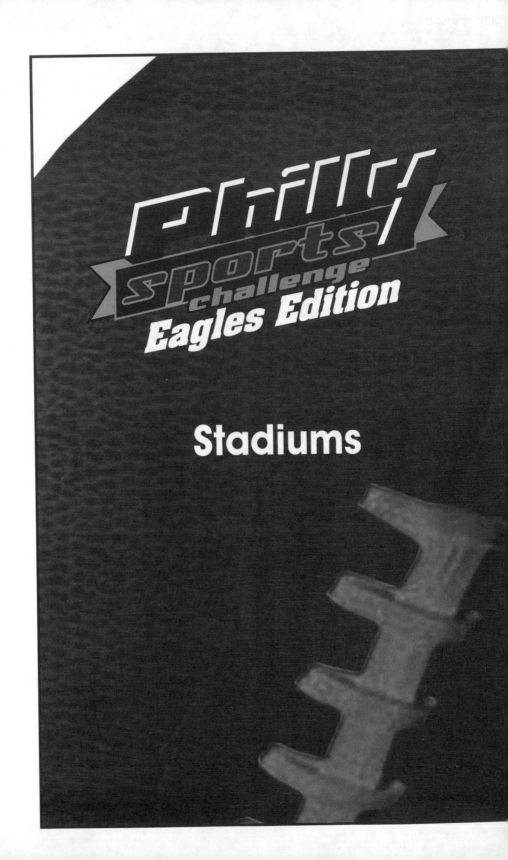

Stadiums

EAGLES AT THE LINC

1. How long was Eagle David Akers's first regular season field goal at the Linc?

    a. 19 yards
    b. 28 yards
    c. 42 yards
    d. Over 50 yards

2. Which Eagles player had the first regular season interception at the Linc?

    a. Troy Vincent
    b. Brian Dawkins
    c. Nate Wayne
    d. Lito Sheppard

3. Who did the Eagles host in the first football game played at the Linc?

    a. Washington Redskins
    b. Seattle Seahawks
    c. New England Patriots
    d. Carolina Panthers

4. Who scored the Eagles' first defensive touchdown at the Linc?

    a. Darwin Walker
    b. Troy Vincent
    c. N.D. Kalu
    d. Ike Reese

5. Which Eagles player had the first regular season sack at the Linc?

    a. Hollis Thomas
    b. Ike Reese
    c. Corey Simon
    d. N.D. Kalu

6. What was the first event held at Lincoln Financial Field?

    a. Eagles game
    b. Soccer match
    c. Rock concert
    d. Temple football game

answers on page 418

EAGLES AT THE VET

1. Who scored the Eagles' last defensive touchdown at Veterans Stadium?

    a. Shawn Barber
    b. Bobby Taylor
    c. Brian Dawkins
    d. Lito Sheppard

2. Who did the Eagles defeat for their first win at Veterans Stadium?

    a. Dallas Cowboys
    b. New York Giants
    c. Washington Redskins
    d. Denver Broncos

3. The very first game the Eagles played at the Vet was a preseason game against which team?

   a. Buffalo Bills
   b. New York Giants
   c. Green Bay Packers
   d. Pittsburgh Steelers

4. Which one of the following NFL teams never played a regular season game against the Eagles at Veterans Stadium?

   a. Jacksonville Jaguars
   b. Carolina Panthers
   c. Kansas City Chiefs
   d. Houston Texans

5. What caused Judge Seamus McCaffrey to set up a small courtroom at Veterans Stadium?

   a. Too many drunks
   b. A flare gun incident
   c. Snowballs being thrown
   d. Too many Dallas fans

6. Which one of the following Eagles coaches did not play his home games at the Vet?

   a. Jerry Williams
   b. Ed Khayat
   c. Fred Bruney
   d. Joe Kuharich

7. Who were the Eagles playing when only 4,074 fans actually attended?

   a. Chicago Bears
   b. Cleveland Browns
   c. Pittsburgh Pirates
   d. Washington Redskins

8. What was the Eagles' record playing at the Vet?

    a. 134-122-1
    b. 144-111-2
    c. 157-98-2
    d. 160-92-3

9. In the last game played at Veterans Stadium, which Eagles player scored the last points ever put on the scoreboard?

    a. Duce Staley
    b. James Thrash
    c. Brian Dawkins
    d. David Akers

10. How did the Eagles score their last defensive touchdown at Veterans Stadium?

    a. Blocked punt return
    b. Fumble recovery return
    c. Safety
    d. Interception return

11. Who was the Eagles kicker who had the first regular season kickoff at Veterans Stadium?

    a. Nick Mike-Mayer
    b. Ove Johansson
    c. Dale Dawson
    d. Mark Moseley

12. How many seasons did the Eagles play at Veterans Stadium?

    a. 32
    b. 35
    c. 37
    d. 40

answers on page 418

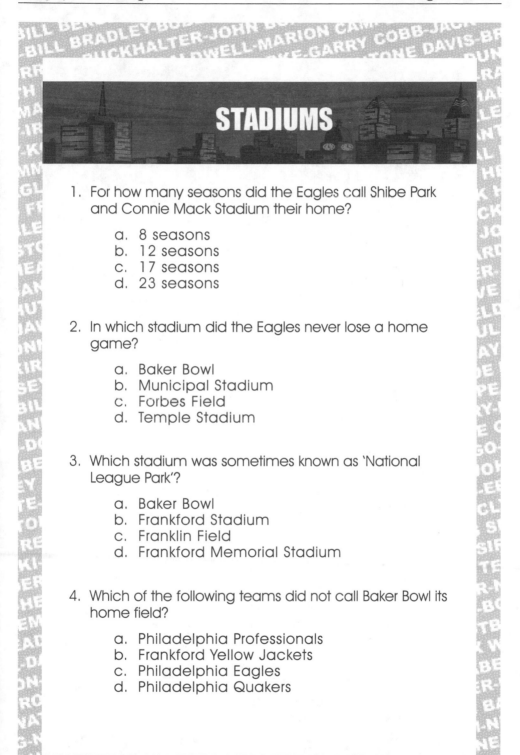

STADIUMS

1. For how many seasons did the Eagles call Shibe Park and Connie Mack Stadium their home?

    a. 8 seasons
    b. 12 seasons
    c. 17 seasons
    d. 23 seasons

2. In which stadium did the Eagles never lose a home game?

    a. Baker Bowl
    b. Municipal Stadium
    c. Forbes Field
    d. Temple Stadium

3. Which stadium was sometimes known as 'National League Park'?

    a. Baker Bowl
    b. Frankford Stadium
    c. Franklin Field
    d. Frankford Memorial Stadium

4. Which of the following teams did not call Baker Bowl its home field?

    a. Philadelphia Professionals
    b. Frankford Yellow Jackets
    c. Philadelphia Eagles
    d. Philadelphia Quakers

5. In which stadium did the Eagles only win one home game?

    a. Forbes Field
    b. Temple Stadium
    c. Baker Bowl
    d. Franklin Field

6. Which one of the following was not one of the names used for 'JFK Stadium'?

    a. Sesquicentennial Stadium
    b. Municipal Stadium
    c. War Veterans Stadium
    d. John F. Kennedy Stadium

7. Which stadium was torn down to make way for the construction of the First Union Center?

    a. Shibe Park
    b. JFK Stadium
    c. Beury Stadium
    d. Cores States Center

8. Which one of the following stadiums was the Eagles' first home field?

    a. Shibe Park
    b. Baker Bowl
    c. Franklin Field
    d. Municipal Stadium

9. Where did the Eagles play their home games from 1958 through 1970?

    a. Connie Mack Stadium
    b. Franklin Field
    c. Municipal Stadium
    d. Veterans Stadium

10. Against whom did the Eagles play their first home game at Franklin Field?

    a. New York Giants
    b. San Francisco 49ers
    c. Washington Redskins
    d. Pittsburgh Steelers

11. Which Philadelphia stadium was nicknamed 'The Hump'?

    a. Franklin Field
    b. JFK Stadium
    c. Baker Bowl
    d. Shibe Park

12. In which one of the following stadiums did the Eagles actually have a winning record from home games played there?

    a. Baker Bowl
    b. Municipal Stadium
    c. Franklin Field
    d. Connie Mack Stadium

13. Which of the following stadiums never hosted an NFL contest?

    a. Franklin Field
    b. Temple Stadium
    c. Frankford Stadium
    d. Baker Bowl

14. In which one of the following stadiums did the Eagles not win any playoff games?

    a. Franklin Field
    b. Connie Mack Stadium
    c. Veterans Stadium
    d. Municipal Stadium

answers on page 419

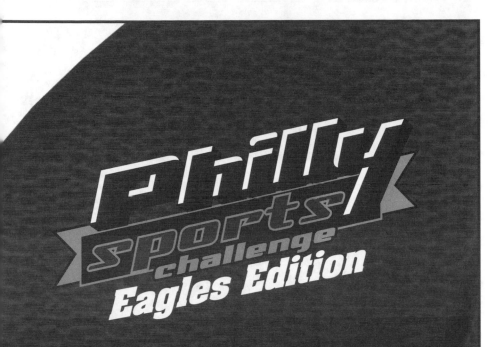

Answers

THE THIRTIES: DEPRESSING EAGLES

Questions on page 13

1.   c. 4
2.   a. 116-9
3.   c. 1937
4.   b. 3
5.   a. New York Giants
6.   c. 6
7.   d. New York Giants
8.   a. Brooklyn Dodgers
9.   a. 1
10. d. Green Bay Packers
11. d. Pittsburgh Pirates
12. c. Hank Reese
13. a. 0
14. a. Threatening weather
15. d. Joe Carter
16. b. 5
17. a. Bill Hewitt
18. b. 18
19. d. Cleveland Rams
20. c. Fifth game
21. c. 1936
22. a. Jack Roberts

THE FORTIES: EAGLES UPLIFTED

Questions on page 17

1.   b. Chicago Bears
2.   d. Detroit Lions
3.   c. 4
4.   a. 1
5.   c. 8
6.   b. Don Looney
7.   b. 1943
8.   c. 14
9.   d. Cliff Patton
10.   a. 5-4-1
11.   c. Al Wistert

THE FIFTIES: FLY EAGLES FLY

Questions on page 22

1.   b. Chicago Cardinals
2.   c. T- formation
3.   b. Pittsburgh Steelers
4.   d. Vince Lombardi
5.   a. Cleveland Browns
6.   c. 141
7.   b. Dallas Texans
8.   c. Chicago Cardinals
9.   b. Tommy McDonald
10.   d. Bobby Walston
11.   b. Cleveland Browns

12.   a. Bucko Kilroy
13.   b. Pittsburgh Steelers
14.   b. 51
15.   c. Tommy McDonald
16.   d. Ken Keller
17.   a. Baltimore Colts

THE SIXTIES: ON THE ROAD TO VICTORY

Questions on page 26

1.   b. Pete Retzlaff
2.   c. 11
3.   a. 0
4.   b. 4
5.   a. 24
6.   d. 1969
7.   c. Cleveland Browns
8.   c. 6
9.   d. Tim Brown
10.   a. Bob Pellegrini
11.   c. Joe Kuharich
12.   d. Tim Brown
13.   c. St. Louis Cardinals
14.   a. Detroit Lions
15.   a. Earl Gros

THE SEVENTIES: EAGLES TAKE A DIVE

Questions on page 30

1. d. 7 games
2. d. Washington Redskins
3. d. Pete Liske
4. c. 20 players
5. a. Washington Redskins
6. d. New York Giants
7. c. 1974
8. c. Fred Hill
9. a. New Orleans Saints
10. a. 3
11. c. Horst Muhlmann
12. c. Adrian Burk
13. c. Tom Sullivan
14. d. 1978
15. c. Detroit Lions

THE EIGHTIES: FLYING IN CIRCLES

Questions on page 35

1. d. Fred Bruney
2. b. 3 games
3. d. Seattle Seahawks
4. b. 1985
5. c. St. Louis Cardinals
6. c. 12
7. d. Los Angeles Rams
8. b. Dallas Cowboys
9. d. Atlanta Falcons
10. c. Atlanta Falcons

11.   d.   Buddy Ryan
12.   a.   St. Louis Cardinals
13.   c.   Luis Zendejas
14.   b.   Dallas Cowboys
15.   c.   Dallas Cowboys

THE NINETIES: WATCH OUR EAGLES SOAR

Questions on page 38

1.   a.   Michael Zordich
2.   d.   1998
3.   b.   Rich Kotite
4.   c.   1995
5.   b.   Seattle Seahawks
6.   b.   1996
7.   a.   396
8.   c.   6
9.   a.   Green Bay Packers
10.   b.   5
11.   c.   14
12.   d.   1998
13.   b.   Rich Kotite
14.   a.   Chicago Bears
15.   b.   Ray Phillips

THE NEW MILLENNIUM
Road to the Super Bowl

Questions on page 43

1.   c.   39
2.   c.   7
3.   c.   Yards per catch
4.   d.   Chad Lewis
5.   a.   0
6.   b.   1993
7.   b.   1
8.   d.   Chad Lewis
9.   b.   Corey Simon
10.   d.   Kevin Mathis
11.   a.   Freddie Mitchell
12.   b.   A.J. Feeley

FRONT OFFICE

Questions on page 47

1.   a.   Director of player relations
2.   d.   Jerry Wolman
3.   b.   Offensive coordinator
4.   b.   1933
5.   c.   Jerry Wolman
6.   d.   1935
7.   d.   Commissioner of Immigration and Naturalization service
8.   b.   Field hockey
9.   b.   Leonard Tose
10.   a.   Jimmy Johnson

11.   b.   Leonard Tose
12.   c.   WCAU
13.   b.   The Eagle's Nest
14.   c.   Fire Commissioner
15.   b.   Team Ambassador
16.   b.   Pete Retzlaff
17.   d.   Phoenix

HEAD EAGLE

Questions on page 52

1.   d.   Cleveland Browns
2.   b.   UCLA
3.   b.   1995
4.   c.   Dick Vermeil
5.   b.   Greasy Neale
6.   d.   Bert bell
7.   b.   Nick Skorich
8.   c.   31 wins
9.   c.   Rich Kotite
10.   a.   Dallas Cowboys
11.   a.   Walt Kiesling
12.   b.   Chicago Bears
13.   b.   51-29-0
14.   b.   Baltimore Colts
15.   a.   39
16.   b.   Joe Kuharich
17.   c.   Bo McMillin
18.   b.   Bert bell
19.   c.   Buck Shaw
20.   d.   15 years
21.   c.   Atlanta Falcons
22.   a.   Arizona Cardinals
23.   b.   3
24.   c.   Green Bay Packers

25.	d.	Cleveland Browns
26.	a.	4
27.	d.	Mike McCormick
28.	c.	Ray Rhodes
29.	a.	Buck Shaw
30.	b.	New York Giants
31.	b.	9

EAGLE COACHES

Questions on page 58

1.	a.	Marty Mornhinweg
2.	a.	Quarterback
3.	c.	Cleveland Browns
4.	a.	Miami of Ohio
5.	d.	San Antonio Gunslingers
6.	c.	Buffalo Bills
7.	a.	Defensive Coordinator
8.	b.	Minnesota Vikings
9.	d.	Bill Walsh
10.	b.	Special Teams
11.	a.	Frank Reagan
12.	d.	Missouri Southern
13.	c.	Line
14.	c.	Emmitt Thomas
15.	c.	Quarterbacks coach
16.	d.	Marty Mornhinweg

CALL OF THE EAGLES

Questions on page 63

1.	d.	1956
2.	c.	1977
3.	a.	Charlie Swift
4.	b.	1998
5.	b.	Joe Pisarcik
6.	d.	Thatcher Longstreth
7.	b.	Andy Musser
8.	c.	Taylor Grant
9.	b.	610 WIP
10.	b.	Tom Brookshier

A BIRD BY ANY OTHER NAME

Questions on page 67

1.	c.	Christian
2.	a.	Stephen
3.	c.	William
4.	d.	Thomas
5.	a.	James
6.	d.	Edwin
7.	a.	Lawrence
8.	b.	Adam
9.	c.	Reno Mahe
10.	b.	Harold
11.	c.	Edwin
12.	b.	Loris
13.	c.	Ron
14.	c.	Earle
15.	d.	Abisha

NICKNAMES FROM THE '30s

Questions on page 70

1.	b.	John Roberts
2.	d.	The Sharon Express
3.	c.	Dave Smukler
4.	d.	Forrest McPherson
5.	a.	Diddie
6.	c.	George Rado
7.	a.	John Cole
8.	b.	Clarence Thomason
9.	d.	Glenn Frey
10.	c.	Bill Hewitt
11.	b.	Tex
12.	c.	Herschel Stockton
13.	a.	Moose
14.	d.	Herbert Roton
15.	c.	Butch

NICKNAMES FROM THE '40s

Questions on page 72

1.	a.	Walter Barnes
2.	c.	Rocco Canale
3.	b.	Foster Watkins
4.	a.	Bosh Pritchard
5.	a.	Al Wistert
6.	d.	Maurice Harper
7.	b.	Elmer hackney
8.	d.	Bob Davis
9.	c.	Albert Johnson
10.	c.	The Golden Greek
11.	b.	Movin' Van

12.   a.   Dick Humbert
13.   b.   Al Thacker
14.   d.   Wes McAfee
15.   a.   Davey O'Brien

NICKNAMES FROM THE '50s

Questions on page 75

1.   c.   Marion Campbell
2.   a.   Bobby Walston
3.   d.   Adrian Burk
4.   a.   The Baron
5.   b.   Wild Man
6.   c.   Big Train
7.   b.   Country
8.   a.   John Ryan
9.   b.   Ken Keller
10.   a.   Billy Barnes
11.   c.   Clyde Scott
12.   a.   Jim Carr
13.   c.   High
14.   a.   Ken Snyder
15.   c.   John Huzvar

NICKNAMES FROM THE '60s

Questions on page 78

1.   d.   Boomer
2.   b.   Chuck Bednarik
3.   d.   Mike Ditka
4.   a.   The Sheriff
5.   c.   Alvin Haymond
6.   b.   Howard Cassady

7.   d.   Stormin'
8.   c.   Don Burroughs
9.   a.   Onside
10.   a.   Bob Freeman
11.   d.   Bye Bye
12.   b.   John Mellekas
13.   b.   Red
14.   d.   Ike

NICKNAMES FROM THE '70s

Questions on page 80

1.   a.   Doug Collins
2.   a.   Popeye
3.   c.   Dennis Harrison
4.   c.   Silky
5.   a.   Joe Lavender
6.   b.   Tree
7.   d.   Richard Harris
8.   c.   Bill Bergey
9.   a.   John Bunting
10.   c.   Artimus Parker

NICKNAMES FROM THE '80s

Questions on page 82

1.   b.   David Alexander
2.   d.   Mike Quick
3.   c.   Henry Williams
4.   b.   Rock'em Back
5.   d.   Dennis Harrison
6.   b.   Harold Carmichael

7. b. Polish rifle
8. a. Gregg Garrity
9. d. Conan
10. b. Cris Carter
11. c. Big Dog
12. a. Face

NICKNAMES FROM THE '90s

Questions on page 84

1. d. Gary Anderson
2. c. Rev
3. a. Eddie Murray
4. b. Eric Allen
5. b. Pretty Boy
6. c. William Perry
7. a. Ed Jasper
8. d. Kelvin Martin
9. a. Wolfman
10. c. Al Harris
11. c. Toast
12. a. Jerome Brown
13. c. Duce Staley

NICKNAMES OF THE 21st CENTURY

Questions on page 87

1. d. Tra Thomas
2. c. Green
3. a. Bumps
4. b. The Freak
5. a. Pooh Bear
6. b. Truck Driver
7. b. Jason Short

8.   d. Mr. Bigglesworth
9.   c. Rod Smart
10. b. Jeremiah Trotter
11. d. Correll Buckhalter
12. a. Horse
13. d. Big Red
14. d. The Eagles Pep Band

LEAVING THE NEST

Questions on page 91

1.   b. Dallas Cowboys
2.   d. Philadelphia Soul
3.   a. New Orleans Saints
4.   c. Miami Dolphins
5.   d. Kansas City Chiefs
6.   d. Philadelphia Eagles
7.   c. Tim Brown
8.   d. Davey O'Brien
9.   c. St. Louis Cardinals
10. c. Boston Patriots
11. a. Washington Redskins
12. a. Cleveland Browns
13. c. Pittsburgh Steelers
14. c. Pittsburgh Pirates
15. b. New York Giants
16. c. Atlanta Falcons
17. a. New York Giants
18. b. Philadelphia Eagles
19. d. New York Giants
20. a. Tampa Bay Buccaneers
21. a. Baltimore Ravens
22. b. Carolina Panthers
23. c. New York Jets
24. a. Phoenix Cardinals
25. c. Oakland Raiders

26. b. Green Bay Packer
27. a. Pittsburgh Pirates
28. c. Philadelphia Eagles
29. d. Baltimore Colts
30. a. Minnesota Vikings
31. a. New York Jets
32. b. San Diego Chargers
33. d. Minnesota Vikings
34. c. Philadelphia Eagles
35. b. Jim Ring

ARE YOU SURE THAT'S MY NUMBER

Questions on page 98

1. a. 57
2. c. Dan Sandifer
3. d. Bosh Pritchard
4. a. 50
5. c. 44
6. d. 55
7. c. 27
8. d. 86
9. c. 97
10. b. 55
11. c. 77
12. b. 8
13. a. 38
14. a. 50
15. c. 11
16. d. Maxie Baughan

BEFORE THE BIRDS

Questions on page 102

1.   d. New Orleans Saints
2.   a. Green Bay Packers
3.   c. Green Bay Packers
4.   d. New England Patriots
5.   a. San Francisco 49ers
6.   c. New England Patriots
7.   a. Detroit Lions
8.   c. Tampa Bay Buccaneers
9.   b. Atlanta Falcons
10. c. Cincinnati Bengals
11. b. Washington Redskins
12. d. Cincinnati Reds
13. b. Green Bay Packers
14. c. Pittsburgh Steelers
15. a. New England Patriots
16. d. Memphis Showboats
17. b. Arizona Cardinals
18. a. San Francisco 49ers
19. d. Tennessee Titans
20. a. Green Bay Packers
21. c. New York Giants
22. a. Baltimore Ravens
23. d. Miami Dolphins
24. c. New York Jets
25. b. New Orleans Saints
26. b. Chicago Bears
27. d. Tennessee Titan
28. c. Green Bay Packers
29. b. Dallas Cowboys

BIRDS OF A DIFFERENT FEATHER

Questions on page 108

1.	b.	Atlanta Falcons
2.	d.	Philadelphia Eagles
3.	d.	Atlanta Falcons
4.	a.	St. Louis Cardinals
5.	c.	St. Louis Cardinals
6.	a.	St. Louis Cardinals
7.	a.	Chicago Cardinals
8.	d.	St. Louis Cardinals
9.	a.	Seattle Seahawks
10.	b.	Seattle Seahawks
11.	a.	Seattle Seahawks
12.	c.	Atlanta Falcons
13.	a.	Atlanta Falcons
14.	b.	Phoenix Cardinals
15.	c.	Atlanta Falcons

BROTHERS

Questions on page 111

1.	a.	Sam
2.	c.	Bob
3.	b.	Steve
4.	d.	Stockar
5.	a.	Don
6.	c.	Alvin
7.	d.	Chris
8.	b.	Bob
9.	a.	Ebert
10.	c.	Stan

COWBOYS WHO LEARNED TO FLY

Questions on page 113

1. b. Keith Adams
2. a. Jimmie Jones
3. b. Broderick Thompson
4. d. George Hegamin
5. c. Roger Ruzek
6. c. Brian Baldinger
7. d. Rodney Peete
8. a. Oliver Ross
9. a. Sam Baker
10. d. Lynn Hoyem

RECRUITED BIRDS

Questions on page 115

1. c. 1992
2. b. Virginia Tech
3. c. Hank Fraley
4. d. Keith Adams
5. a. L.J. Smith
6. b. Green Bay Packers
7. c. San Jose State
8. b. Dartmouth
9. c. North Illinois
10. a. Michigan State

EAGLES FIRST ROUND

Questions on page 119

1.   d.   Jerome McDougle
2.   c.   Jay Berwanger
3.   a.   Clarence Peaks
4.   b.   Kevin Allen
5.   d.   Jermane Mayberry
6.   c.   1987
7.   d.   Leonard Mitchell
8.   a.   Leonard Mitchell
9.   d.   Brian Dawkins
10.   c.   Siran Stacy
11.   b.   1945
12.   d.   Norm Snead
13.   a.   Ben Smith
14.   c.   11
15.   d.   Jon Harris

EUROPEAN BIRDS

Questions on page 122

1.   d.   Berlin Thunder
2.   a.   Barcelona Dragons
3.   c.   Rhien Fire
4.   d.   Josh Parry
5.   b.   Rhein Fire
6.   b.   Kori Dickerson
7.   d.   Detroit Lions
8.   b.   91
9.   c.   Siran Stacy
10.   c.   54 yards

EAGLES TRAINING CAMPS

Questions on page 124

1.	a.	Atlantic City
2.	b.	Reading
3.	b.	West Chester State
4.	b.	1939
5.	c.	1996
6.	d.	15
7.	d.	Delaware
8.	b.	Cherry Hill Inn
9.	a.	Widener College

NUMBERED EAGLES

Questions on page 126

1.	b.	5, 18
2.	b.	Mark Simoneau
3.	c.	14
4.	a.	Roger Ruzek
5.	a.	50
6.	b.	Billy McMullen
7.	d.	75
8.	d.	Bosh Pritchard
9.	d.	83
10.	a.	57
11.	c.	Dan Sandifer
12.	d.	Al Davis
13.	a.	Tommy Thompson
14.	c.	78
15.	b.	Jack Concannon
16.	d.	Bob Holly

EAGLES WHO BECAME COWBOYS

Questions on page 131

1.   b. Garry Cobb
2.   d. Randall Cunningham
3.   a. Mike Ditka
4.   b. Walt Kowalczyk
5.   a. Junior Tautalatasi
6.   c. Dick Bielski
7.   a. Tommy McDonald
8.   b. Jerry Norton
9.   d. Terrell Owens

JERSEY NUMBERS HISTORY

Questions on page 133

1.   c. 92
2.   a. Happy Feller
3.   d. Joe Kresky
4.   b. Roy Zimmerman
5.   c. Tommy Thompson
6.   a. Lee Woodruff
7.   c. John Lipski
8.   a. Osborne Willson
9.   d. Joe Carter
10.   b. Ed Manske
11.   a. Don Miller
12.   d. Alabama Pitts
13.   c. Gerry Huth
14.   b. Frank Bausch
15.   a. Bill Hewitt

16.   c.   Joseph Wendlick
17.   b.   John Wyhonic
18.   c.   Dave DiFilippo
19.   d.   Ed Kasky
20.   a.   Bill Halverson
21.   a.   Granville Harrison
22.   c.   Dick Humbert
23.   c.   John Durko
24.   b.   John Sodaski
25.   b.   Mike Ditka

REVERSE UNIFORMS 2004 SEASON

Questions on page 139

1.   d.   Ian Allen
2.   b.   Jeff Thomason
3.   d.   Correll Buckhalter
4.   a.   Dorsey Levens
5.   b.   Paul Grasmanis
6.   c.   Alonzo Ephraim
7.   c.   Hank Fraley
8.   c.   Josh Parry

REVERSE UNIFORMS 2005 SEASON

Questions on page 141

1.   b.   Juqua Thomas
2.   d.   Todd Pinkston
3.   b.   Mike Labinjo
4.   a.   L.J. Smith
5.   d.   Sean Considine
6.   c.   Brian Westbrook
7.   c.   Jeremy Thornburg

8.   a.   Trent Cole
9.   c.   Todd Herremans
10.   a.   Ryan Moats
11.   d.   Quintin Mikell
12.   c.   Jon Runyan

ROOKIE SEASONS

Questions on page 143

1.   a.   Jevon Kearse
2.   b.   Correll Buckhalter
3.   d.   Maxie Baughan
4.   c.   Vince Papale
5.   d.   Calvin Williams
6.   a.   Mike Quick
7.   d.   Correll Buckhalter
8.   b.   41
9.   a.   Calvin Williams
10.   b.   8 interceptions
11.   d.   41
12.   a.   Barry Gardner
13.   c.   Mike Boryla

BIRDS THAT FLEW THE COOP

Questions on page 146

1.   a.   Kansas City Chiefs
2.   d.   New York Jets
3.   c.   Washington Redskins
4.   a.   Garry Cobb
5.   c.   Cincinnati Bengals
6.   a.   San Francisco 49ers

7.	b.	Pittsburgh Steelers
8.	b.	Washington Redskins
9.	d.	Brandon Whiting
10.	a.	Charlie Young
11.	c.	Andy Harmon
12.	b.	Reggie Brown
13.	d.	Green Bay Packers
14.	a.	New England Patriots
15.	c.	Joe Jones
16.	c.	1987
17.	b.	Pittsburgh Steelers

UNUSUAL BIRTHPLACES

Questions on page 149

1.	a.	Honduras
2.	c.	Max Padlow
3.	b.	Tonga
4.	d.	South Africa
5.	a.	Mexico
6.	c.	Liberia
7.	b.	Italy

BIG FOOT

Questions on page 153

1.	b.	276
2.	d.	Tony Franklin
3.	c.	50 yards
4.	d.	Tony Franklin
5.	a.	5
6.	a.	New England Patriots
7.	b.	Randall Cunningham
8.	b.	9

BIG HITS

Questions on page 155

1. b. Mike Morgan
2. d. Ike Hilliard
3. c. Frank Gifford
4. d. Bill Bergey
5. c. Jim Taylor
6. a. Jeff Fisher
7. c. Doug Dennison

BIRDS ON THE FIELD

Questions on page 157

1. d. Tackle
2. c. Halfback
3. b. Running back
4. a. Tackle
5. a. Safety
6. d. Tackle
7. b. Linebacker
8. c. Linebacker
9. a. Guard
10. b. Cornerback
11. a. Guard
12. c. Linebacker
13. d. End
14. a. Mike Ditka
15. a. Tight end

BROKEN EAGLES

Questions on page 160

1.   c. Washington Redskins
2.   b. Cracked ribs
3.   d. Broken arm
4.   c. Washington Redskins
5.   b. Dallas Cowboys
6.   c. New Orleans Saints
7.   b. St. Louis Cardinals
8.   c. Minnesota Vikings
9.   a. Rodney Parker

EAGLES CELEBRATIONS

Questions on page 163

1.   b. Jeremiah Trotter
2.   a. Dhani Jones
3.   c. Jevon Kearse
4.   d. Jeff Thomason
5.   a. Herb Lusk
6.   b. Sam Rayburn
7.   d. Harold Carmichael
8.   c. Koy Detmer
9.   b. Via Sikahema

EAGLES LORE

Questions on page 165

1. d. Washington Redskins
2. c. Herman Edwards
3. c. Minnesota Vikings
4. d. Chicago Bears
5. b. Snow Game
6. c. Houston Oilers
7. c. 1947-49
8. b. 74 double go
9. b. Jim Taylor

EAGLES RUNNING BACKS

Questions on page 167

1. b. 1992
2. b. 8 touchdowns
3. d. Heath Sherman
4. b. Timmy Brown
5. d. 1,618 yards
6. a. Steve Van Buren
7. a. Ricky Watters
8. a. 1977
9. c. 69
10. c. Louie Gammona
11. b. Charlie Garner
12. a. Steve Van Buren
13. b. Ricky Watters
14. b. 4 games
15. c. Pittsburgh Steelers
16. a. Herschel Walker

EAGLES STARTS

Questions on page 172

1.   a. New England Patriots
2.   d. Pass to Lewis
3.   a. Dallas Cowboys
4.   d. 1993
5.   a. Todd Heremans
6.   c. 1953
7.   a. Dallas Cowboys
8.   c. Green Bay Packers

EAGLES DEBUT

Questions on page 173

1.   b. Left guard
2.   c. Washington Redskins
3.   d. Washington Redskins
4.   d. Tampa Bay Buccaneers
5.   b. New York Giants
6.   c. Torrance Small
7.   b. New York Giants
8.   a. San Francisco 49ers
9.   c. New York Giants
10.   c. Washington Redskins
11.   c. Tampa Bay Buccaneers
12.   a. New York Jets

EAGLES QBs

Questions on page 176

1.   a.   Norm Van Brocklin
2.   b.   Doug Pederson
3.   b.   Randall Cunningham
4.   b.   Jeff Graham
5.   b.   Sonny Jurgensen
6.   b.   2 touchdowns
7.   d.   Randall Cunningham
8.   a.   Bobby Thomason
9.   d.   Randall Cunningham
10.   b.   32
11.   b.   Randall Cunningham
12.   b.   Sonny Jurgensen
13.   d.   Adrian Burk
14.   b.   Ron Jaworski
15.   c.   Sonny Jurgensen
16.   b.   Reggie Brown
17.   d.   4-1
18.   b.   Sonny Jurgensen
19.   b.   5
20.   a.   Jeff Blake
21.   b.   Vince Papale
22.   a.   1961
23.   c.   1976-77
24.   d.   Mike Boryla
25.   b.   Don McPherson
26.   a.   0
27.   a.   1985
28.   b.   Green Bay Packers
29.   b.   4
30.   c.   Bill Mackrides
31.   b.   Dallas Cowboys

EAGLES RECEPTIONS

Questions on page 184

1.   d.   Irving Fryar
2.   c.   Brian Westbrook
3.   d.   52 yards
4.   b.   James Thrash
5.   b.   Swede Hansen
6.   b.   79
7.   a.   Tommy McDonald
8.   c.   Billy McMullen
9.   d.   San Francisco 49ers
10.   d.   Pete Retzlaff
11.   a.   Reggie Brown
12.   c.   Terrell Owens
13.   d.   Brian Westbrook
14.   a.   Torrance Small
15.   d.   Fred Barnett
16.   a.   Mike Quick
17.   b.   San Diego Chargers
18.   d.   1979
19.   a.   Pete Retzlaff
20.   c.   Irving Fryar
21.   c.   80 yarder
22.   b.   Seven
23.   d.   Chad Lewis
24.   a.   Herschel Walker
25.   b.   24
26.   b.   Oakland Raiders
27.   b.   59 yards
28.   b.   47
29.   a.   6

EAGLES SACK ATTACK

Questions on page 190

1.   d.   Hugh Douglas
2.   a.   Oakland Raiders
3.   b.   31.5
4.   c.   Corey Simon
5.   a.   Mike Mamula
6.   b.   9.5 sacks
7.   d.   Reggie White
8.   b.   Hugh Douglas
9.   a.   236
10.   b.   124
11.   c.   Dennis Harrison
12.   b.   47
13.   b.   62
14.   b.   1987
15.   c.   Detroit Lions
16.   b.   Clyde Simmons
17.   b.   4
18.   d.   Phil Simms
19.   c.   Detroit Lions
20.   c.   Jeremiah Trotter

E-A-G-L-E-S TOUCHDOWNS

Questions on page 196

1.   b.   6
2.   b.   Swede Hanson
3.   a.   Tim Brown
4.   d.   Terrell Owens
5.   c.   Brian Dawkins
6.   d.   Herschel Walker

7.   b.   Steve Van Buren
8.   d.   Steve Van Buren
9.   b.   79
10.   c.   9
11.   a.   Emmett Mortel
12.   c.   Joe Carter
13.   b.   Brian Westbrook
14.   d.   Lito Sheppard
15.   a.   Calvin Williams
16.   b.   Miami Dolphins
17.   d.   Green Bay Packers
18.   b.   Brian Westbrook
19.   d.   Bosh Pritchard
20.   d.   San Diego Chargers

EAGLES-COWBOYS INJURIES

Questions on page 200

1.   a.   Clyde Simmons
2.   c.   Dennis Thurman
3.   c.   Roy Williams
4.   d.   Tim Hauck
5.   b.   Mel Tom
6.   d.   Jessie Small
7.   a.   Tony Tolbert

INTERCEPTIONS

Questions on page 202

1.   b.   Joe Scarpati
2.   a.   Bill Bradley
3.   c.   Eric Allen
4.   b.   Bill Bradley

5.   b. Seattle Seahawks
6.   c. Eric Allen
7.   c. Eric Allen
8.   b. Russ Craft
9.   b. Los Angeles Rams
10.   b. 11
11.   d. 101 yards
12.   c. Bill Bradley
13.   c. Troy Vincent
14.   a. Bill Bradley
15.   b. William Thomas
16.   b. 2

KICKERS

Questions on page 206

1.   a. Joe Scarpati
2.   a. David Akers
3.   b. Chad Lewis
4.   b. 13
5.   b. 9 different kickers
6.   a. David Jacobs
7.   a. Kick off with the new commissioner's ball
8.   c. Bobby Walston
9.   c. Tony Franklin and Paul McFadden
10.   a. John Teltschik
11.   c. 108
12.   a. 12
13.   d. Dallas Cowboys
14.   c. David Akers
15.   b. 2001
16.   a. Houston Oilers
17.   a. 80
18.   b. 309
19.   a. Roger Ruzek
20.   d. St. Louis Cardinals

PLAYERS' STRIKE

Questions on page 211

1.   d. Jerry Sisemore
2.   c. 20 players
3.   d. Walter Abercrombie
4.   a. Randy Logan
5.   d. 0-3
6.   b. New Orleans Saints

PUNT RETURNS

Questions on page 213

1.   d. Vai Sikahema
2.   c. Larry Marshall
3.   a. Brian Westbrook
4.   a. Ernie Steele
5.   b. Allen Rossum
6.   c. Larry Marshall

PUNTERS

Questions on page 214

1.   a. Philadelphia Stars
2.   c. 108
3.   a. John Teltschik
4.   b. Randall Cunningham
5.   c. New York Giants

SEASON OPENERS

Questions on page 215

1.   c. Green Bay Packers
2.   d. Green Bay Packers
3.   b. Cleveland Browns
4.   a. Cleveland Browns
5.   b. Dallas Cowboys
6.   c. Denver Broncos
7.   b. New York Giants
8.   a. Tampa Bay Buccaneers
9.   b. Dallas Cowboys

SPECIAL TEAMS

Questions on page 217

1.   d. Jeremiah Trotter
2.   d. Ken Rose
3.   c. Brian Mitchell
4.   a. Timmy Brown
5.   b. Darwin Walker
6.   d. 79 yards
7.   a. Ike Reese
8.   c. Jevon Kearse
9.   d. Al Nelson

TWO TIMES

Questions on page 219

1. c. 27 points
2. a. Ike Reese
3. d. Simon/Walker
4. b. Charles Young/Jerry Sisemore
5. b. San Francisco 49ers
6. b. Seattle Seahawks
7. a. 0
8. c. '35/'37

EAGLES PRO BOWLERS

Questions on page 223

1.   c. 1964
2.   d. Barry Gardner
3.   c. Norm Snead
4.   c. Bobby Taylor
5.   d. Chuck Bednarik
6.   b. 1971
7.   a. Chuck Bednarik
8.   c. Reggie White
9.   a. Brian Dawkins
10. d. Reggie White
11. b. 1959

EAGLES HONORS

Questions on page 225

1.   b. 1987
2.   a. Sean Morey
3.   d. Brian Dawkins
4.   c. 1991
5.   b. Troy Vincent
6.   c. Donovan McNabb
7.   d. Ron Heller
8.   a. Chicago Bears
9.   c. Norm Van Brocklin

EAGLES PRO BOWLS

Questions on page 227

1.   c. 7 games
2.   d. Mike Quick
3.   a. 1 player
4.   d. 2003
5.   b. 1971
6.   d. Frank LeMaster
7.   b. Jeremiah Trotter
8.   d. Irving Fryar
9.   b. Tommy McDonald
10. a. Bobby Taylor
11. d. Russ Craft
12. c. Floyd Peters
13. b. 1938
14. c. Eric Allen
15. c. 2004
16. b. 1989
17. d. Brenard Wilson

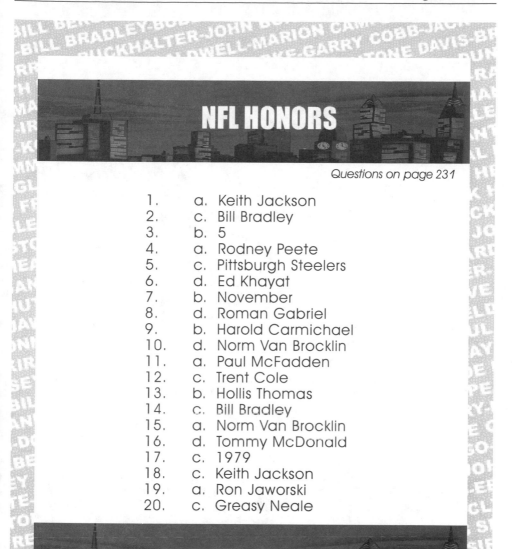

NFL HONORS

Questions on page 231

1.   a. Keith Jackson
2.   c. Bill Bradley
3.   b. 5
4.   a. Rodney Peete
5.   c. Pittsburgh Steelers
6.   d. Ed Khayat
7.   b. November
8.   d. Roman Gabriel
9.   b. Harold Carmichael
10. d. Norm Van Brocklin
11. a. Paul McFadden
12. c. Trent Cole
13. b. Hollis Thomas
14. c. Bill Bradley
15. a. Norm Van Brocklin
16. d. Tommy McDonald
17. c. 1979
18. c. Keith Jackson
19. a. Ron Jaworski
20. c. Greasy Neale

RETIRED JERSEYS

Questions on page 236

1. b. Bob Suffridge
2. d. Mel Tom
3. b. Laf Russell
4. c. Jim Skaggs
5. d. Frank Emmons
6. a. Charles Newton
7. c. Smiley Creswell

EAGLES POSTSEASONS

Questions on page 252

1.   a.   Pittsburgh Steelers
2.   d.   Chicago Cardinals
3.   b.   Chicago Bears
4.   b.   Randall Cunningham
5.   b.   11
6.   a.   Detroit Lions
7.   d.   Wilbert Montgomery
8.   d.   Tommy McDonald
9.   c.   Ted Dean
10.   b.   Keith Jackson
11.   d.   Mike Michel
12.   b.   Chicago Bears
13.   c.   Wally Henry
14.   b.   194 yards
15.   c.   Anthony Toney
16.   d.   Jim McMahon
17.   b.   Detroit Lions
18.   a.   Detroit Lions
19.   a.   Tampa Bay Buccaneers
20.   d.   1988
21.   c.   Green Bay Packers
22.   b.   Duce Staley
23.   c.   107 yards
24.   c.   28 yards
25.   c.   16
26.   b.   31 yard line
27.   c.   33 yards
28.   a.   Freddie Mitchell
29.   a.   1 catch
30.   c.   101 yards
31.   c.   Dorsey Levens
32.   b.   24
33.   b.   17

34.   d.   Chad Lewis
35.   b.   10 games
36.   b.   15

SUPER BOWL

Questions on page 260

1.   a.   Leroy Harris
2.   d.   Charlie Smith
3.   d.   Keith Krepfle
4.   b.   24-21
5.   d.   L.J. Smith
6.   a.   40 yards
7.   b.   Mike Bartrum
8.   c.   Greg Lewis
9.   b.   9
10.   c.   Jeff Thomason
11.   b.   Dallas Cowboys
12.   c.   Derrick Burgess
13.   a.   Eagles by 3

EAGLES HIGHS AND LOWS

Questions on page 265

1.   a.   Dallas Cowboys
2.   d.   Cincinnati Reds
3.   a.   Brooklyn Dodgers
4.   a.   Tampa Bay Buccaneers
5.   c.   Green Bay Packers
6.   b.   105 points
7.   a.   1934
8.   d.   New York Giants
9.   b.   Dallas Cowboys
10.   b.   Washington Redskins

11. a. New York Giants
12. a. 1948
13. a. Tampa Bay Buccaneers
14. b. 96 points

STREAKING EAGLES

Questions on page 268

1.   c. 127 games
2.   d. 99 games
3.   c. 8
4.   a. Dan Abramowicz
5.   b. 9 games
6.   c. 144
7.   c. 8 seasons
8.   c. Steve Van Buren
9.   c. 88
10. c. Dallas Cowboys
11. a. Randy Logan
12. b. 7
13. b. 14
14. b. 3
15. b. 1949
16. d. 2003
17. b. 8
18. b. 162
19. c. 116 games

EAGLES FIRSTS

Questions on page 272

1.　b. Cleveland Browns
2.　d. Timmy Brown
3.　b. Swede Hansen
4.　a. Cincinnati Reds
5.　a. Rams
6.　b. 25-0
7.　a. George Kenneally
8.　b. Cincinnati Reds
9.　b. 4
10.　d. Washington Redskins
11.　d. Bud Grant
12.　d. Washington Redskins
13.　d. Swede Hanson
14.　c. Guy Turnbow
15.　c. Davey O'Brien
16.　d. New York Giants
17.　d. Chad Lewis
18.　d. Bobby Herbert
19.　a. Pittsburgh Steelers
20.　b. Buffalo Bills
21.　b. New York Giants
22.　c. 3
23.　b. 5-11
24.　c. Mark Brunell
25.　a. Washington Redskins
26.　a. New York Giants
27.　c. Brooklyn Dodgers
28.　b. Portsmouth Spartans
29.　a. 1949

EAGLES TEAM RECORDS

Questions on page 278

1. b. 35
2. c. 59 yards
3. c. Tom Dempsey
4. c. New York Giants
5. c. Adrian Burk
6. d. Wally Henry
7. c. Bobby Thomason
8. b. Cleveland Browns
9. a. Brooklyn Dodgers
10. c. Harold Carmichael
11. d. Bobby Walston
12. d. 569
13. b. Punt-return average
14. c. Victor Bailey
15. b. Andy Harmon
16. a. Pittsburgh Steelers
17. c. Joe Lavender
18. b. Wilbert Montgomery
19. d. Bubby Brister
20. c. Don Looney
21. d. Tommy McDonald
22. a. Calvin Williams
23. c. Victor Bailey
24. a. Duce Staley
25. d. Timmy Brown
26. c. Chicago Bears
27. c. 25
28. d. San Diego Chargers
29. b. Houston Texans
30. d. Oakland Raiders
31. c. 153
32. a. 121
33. c. Brooklyn Dodgers

FIRST TIME OPPONENTS

Questions on page 285

1. c. 1966
2. b. 1937
3. d. 1997
4. d. 1973
5. c. 1950
6. a. 1973
7. c. 1973
8. b. 1971
9. a. 1972
10. c. 1950
11. b. 1997
12. d. 1971
13. d. 2002

NFL RECORDS

Questions on page 288

1. b. 17
2. a. 8
3. b. 1939
4. b. Mike Quick
5. c. 227 passes
6. b. 2
7. b. 72
8. d. Dallas Cowboys

DRAFT SELECTIONS

Questions on page 292

1.   b.   Ricky Williams
2.   c.   7
3.   a.   Deauntae Brown
4.   d.   Antone Davis
5.   d.   Never drafted
6.   a.   Tommy Thompson
7.   d.   Hollis Thomas
8.   b.   Kevin Allen
9.   b.   Corey Simon
10.   a.   Jerry Sisemore
11.   c.   Texas A&M
12.   d.   Seventh
13.   a.   Chris T. Jones
14.   a.   Bill Mackrides
15.   d.   1988

EAGLES SMARTS

Questions on page 295

1.   a.   Arkansas
2.   c.   Illinois
3.   a.   Penn State
4.   b.   Wake Forest
5.   b.   University of Miami
6.   a.   Louisville
7.   c.   South Carolina
8.   b.   Ohio State
9.   c.   Youngstown State
10.   d.   UCLA

11.   b.   Brigham Young
12.   a.   Colorado
13.   d.   University of Tennessee
14.   a.   Tackle/Guard
15.   c.   Duke
16.   c.   Syracuse
17.   b.   Georgia State
18.   d.   Oklahoma
19.   c.   Marshall
20.   a.   Central State

LOCAL COLLEGES

Questions on page 299

1.   d.   George Savitsky
2.   a.   Kevin Reilly
3.   b.   Zachary Dixon
4.   d.   Mike Sebastian
5.   a.   Chuck Weber
6.   a.   John Cole
7.   d.   Temple
8.   a.   20
9.   b.   Andre Waters

COLLEGE HONORS

Questions on page 301

1.   b.   Brian Mitchell
2.   d.   2003
3.   d.   Chuck Bednarik
4.   c.   Bobby Hoying
5.   d.   Jeremiah Trotter
6.   b.   Reb Russell

EAGLES IN PRINT

Questions on page 304

1.   a.   Merrill Reese: *It's Gooooood!*
2.   c.   Tommy McDonald
3.   d.   Chuck Bednarik
4.   b.   *Sunday's Warriors*
5.   b.   *Catch This!*
6.   b.   *Eagles Pride, More Than a Game!*
7.   d.   Randall Cunningham
8.   a.   Donovan McNabb
9.   b.   Ray Didinger
10.   d.   Anthony Gargano

EAGLES IN HOLLYWOOD

Questions on page 306

1.   b.   *The Waterboy*
2.   a.   *Kicking and Screaming*
3.   c.   *Johnny be Good*
4.   b.   *The Longest Yard*
5.   d.   *Travelin' On*
6.   b.   Don Chuy
7.   a.   *Jerry Maguire*
8.   d.   Bobby Taylor
9.   b.   Reb Russell
10.   a.   Tim Rossovich
11.   d.   Darnell Autry

EAGLES ON TV

Questions on page 308

1.   a. Hollis Thomas
2.   a. *Scramble*
3.   b. Jeremiah Trotter
4.   c. Vaughn Hebron
5.   a. Mike Caldwell
6.   b. TNT
7.   b. Dhani Jones
8.   d. Jevon Kearse

MAGAZINES

Questions on page 310

1.   d. GQ *Magazine*
2.   b. Bobby Hoying
3.   a. 2
4.   d. Norm Van Brocklin
5.   a. Bobby Hoying
6.   d. Randall Cunningham
7.   b. Jeremiah Trotter
8.   d. Vyto kab
9.   b. *Pro Football Scene*
10. d. Wayne Robinson

MONDAY NIGHT FOOTBALL

Questions on page 312

1.   c.   Baltimore Ravens
2.   c.   61
3.   d.   Seattle Seahawks
4.   a.   New York Giants
5.   c.   New York Giants
6.   c.   7
7.   b.   Baltimore Ravens
8.   b.   Tampa Bay Buccaneers
9.   d.   San Francisco 49ers
10.   c.   John Walton
11.   a.   Dallas Cowboys
12.   b.   23
13.   a.   6

DATES, DATES AND MORE DATES

Questions on page 317

1.   d.   1947
2.   c.   1996
3.   c.   2001
4.   b.   1994
5.   c.   1969
6.   c.   1968
7.   c.   1939
8.   b.   1938
9.   c.   1936
10.   c.   1943
11.   a.   1949
12.   c.   1971
13.   b.   1987

DID YOU KNOW?

Questions on page 320

1.	b.	Rod Hood
2.	d.	John Carlos
3.	c.	Bill Bergey
4.	a.	William Thomas
5.	d.	Donovan McNabb
6.	d.	Airport Marriott
7.	c.	Seattle Seahawks
8.	b.	Darwin Walker
9.	c.	Bill Hewitt
10.	d.	Alabama Pitts
11.	c.	5
12.	a.	Tommy Thompson
13.	b.	13
14.	d.	53 yds
15.	d.	169 games
16.	a.	New York Giants
17.	a.	James Thrash
18.	c.	4
19.	b.	133
20.	c.	5
21.	b.	Al Wistert
22.	d.	Chicago Bears
23.	c.	Thinking Man
24.	c.	Hank Fraley
25.	a.	Norm Bulaich
26.	d.	New Hanover High School

DO YOU REMEMBER?

Questions on page 326

1.	d.	Frank Olivo
2.	a.	Plage Tahiti
3.	b.	Second game of the season
4.	b.	1991
5.	d.	McNabb sacked
6.	a.	Washington Redskins
7.	b.	Mayor Tate
8.	b.	Terrell Owens
9.	d.	Atlanta Falcons
10.	b.	23 yards
11.	a.	Ray Didinger
12.	d.	Jerome McDougle
13.	c.	1997
14.	d.	Cleveland Browns
15.	c.	All he can do is score touchdowns
16.	b.	7
17.	a.	Stephen Spach
18.	b.	5
19.	a.	Ernie Steele
20.	a.	Michael Haddix
21.	a.	Denver Broncos
22.	a.	3

FUN FACTS

Questions on page 331

1.	b.	University of Miami
2.	b.	Sinbad
3.	a.	Troy Vincent
4.	d.	Dhani Jones

5.   c. Swoop
6.   a. Shawn Andrews
7.   b. New Deal's National Recovery Act
8.   a. Chase Utley
9.   a. Provo Daily Herald
10.   b. San Diego
11.   b. Tra Thomas
12.   a. Dhani Jones
13.   d. Jon Runyan
14.   b. Minnesota Vikings
15.   b. Steagles
16.   c. 1970
17.   b. Eaglettes
18.   d. 22
19.   b. Atlanta Falcons
20.   c. 15
21.   c. WIP
22.   a. Touchdown Sundae
23.   d. Marty Mornhinweg
24.   c. 00
25.   a. Eric Bieniemy
26.   b. Tra Thomas
27.   c. $130,000
28.   c. Sacramento Kings
29.   b. 42 players

REMEMBER THIS?

Questions on page 337

1.   a. Tampa Bay Buccaneers
2.   d. Chickie's and Pete's
3.   b. Pickle juice
4.   c. Pittsburgh Steelers
5.   b. 26 days
6.   c. Stephen Burbank
7.   a. Coastal Airline
8.   c. 1992

9.   d. Daily News
10.   a. Frito-Lay
11.   b. 6
12.   d. Tim Brown
13.   a. 1972
14.   b. Harry Kalas
15.   c. Tommy McDonald
16.   c. 1982
17.   c. Andy Hall
18.   b. Clyde Simmons

WHAT A STAT!

Questions on page 342

1.   b. 41 games
2.   c. 1,018 games
3.   c. Frank Giddens
4.   b. 1950
5.   b. 105 points
6.   b. 59 games
7.   d. Fourth
8.   c. 9
9.   d. 36
10.   a. 30
11.   a. Oakland Raiders
12.   a. 1934
13.   c. 56-23
14.   c. Dallas Texans
15.   b. Green Bay Packers
16.   b. Cleveland Browns
17.   c. Herschel Walker
18.   b. 26,963
19.   b. 7
20.   a. 59
21.   a. 139
22.   c. 14-14
23.   a. 1/6

24.   a.   3
25.   d.   San Diego Chargers
26.   b.   1987
27.   a.   8 Times
28.   b.   17
29.   b.   81
30.   a.   40.9%
31.   b.   Andy Reid
32.   a.   1,618 yards
33.   c.   22
34.   d.   −33 yards
35.   c.   1947

WHICH EAGLES PLAYER

Questions on page 349

1.   a.   Steve Van Buren
2.   d.   Ben Hawkins
3.   d.   Ralph Goldston
4.   a.   N.D. Kalu
5.   d.   Invincible
6.   b.   Bill Bergey
7.   b.   Paul Grasmanis
8.   c.   Seattle Mariners

OTHER PHILLY FOOTBALL TEAMS

Questions on page 351

1.   c.   Stars
2.   b.   1924
3.   a.   Punk Berryman
4.   b.   1925
5.   c.   Jim Mora
6.   d.   Kelvin Bryant

7.   b.   Pottsville Maroons
8.   a.   Gary Anderson
9.   a.   2
10.   c. Atlantic
11.   d.   New Orleans Voodoo
12.   b.   Michigan Panthers

EAGLES AT THE LINC

Questions on page 355

1.   d.   Over 50 yards
2.   a.   Troy Vincent
3.   c.   New England Patriots
4.   c.   N.D. Kalu
5.   b.   Ike Reese
6.   b.   Soccer match

EAGLES AT THE VET

Questions on page 356

1.   b.   Bobby Taylor
2.   b.   New York Giants
3.   a.   Buffalo Bills
4.   a.   Jacksonville Jaguars
5.   b.   A flare gun incident
6.   d.   Joe Kuharich
7.   a.   Chicago Bears
8.   b.   144-111-2
9.   d.   David Akers
10.   d.   Interception return
11.   d.   Mark Moseley
12.   a.   32

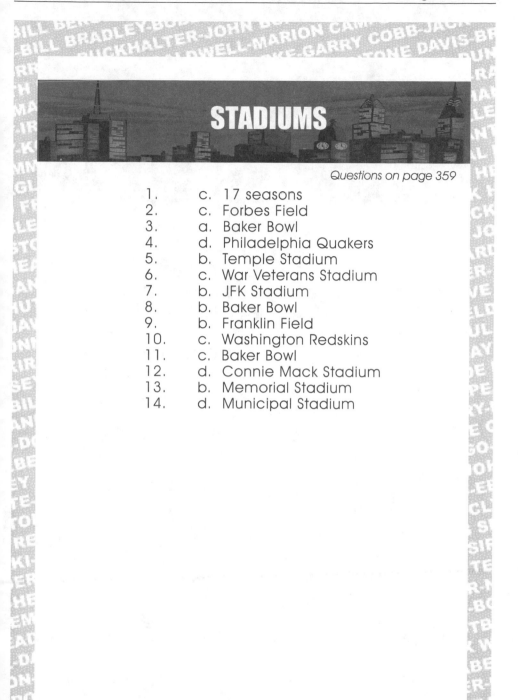

STADIUMS

Questions on page 359

1.   c. 17 seasons
2.   c. Forbes Field
3.   a. Baker Bowl
4.   d. Philadelphia Quakers
5.   b. Temple Stadium
6.   c. War Veterans Stadium
7.   b. JFK Stadium
8.   b. Baker Bowl
9.   b. Franklin Field
10. c. Washington Redskins
11. c. Baker Bowl
12. d. Connie Mack Stadium
13. b. Memorial Stadium
14. d. Municipal Stadium

Puzzle on page 21

PUZZLES

'50s PRO BOWLERS

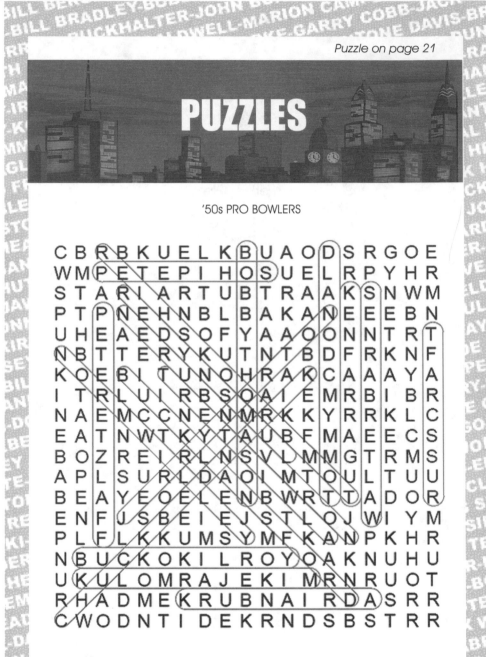

```
C B R B K U E L K B U A O D S R G O E
W M P E T E P I H O S U E L R P Y H R
S T A R I A R T U B T R A A K S N W M
P T P N E H N B L B A K A N E E E B N
U H E A E D S O F Y A A O N N T R T
N B T T E R Y K U T N T B D F R K N F
K O E B I T U N O H R A K C A A A Y A
I T R L U I R B S O A I E M R B I B R
N A E M C C N E N M R K K Y R R K L C
E A T N W T K Y T A U B F M A E E C S
B O Z R E I R L N S V L M M G T R M S
A P L S U R L D A O I M T O U L T U U
B E A Y E O E L E N B W R T T A D O R
E N F J S B E I E J S T L O J W I Y M
P L F L K K U M S Y M F K A N P K H R
N B U C K O K I L R O Y O A K N U H U
U K U L O M R A J E K I M R N R U O T
R H A D M E K R U B N A I R D A S R R
C W O D N T I D E K R N D S B S T R R
```

AdrianBurk	AlWistert	BobbyThomason	BuckLansford
BuckoKilroy	ChuckBednarik	JerryNorton	KenFarragut
LumSnyder	MikeJarmoluk	NormVanBuren	NormWilley
PetePihos	PeteRetzlaff	RussCraft	TomBrookshier
TommyMcDonald	WalterBarnes		

Puzzle on page 29

PUZZLES

'60s NICKNAMES

Baron	Blade	Bruno
Bullet	ConcreteCharlie	Dutchman
GoldenGreek	Goose	Gummy
High	Hopalong	King
Messiah	Sheriff	SwampFox

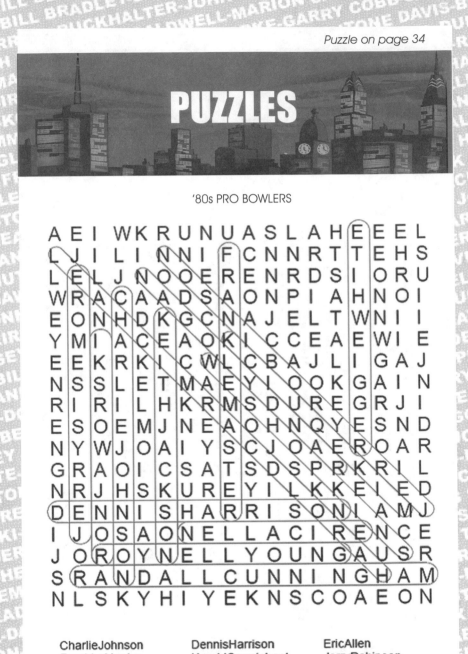

Puzzle on page 34

PUZZLES

'80s PRO BOWLERS

A	E	I	W	K	R	U	N	U	A	S	L	A	H	E	E	E	L
L	J	I	L	I	N	N	I	F	C	N	N	R	T	T	E	H	S
L	E	L	J	N	O	O	E	R	E	N	R	D	S	I	O	R	U
W	R	A	C	A	A	D	S	A	O	N	P	I	A	H	N	O	I
E	O	N	H	D	K	G	C	N	A	J	E	L	T	W	N	I	I
Y	M	I	A	C	E	A	O	K	I	C	C	E	A	E	W	I	E
E	E	K	R	K	I	C	W	L	C	B	A	J	L	I	G	A	J
N	S	S	L	E	T	M	A	E	Y	I	O	O	K	G	A	I	N
R	I	R	I	L	H	K	R	M	S	D	U	R	E	G	R	J	I
E	S	O	E	M	J	N	E	A	O	H	N	Q	Y	E	S	N	D
N	Y	W	J	O	A	I	Y	S	C	J	O	A	E	R	O	A	R
G	R	A	O	I	C	S	A	T	S	D	S	P	R	K	R	I	L
N	R	J	H	S	K	U	R	E	Y	I	L	K	K	E	I	E	D
D	E	N	N	I	S	H	A	R	R	I	S	O	N	I	A	M	J
I	J	O	S	A	O	N	E	L	L	A	C	I	R	E	N	C	E
J	O	R	O	Y	N	E	L	L	Y	O	U	N	G	A	U	S	R
S	R	A	N	D	A	L	L	C	U	N	N	I	N	G	H	A	M
N	L	S	K	Y	H	I	Y	E	K	N	S	C	O	A	E	O	N

CharlieJohnson	DennisHarrison	EricAllen
FrankLeMaster	HaroldCarmichael	JerryRobinson
JerrySisemore	KeithJackson	MikeQuick
RandallCunningham	RandyLogan	ReggieWhite
RonJaworski	RoynellYoung	WesHopkins

422

Puzzle on page 42

PUZZLES

'90s NICKNAMES

```
Y B R I Y S F A G K A A O E E Y
N B G H Y A S B M V A Y D N S R
L R F K T A B U S U D E S I N E
R T F F B F Y B U D D Y L E E E
R F E L K R S I U L O K W A F E
I R M T M O N M S B N F L A E D
R R A B B T D J Y A B H D I D N
O U G N I A R T H G I E R F A
H E B N R R T A T N A M F L O W
B N F C H E E S E B U R G E R R
G R E I R G M T T Y E E U B E F
A M H P I I R O T V A G R G T I
C R L R A R K A N A S H F T S A
R L H I R F J S S E E R A E I R
E E E R O E A T A L Y N O G N F
A T I R F R X D B F R A B I I L
L T E E C U E F R O M A F E M A
```

Arkanas	Bubba	BuddyLee
Cheeseburger	Flea	FreightTrain
Kjax	MinisterofDefense	Money
Muddy	PrettyBoy	Refrigerator
Rev	Silk	Tank
Toast	Tra	Wolfman

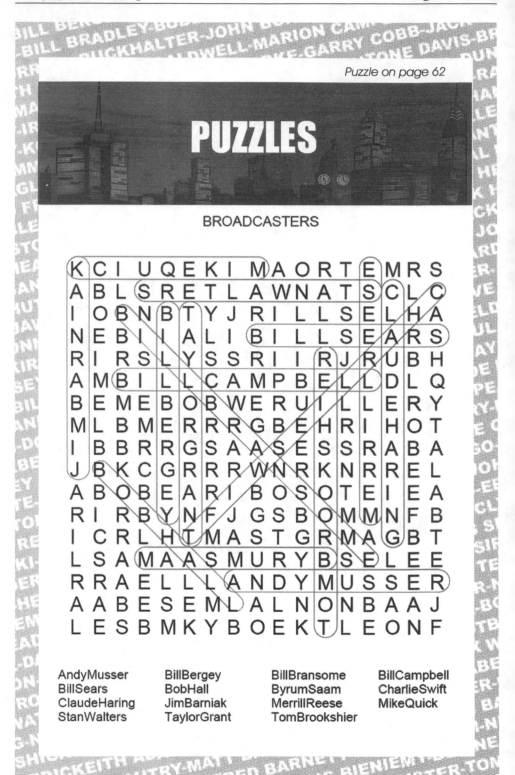

Puzzle on page 62

PUZZLES

BROADCASTERS

```
K C I U Q E K I M A O R T E M R S
A B L S R E T L A W N A T S C L C
I O B N B T Y J R I L L S E L H A
N E B I I A L I B I L L S E A R S
R I R S L Y S S R I I R J R U B H
A M B I L L C A M P B E L L D L Q
B E M E B O B W E R U I L L E R Y
M L B M E R R R G B E H R I H O T
I B B R R G S A A S E S S R A B A
J B K C G R R R W N R K N R R E L
A B O B E A R I B O S O T E I E A
R I R B Y N F J G S B O M M N F B
I C R L H T M A S T G R M A G B T
L S A M A A S M U R Y B S E L E E
R R A E L L A N D Y M U S S E R
A A B E S E M L A L N O N B A A J
L E S B M K Y B O E K T L E O N F
```

AndyMusser	BillBergey	BillBransome	BillCampbell
BillSears	BobHall	ByrumSaam	CharlieSwift
ClaudeHaring	JimBarniak	MerrillReese	MikeQuick
StanWalters	TaylorGrant	TomBrookshier	

Puzzle on page 130

PUZZLES

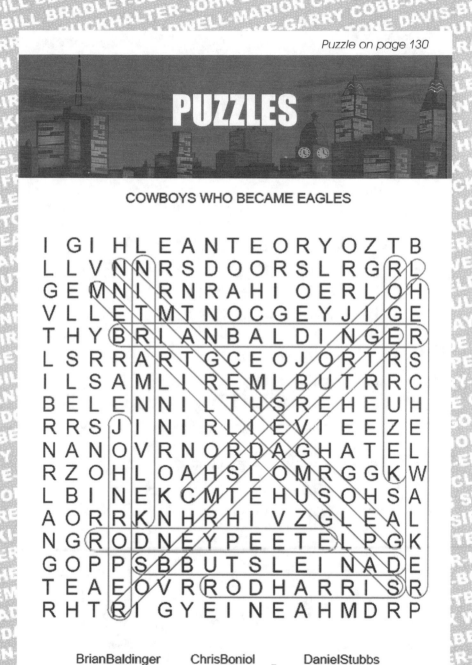

COWBOYS WHO BECAME EAGLES

```
I  G I  H L E A N T E O R Y O Z T B
L  L V N N R S D O O R S L R G R L
G  E M N I R N R A H I O E R L O H
V  L L E T M T N O C G E Y J I G E
T  H Y B R I A N B A L D I N G E R
L  S R R A R T G C E O J O R T R S
I  L S A M L I R E M L B U T R R C
B  E L E N N I L T H S R E H E U H
R  R S J I N I R L I E V I E E Z E
N  A N O V R N O R D A G H A T E L
R  Z O H L O A H S L O M R G G K W
L  B I N E K C M T E H U S O H S A
A  O R R K N H R H I V Z G L E A L
N  G R O D N E Y P E E T E L P G K
G  O P P S B B U T S L E I N A D E
T  E A E O V R R O D H A R R I S R
R  H T R I G Y E I N E A H M D R P
```

BrianBaldinger	ChrisBoniol	DanielStubbs
GeorgeHegamin	HerschelWalker	JohnRoper
KelvinMartin	MerrillDouglas	RobertLavette
RodHarris	RodneyPeete	RogerRuzek

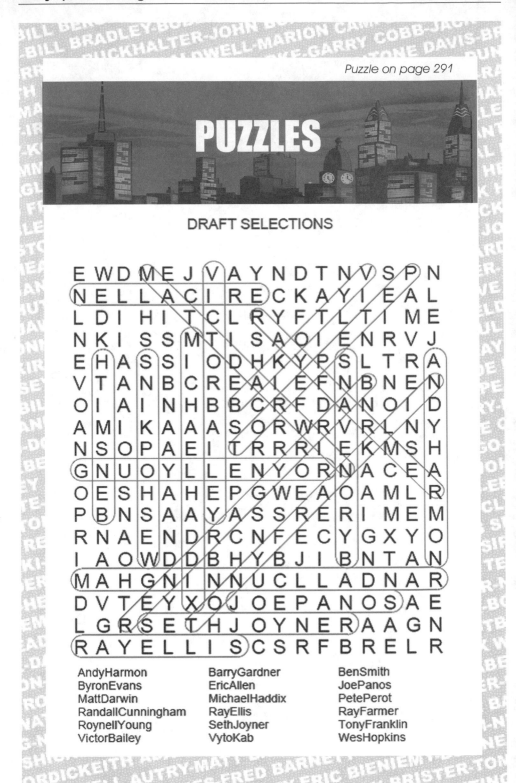

Puzzle on page 291

PUZZLES

DRAFT SELECTIONS

AndyHarmon	BarryGardner	BenSmith
ByronEvans	EricAllen	JoePanos
MattDarwin	MichaelHaddix	PetePerot
RandallCunningham	RayEllis	RayFarmer
RoynellYoung	SethJoyner	TonyFranklin
VictorBailey	VytoKab	WesHopkins

Puzzle on page 51

PUZZLES

EAGLES HEAD COACHES

AndyReid	BertBell	BuckShaw
BuddyRyan	DickVermeil	EdKhayat
GreasyNeale	HughDevore	JerryWilliams
JimTrimble	JoeKuharich	LudWray
MarionCampbell	MikeMcCormack	NickSkorich
RayRhodes	RichKotite	WayneMillner

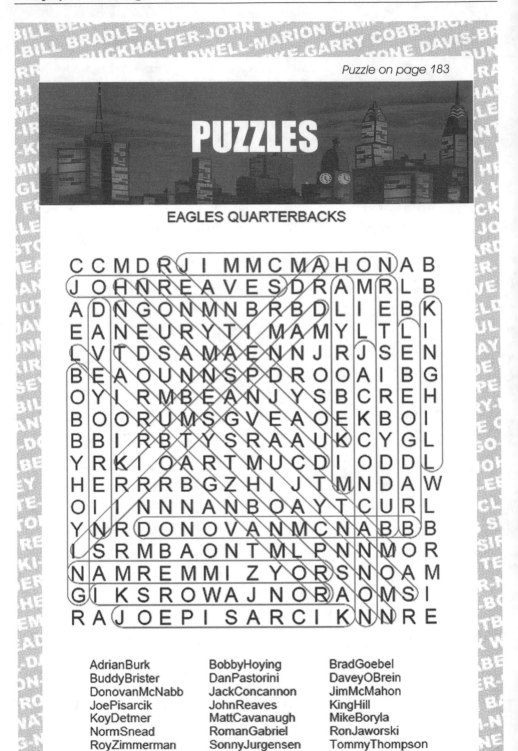

Puzzle on page 183

PUZZLES

EAGLES QUARTERBACKS

AdrianBurk	BobbyHoying	BradGoebel
BuddyBrister	DanPastorini	DaveyOBrein
DonovanMcNabb	JackConcannon	JimMcMahon
JoePisarcik	JohnReaves	KingHill
KoyDetmer	MattCavanaugh	MikeBoryla
NormSnead	RomanGabriel	RonJaworski
RoyZimmerman	SonnyJurgensen	TommyThompson

Puzzle on page 118

PUZZLES

FIRST ROUND PICKS

ArtJones	BobPellegrini	HarryGrant	HarryJones
JeromeBrown	JerrySisemore	JessieSmall	JoeMuha
JohnYonaker	MikeMamula	MikeQuick	NeilWorden
PeteCase	RonBurton	SamFrancis	ShawnAndrews
SiranStacy	SkipSharp	SteveZabel	TraThomas

Puzzle on page 250

PUZZLES

HALL OF FAMERS

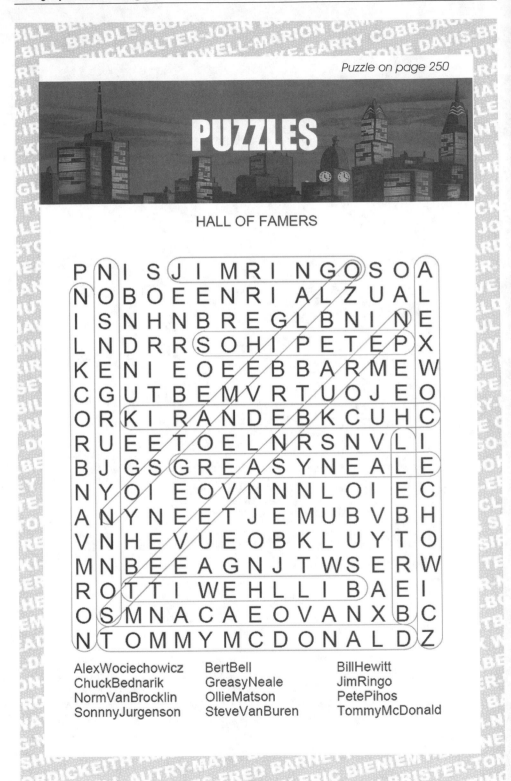

P	N	I	S	J	I	M	R	I	N	G	O	S	O	A
N	O	B	O	E	E	N	R	I	A	Z	U	A	L
I	S	N	H	N	B	R	E	G	L	B	N	I	N	E
L	N	D	R	R	S	O	H	I	P	E	T	E	P	X
K	E	N	I	E	O	E	E	B	B	A	R	M	E	W
C	G	U	T	B	E	M	V	R	T	U	O	J	E	O
O	R	K	I	R	A	N	D	E	B	K	C	U	H	C
R	U	E	E	T	O	E	L	N	R	S	N	V	L	I
B	J	G	S	G	R	E	A	S	Y	N	E	A	L	E
N	Y	O	I	E	O	V	N	N	N	L	O	I	E	C
A	N	Y	N	E	E	T	J	E	M	U	B	V	B	H
V	N	H	E	V	U	E	O	B	K	L	U	Y	T	O
M	N	B	E	E	A	G	N	J	T	W	S	E	R	W
R	O	T	T	I	W	E	H	L	L	I	B	A	E	I
O	S	M	N	A	C	A	E	O	V	A	N	X	B	C
N	T	O	M	M	Y	M	C	D	O	N	A	L	D	Z

AlexWociechowicz   BertBell   BillHewitt
ChuckBednarik   GreasyNeale   JimRingo
NormVanBrocklin   OllieMatson   PetePihos
SonnnyJurgenson   SteveVanBuren   TommyMcDonald

Puzzle on page 191

PUZZLES

RECEIVERS

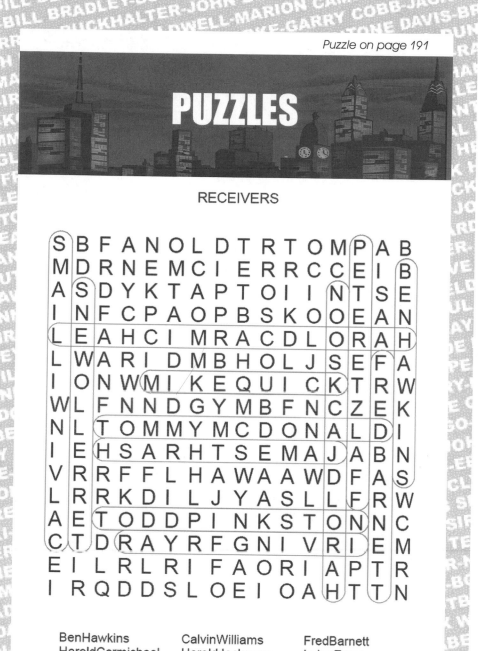

BenHawkins	CalvinWilliams	FredBarnett
HaroldCarmichael	HaroldJacksoon	IrvingFryar
JamesThrash	MikeQuick	PeteRetzlaff
TerrellOwens	ToddPinkston	TommyMcDonald

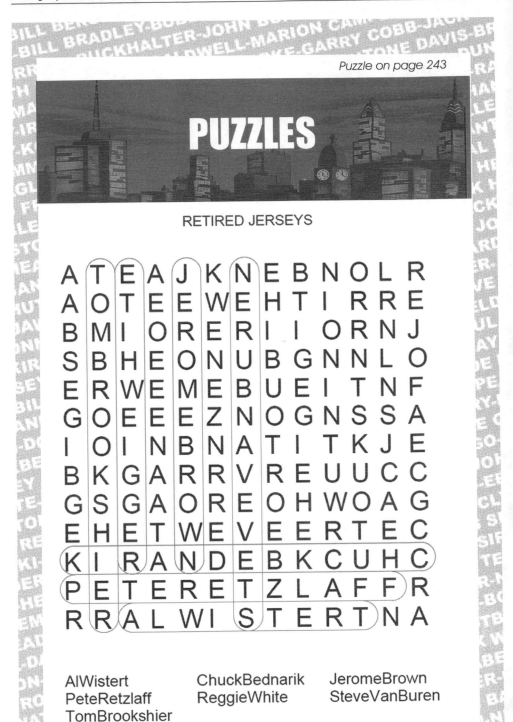

Puzzle on page 243

PUZZLES

RETIRED JERSEYS

```
A T E A J K N E B N O L R
A O T E E W E H T I R R E
B M I O R E R I I O R N J
S B H E O N U B G N N L O
E R W E M E B U E I T N F
G O E E E Z N O G N S S A
I O I N B N A T I T K J E
B K G A R R V R E U U C C
G S G A O R E O H W O A G
E H E T W E V E E R T E C
K I R A N D E B K C U H C
P E T E R E T Z L A F F R
R R A L W I S T E R T N A
```

AlWistert   ChuckBednarik   JeromeBrown
PeteRetzlaff   ReggieWhite   SteveVanBuren
TomBrookshier

Puzzle on page 171

PUZZLES

RUNNING BACKS

Y	D	A	L	M	H	T	R	Z	E	E	N	I	T	H	E	T
S	J	U	A	N	I	S	I	A	S	K	Y	N	S	K	G	K
R	O	R	C	J	E	K	R	M	D	S	O	C	E	T	O	H
D	H	K	I	E	A	O	E	D	B	P	O	N	T	O	T	E
R	N	A	R	C	S	M	A	H	O	R	K	H	R	N	O	R
U	H	I	E	R	K	T	E	J	O	E	O	B	I	A	M	S
E	U	H	O	A	N	Y	A	S	L	G	T	W	I	E	S	C
S	Z	I	L	A	A	M	W	L	J	S	A	N	N	T	U	H
R	V	E	A	M	E	H	E	A	E	O	P	N	K	B	L	E
A	A	R	E	S	E	R	A	W	T	Y	S	S	A	J	L	L
Y	R	E	M	O	G	T	N	O	M	T	R	E	B	L	I	W
B	I	L	L	Y	B	A	R	N	E	S	E	A	P	R	V	A
H	E	L	K	N	I	H	K	C	A	J	R	R	B	H	A	L
T	C	L	A	R	E	N	C	E	P	E	A	K	S	W	N	K
I	B	R	B	N	O	S	N	A	H	E	D	E	W	S	W	E
E	R	B	D	B	M	D	A	V	E	S	M	U	K	L	E	R
K	E	C	E	A	H	E	N	N	V	A	R	O	E	T	P	A

BillyBarnes	BrianWestbrook	ClarencePeaks
DaveSmukler	DuceStaley	HerschelWalker
JackHinkle	JamesJoseph	JohnHuzvar
KeithByars	KenKeller	MikeHogan
PoJames	RickyWatters	SwedeHanson
TimBrown	TomSullivan	WilbertMontgomery

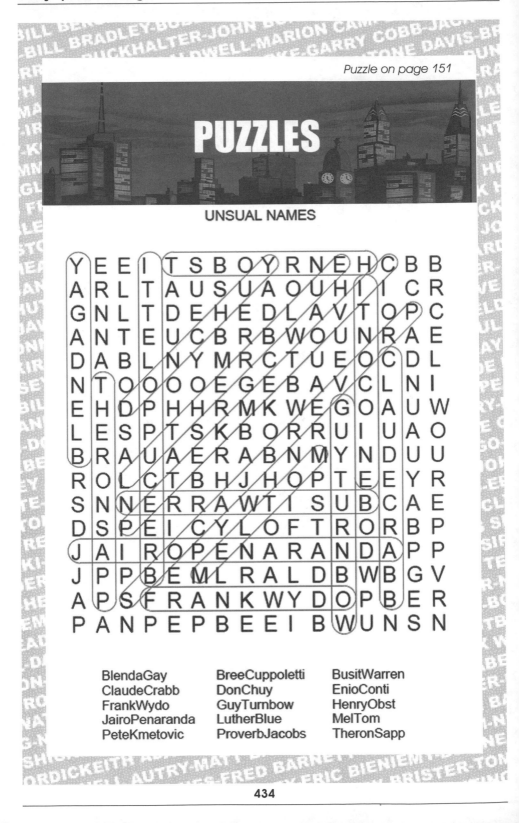

Puzzle on page 151

PUZZLES

UNSUAL NAMES

BlendaGay   BreeCuppoletti   BusitWarren
ClaudeCrabb   DonChuy   EnioConti
FrankWydo   GuyTurnbow   HenryObst
JairoPenaranda   LutherBlue   MelTom
PeteKmetovic   ProverbJacobs   TheronSapp

BIBLIOGRAPHY

Books

Didinger, Ray and Robert S. Lyons. *The Eagles Encyclopedia*. Philadelphia: Temple University Press, 2005.

Macnow, Glen, and Anthony L. Gargano. *The Great Philadelphia Fan Book*. Moorestown, NJ: Middle Atlantic Press, 2003.

Maxymuk, John. *EAGLES by the Numbers*. Philadelphia: Camino Books, 2005.

Newspapers/Periodicals

The FAN magazine
Philadelphia Daily News
Philadelphia Eagles Media Guides
Philadelphia Evening Bulletin
Sports Illustrated

Web Sites

Draft History,
http://www.drafthistory.com/teams/eagles.html

Eagles Team Histories,
http://www.jt-sw.com/football/pro/teams.nsf/histories/eagles

National Football League, http://www.nfl.com

Official Eagles Team Site, http://www.philadelphiaeagles.com